A WEEK IN YELLOWSTONE'S THOROFARE

A Week in Yellowstone's Thorofare

A JOURNEY THROUGH THE REMOTEST PLACE

Michael J. Yochim

Oregon State University Press   Corvallis

Library of Congress Cataloging-in-Publication Data

Names: Yochim, Michael J., author.
Title: A week in Yellowstone's Thorofare : a journey through the remotest place /
    Michael J. Yochim.
Description: Corvallis : Oregon State University Press, 2016. | Includes
    bibliographical references and index.
Identifiers: LCCN 2015051064 | ISBN 9780870718564 (paperback)
Subjects: LCSH: Yellowstone National Park—Description and travel. | Wilderness
    areas—Yellowstone National Park—Management. | Nature conservation—
    Yellowstone National Park. | Yochim, Michael J.—Travel—Yellowstone
    National Park. | BISAC: NATURE / Environmental Conservation & Protection.
    | NATURE / Regional. | BIOGRAPHY & AUTOBIOGRAPHY / Personal
    Memoirs.
Classification: LCC F722 .Y633 2016 | DDC 978.7/52—dc23
LC record available at http://lccn.loc.gov/2015051064

♾ This paper meets the requirements of ANSI/NISO Z39.48-1992 (Permanence
of Paper).

Oregon State University Press
121 The Valley Library
Corvallis, OR 97331-4501
541-737-3166 • fax 541-737-3170
www.osupress.oregonstate.edu

For all those whose lives are affected by ALS: may the day soon come where the world is free of this disease. Toward that end, at least half of the proceeds from the sale of this book will be donated to the ALS Association.

Contents

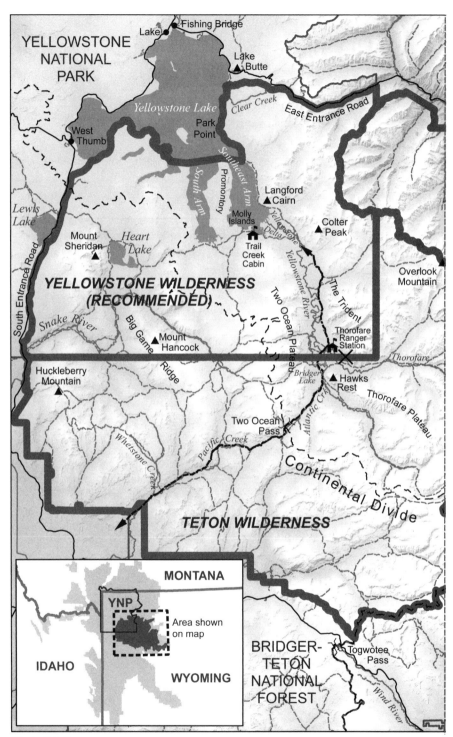

YELLOWSTONE NATIONAL PARK

Lake
Fishing Bridge
Lake Butte
Yellowstone Lake
Clear Creek
East Entrance Road
West Thumb
Park Point
Southeast Arm
South Arm
Promontory
Langford Cairn
Yellowstone Delta
Colter Peak
Lewis Lake
Mount Sheridan
Heart Lake
Molly Islands
Trail Creek Cabin
Yellowstone River
The Trident
Overlook Mountain

YELLOWSTONE WILDERNESS (RECOMMENDED)

Snake River
Big Game Ridge
Mount Hancock
Two Ocean Plateau
Thorofare Ranger Station
Thorofare

South Entrance Road

Huckleberry Mountain
Bridger Lake
Hawks Rest
Thorofare Plateau

Two Ocean Pass
Atlantic Creek

Whetstone Creek
Pacific Creek

Continental Divide

TETON WILDERNESS

MONTANA
YNP
Area shown on map

IDAHO
WYOMING

BRIDGER-TETON NATIONAL FOREST

Togwotee Pass

Wind River

Map by Eric Compas

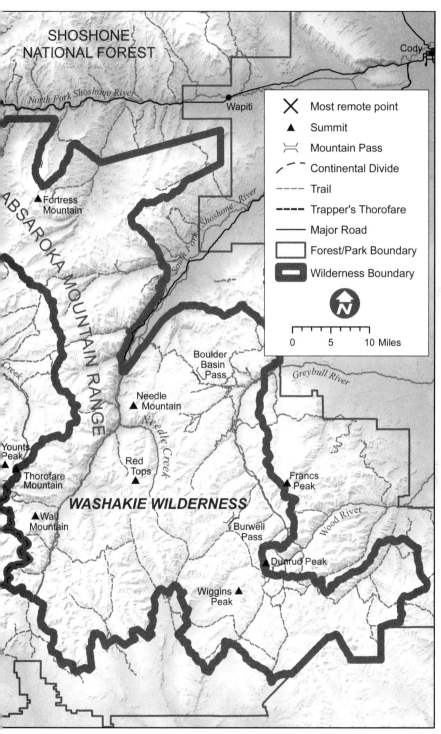

✕	Most remote point	
▲	Summit	
⋈	Mountain Pass	
	Continental Divide	
	Trail	
	Trapper's Thorofare	
	Major Road	
	Forest/Park Boundary	
	Wilderness Boundary	

SHOSHONE NATIONAL FOREST

Cody

North Fork Shoshone River

Wapiti

South Fork Shoshone River

ABSAROKA MOUNTAIN RANGE

▲Fortress Mountain

Creek

Greybull River

Boulder Basin Pass

Needle ▲ Mountain

Needle Creek

Younts Peak
▲

▲ Thorofare Mountain

Red Tops

Francs Peak

Wood River

▲Wall Mountain

WASHAKIE WILDERNESS

Burwell Pass

▲ Dunrud Peak

Wiggins ▲ Peak

0   5   10 Miles

The Thorofare Wilderness Complex

PREFACE A Place Called the Thorofare

In wildness is the preservation of the world.
—Henry David Thoreau, 1862

It is an unlikely name for the most remote point in the contiguous forty-eight states: the Thorofare.[1] About twenty miles as the crow flies to the nearest road in any direction, the point is at the center of a wilderness complex that includes the southeast corner of Yellowstone National Park, the Teton Wilderness within the adjacent Bridger-Teton National Forest, and the Washakie Wilderness within the Shoshone National Forest bordering both on the east. A fur trapper's thoroughfare it was, from the Jackson Hole area onto the Yellowstone Plateau, and before that, a Native American trail.[2] Today it is more a thoroughfare for moose, elk, grizzly bears, and wolves than it is for people, though there are plenty of hikers tramping the trails in the area, anglers fishing its many streams, and hunters tracking their quarry outside the park.

Perhaps surprisingly, this singular area has seen almost nothing published about it: only a book called *Hawk's Rest* by Gary Ferguson, more a (mostly deserved) critique of outfitters and their packstock mismanagement than a survey or history of the Thorofare.[3] Otherwise, only a few obscure popular press articles and passing mentions are found in other literature, including the voluminous scholarship on Yellowstone's natural and cultural history.[4] In contrast, literature on the idea of wilderness and the history of its protection in America is abundant. Writers have chronicled the evolution of the wilderness preservation movement, from its origins attempting to keep roads and automobiles out of America's remaining wildlands to its maturity adeptly using the

Wilderness Act in shifting political climates to protect those lands.[5] They have interpreted its diverse and evolving meanings, showing that wilderness represents, for us, everything from haunt of evil to sacred nature temple, from resource reserve to evolutionary laboratory, from playground to wellspring of rugged individualism and national character.[6] Some have criticized the commonly held idea that wilderness lands have never seen the influence of humanity, arguing instead that Native Americans actively managed most or all of North America's landscapes, so true wilderness never existed and, according to two authors, is a dead concept.[7] In response, others have extolled wilderness as vibrant and relevant, both on the ground and as an idea, supporting their claim with some of the same data as the critics.[8] While significant disagreements remain among these writers, they do agree that the idea of wilderness has a powerful hold on the American imagination. Furthermore, even the critics agree that wilderness has value for us, from providing utilitarian ecosystem services (like clean water) to venues for recreation and contemplation (like hiking, hunting, and writing). Missing from this impressive body of literature, however, is a substantive discussion of the most fundamental attribute of wilderness, its wildness. This is the very foundation of wilderness and the wilderness experience, and yet most of these authors give it only passing mention, providing an incomplete picture of its richness and our relationship to it. For example, Michael L. Johnson devotes an entire book, *Hunger for the Wild*, to exploring the meanings of western wildness to Americans, but spends little time on the significance of wildness in a wilderness context (he also obscures his contribution in dense academic prose). In contrast, Thomas R. Vale's *Fire, Native Peoples, and the Natural Landscape* much more intelligibly explores an attribute of wildness in a landscape: human presence in, and influence on, it. Vale's main objective, however, is to illustrate that some areas of North America had no or minimal human influence; he does not systematically explore other attributes necessary for a landscape to be wild (or not). Similarly, Doug Peacock argues in *The Grizzly Years* that an important component of landscape wildness is the presence of native fauna, especially grizzly bears. Like Vale, though, his main point is not to characterize wildness, but rather (in his case) to illustrate the healing qualities of natural landscapes, as seen through his experience.[9] As illustrated by these authors, then, wilderness writing illuminates some of the conditions necessary for wildness to be present in a landscape, but stops short of providing a comprehensive review of those conditions. In other words, we are left without a complete picture of what puts the "wild" into wilderness, how we react to that wildness, and how that relationship has evolved over time.

This book attempts to fill that void. It is a history and celebration of wildness in the Thorofare, set within a lengthy canoe trip through the area in 2014. Through historic vignettes, descriptions of the Thorofare and its resources, and some of my personal experiences there (on this trip and in past trips), the book shows that the area is defined by wildness. Recognizing both the value and the fragility of that elusive condition, the men and women of the National Park Service and US Forest Service, who manage the area, have struggled on many stages and across many eras to protect it. This book chronicles several of these struggles, including two extended policy battles. These struggles have given us a wild and beautiful Thorofare to enjoy today, a place to forge and solidify bonds between and among each other and nature's inhabitants. Finally, this story provides insight into the passions that motivate those who manage, defend, and journey through the area. Many of us share these passions, so the Thorofare and places like it are important for all of us as venues for coming into contact with a fundamental part of the human experience.

This book draws primarily on archival documents, published literature, select Internet sites, and my own experiences exploring the Thorofare over half a lifetime. Such experiences are a form of "data" rarely utilized by wilderness writers, sometimes because of the problems inherent with such data (they represent only one person's experiences and are interpreted through that person's life lenses) and sometimes because other writers simply do not have such data. Indeed, few other writers—especially, it seems, wilderness critics—have acquired the robust set of field experience data that I have been blessed to enjoy, gathered by hiking almost all Thorofare trails and climbing over forty of its peaks. Such experiences give me a firsthand familiarity with the area and help me avoid embarrassing mistakes like that made by two critics, for example, in describing a fabled lake with two outlets flowing to different oceans at Two Ocean Pass in the Thorofare.[10] No such lake exists; rather, a creek tumbles down a hillside and then splits on the Continental Divide, the two forks never to rejoin and each named for the ocean that will receive its waters (figure P.1).

More important, my Thorofare explorations are *experiential* data that confer rich insight into the significance of something that, to be fully understood, must itself be experienced: the wildness of wilderness. Experiential data like this can be gathered, to some extent, through social science surveys and related analytical tools, but no such survey can approximate the temporal and geographic depth of understanding coming from twenty-eight years methodically exploring the deep recesses and far-flung expanses of this one unique place. Not only do my experiences argue for wildness as the Thorofare's most essential resource, but they also suggest that its beauty and its platform to nurture community go hand-in-hand with its wildness to make it a truly exceptional place.

P.1. Parting of the Waters, Two Ocean Pass, 2002. View is downstream, showing the split in the stream. Sean Miculka (left) points at Atlantic Creek, while Mike Stevens does the same for Pacific Creek. The sign on the tree between them gives the distance to the Atlantic Ocean as 3,488 miles and the Pacific Ocean as 1,353 miles. Author photo.

Because travel through the Thorofare has always been fundamental to experiencing it (as its name implies), the story in these pages uses our weeklong journey as the stepping-off point for a series of vignettes about the Thorofare. Just as no hike to an area this vast can take in every trail or vista, the book cannot relate every historically significant event, every ranger's epic journey, or every contemporary management dilemma. In part, that is a reflection of the area's size and long history, but it is also a reflection of my own physical inability to research every nuance of the area's past and present. For a similar reason, the book is mainly about that portion of the Thorofare within Yellowstone National Park: the park's archives are housed in a state-of-the-art, highly accessible, and organized facility in my home town, whereas the records from the Teton and Washakie Wildernesses are much more scattered and difficult to review. However, in my research, I did not come across a single passing reference to a historically significant event or controversy involving those wildernesses of which I was not already aware, so I am reasonably certain there are no huge oversights herein. Moreover, I drew as heavily on my personal experiences in the two wildernesses as I did on my Yellowstone Thorofare experience. So, just as a well-planned trip provides the traveler a representative cross-section of a region or country, this story provides that for the Thorofare, despite my limitations.

That cross-section begins with a tour of what makes this place wild. Some of these attributes we will see from our boats early in the trip, while others are best illustrated in stories from my twenty-eight years of exploring this area. As we paddle deeper into the Thorofare, we will encounter signs that this area's riches have not come to us easily. Time and again, on the ground and in two national policy battles in the 1900s, the people protecting the Thorofare have stuck their necks out to ensure that it remains a place of incredible wildness and beauty—the reasons we are here today. Later in the journey we will see signs of some present-day Thorofare management struggles, reminders that wildness and beauty require ongoing protection. Woven through all these stories are hints of the values and beliefs held by many of the Thorofare's defenders and explorers: deep-seated, visceral feelings that give rise to loves of wildness, beauty, and community. Thanks to the actions of land stewards to promote and defend those passions, the Thorofare remains a place dominated by nature's forces and randomness, a place of rugged and enduring natural beauty, and a place to forge and cement lifetime bonds with each other and the natural world.[11]

As our week in the wild draws to a close, we will pause to reflect on the meaning and significance of what we have experienced. A look back on some of my own experiences in the Thorofare gives cause to celebrate our success in preserving it largely intact, a land of fierce beauty, great wildness, and abiding community. But a look ahead is not as sanguine, for human-caused global warming may well dilute the wildness and beauty that we have been fortunate to enjoy for a week. Indeed, all who journey through wilderness, whether in person, on paper, or from an ivory tower, would be well advised to focus on the calamity global warming promises for the Thorofare, for wilderness everywhere, for wildness and beauty anywhere, and for humanity in general. Wildness, the very heart and soul of wilderness so often overlooked by wilderness writers, may be so reduced that natural forces no longer dominate, overwhelmed by anthropogenic global warming.[12] Whatever meaning and value we find in wilderness—and we all find something there—will diminish as more and more of the wild erodes from wilderness. Our reflections—and our wilderness journey—then close with a possible path forward, one that would reduce our carbon footprint, preserve more wildness, and retain our place in the world, as Thoreau suggested long ago.

DAY 1 Of Wilds and Men

A friend may well be reckoned the masterpiece of nature.
— Ralph Waldo Emerson, 1847

The Thorofare is a sprawling wilderness, a place of remarkable wildness and beauty. Wilderness explorers have long been drawn to experience those attributes, just as we are today, August 22, 2014. Three friends and I are embarking on a journey through the Thorofare; each of them has explored this area with me before, though we have never done a trip like this together. United by our individual passion for this area and our collective desire to help one of us overcome a new disability and get into the wild once more, we will spend the next week exploring the northern fringes of the Thorofare. Two boats and our paddles will be our mode of transportation, and the waters of Yellowstone Lake our aquatic path through the wilderness.

Yesterday we packed our meals and gear and loaded the boats onto our cars for the two-hour drive to the Bridge Bay Marina. As we made that drive this morning, we saw the forecast of a 70 percent chance of rain become reality, although the shower did not last long. Clouds still fill the sky, and we know the chance of rain will stay with us for the whole first half of the trip. Rain or shine, though, we are thrilled to be the Thorofare's most recent explorers, paddling our way down the wildest part of Yellowstone Lake, its Southeast Arm. We will only approach the most remote point by about fifteen miles, but we will nonetheless paddle well away from civilization, into the Thorofare.

⟨

At 1:00 p.m., the shuttle boat departs the marina with our boats on top and us inside. We ride the boat about fifteen miles across the main body of the lake to the tip of the Promontory, the peninsula separating the lake's South and Southeast Arms. The overcast skies are not accompanied by much wind and rough water, so we make good time and land on a small rocky beach an hour later. The beach is soon covered by our boats and gear, and we watch the shuttle back out of the cove, turn around, and take off back to the marina. It is the last motorized vehicle—and the last person, but for two other small parties of canoeists—we will see or hear for the next three days.

The dry run loading our boats (a canoe and a kayak) that we did yesterday pays off today as we quickly uncover the beach. About 3:00 p.m. we push off from the shore, the sky remaining gray but dry and the temperature cool enough for jackets and long pants. We quickly round the tip of the Promontory and turn south, into the Southeast Arm (figure 1.1). A wilderness panorama opens up to us: the broad waters of the lake's largest arm, bounded by the Absaroka Mountain Range (the peaks partially obscured by clouds) across the arm to our left and the northern flanks of the Two Ocean Plateau rising above the arm's southern end, directly ahead of us (figure 1.2). Bridging the view between them

is the Trident, a high plateau whose western face is dissected into three ridges, each terminating in thousand-foot cliffs above the Yellowstone River (whose mouth we will pass a few days hence). The southernmost of the Trident's spears is just a hop, skip,

1.1. Rounding the tip of the Promontory, 2014. In so doing, we entered the Southeast Arm of Yellowstone Lake, its wildest reach. Photo by Eric Compas. Used with permission.

1.2. Eric Compas and the author on the Promontory, 2003. The background is similar to that which we enjoyed eleven years later: above the Southeast Arm rises the Two Ocean Plateau (top right), with the Trident the long and partly snow-covered plateau in the distance. Eric is at left. Author photo.

and a jump from the most remote point. While that point is out of view to us today, the northernmost of the Trident's ridges is easy to pick out because it holds on to a bank of snow several hundred feet long, several feet deep, and visible from miles away. This year, that snowfield will not melt out; in other warmer and drier summers it will, though not usually till August.

Our view is only a peek into the massive wild area embracing the Thorofare. Follow the route of the trapper's thoroughfare up the broad valley of the Yellowstone (figure 1.3) and then up Atlantic Creek and one is in the Snake River's headwaters in the Teton Wilderness. It is a gentle mountain landscape of forested ridges, open valleys, and the iconic Two Ocean Pass (figures 1.4 and 1.5). Or stay on the Yellowstone, climbing higher and higher until the trees are left behind; this headwaters area is a land of high plateaus and higher mountains (figures 1.6 and 1.7). Continuing east, one enters the Washakie Wilderness, where the valleys get deeper while the mountains get higher still, topping out at 13,158 feet on Francs Peak. This is a land of rugged, naked mountains soaring a mile or more above the rivers that drain them, the gathering place of the Shoshone, Greybull, Wood, and Wind Rivers (figures 1.8 and 1.9). The entire wilderness is such a fountainhead because winter is its dominant season, as even the low elevations top 6,000 feet. At that elevation, accumulating snows begin in October and persist into April or May;

1.3. *The fur trapper's thoroughfare, 2001. As seen from Yellowstone Point in the Teton Wilderness (looking north into Yellowstone National Park) the route entered the Yellowstone River Valley from Two Ocean Pass (lower left, out of sight) and proceeded down the valley to Yellowstone Lake. Author photo.*

on the mountaintops, winter is a month longer on both ends. Though the snowfall is enough to spawn many rivers, it is not enough to create any glaciers. Nonetheless, the Thorofare wilderness is a headwaters of mountain and water, the heart and crest of the Absaroka Range.

And it is wild country. Only hiking and horsepacking trails penetrate this land the size of Delaware, sticking to the major drainages, avoiding some entirely, and rarely venturing to mountaintops. In part for that reason, human use is modest. The area's distance from major population centers also helps explain its emptiness, as both Salt Lake City and Denver are at least a half day's drive away, and both areas have closer mountains tempting weekend warriors. Still another reason is the relative scarcity of lakes here; the crumbly volcanic rock underlying these mountains makes for few of such popular hiker destinations. Many wilderness explorers go instead to the nearby Teton, Beartooth, and Wind River mountain ranges, where lakes are more common (figure 1.10). That volcanic rock does make fertile soils here, however, sustaining a rich vegetative cover—where the land is not vertical—and animals that benefit from such, along with the predators that in turn eat them. Elk, moose, deer, and bighorn sheep are common, as are canine, feline, avian, and mustelid predators. Grizzly bears, though, reign supreme here;

1.4. The author at Two Ocean Pass, 1997. The Parting of the Waters is across the valley and out of sight, behind the author. Author photo.

1.5. Beaver dam on Mink Creek, 2002. Beaver find the lower relief and abundance of willows in the Teton Wilderness to their liking. Author photo.

1.6: Josh Becker at the headwaters of the Yellowstone, 2003. Younts Peak is in the background, 12,156 feet above sea level. Author photo.

1.7. Rolling plateaus of wildflowers around the headwaters of the Yellowstone, 1998. This one ends atop Wall Mountain, in the distance. Author photo.

1.8. The view from 13,158-foot Francs Peak, 2002. Francs is the highest peak in the Absaroka Mountains and in the Thorofare Wilderness Complex. Author photo.

1.9. Bald mountains at the headwaters of Needle Creek, 2002. The peak in the center is crowned with red rock, giving it the name "Red Tops." Author photo.

one can hardly venture into the Thorofare without seeing them or their sign. In their presence, with the vastness, solitude, and abundant ungulates heightening the feeling, one senses the Thorofare's single greatest resource: wildness. It defines the Thorofare.

With that wild country awakening our senses, we continue paddling south, always staying within a hundred yards of the shore, and often closer. On a lake of this size (139 square miles) and this elevation (7,733 feet) in the northern Rockies, the weather can change quickly, with gale-force winds producing waves that can easily swamp a canoe. Knowing that, and that drowning in this lake is the most common way people become part of the food chain in Yellowstone, we illustrate the wisdom that comes from being in our forties by keeping close to shore.

In the bow of the canoe is Sean Miculka, who, like me, works in Yellowstone for the National Park Service (NPS). He is a winterkeeper in the snow season, shoveling the white stuff from building roofs to keep them from collapsing. In the summer he constructs the boardwalks that guide visitors safely through the geyser basins, while I work year-round in park planning, writing management plans. Sean and his wife Missy rented a room to me for two of my grad-school summers in the early 2000s so I could work in Yellowstone and earn some tuition money. They live a block from me in Gardiner, Montana, with their two young children, and Sean and I regularly do weekend outings. Josh Becker, in the canoe's stern, and Eric Compas, in the kayak, are both friends from my time at the University of Wisconsin–Madison. Josh now lives in Minnesota and works in a lab manufacturing eyeglass lenses. He and I have a fourteen-year track record of meeting up annually for a week of tramping in the West, backpacking on the Colorado Plateau or in the northern Rockies. Over that time, we have done overnight hikes—the best way to know a place—in many of the West's fabled wildlands: Zion, Capitol Reef, Escalante, the Grand Canyon, the Bob Marshall Wilderness, Glacier National Park, the Wind River Mountains, and here, in the Thorofare. After I left Madison, Eric took his wife and two kids to Australia for a temporary teaching position. Not long after hosting me on a three-week visit and backpacking through Tasmania with me, he brought his family back to Wisconsin, where he is now a geography

1.10. *Lake in Five Pockets area, 2004. The few lakes in the Absaroka Mountains tend to be found in headwaters areas, where the input of sediment from the easily eroded andesite substrate is minimal. Farther from headwater areas, most lakes are now meadows, having been filled in with such sediment since glaciers receded from the region ten thousand years ago. Author photo.*

professor. He is also the photographer of our current group, doing more with his iPhone than I thought possible, a reflection of the fact that he is more tech-savvy than the other three of us combined.

Our introduction to paddling the lake is brief today, for we pull into our campsite for the night after only an hour of paddling. Our campsite is in a lovely lakeside meadow, covered in drying grasses and late summer flowers that are still blooming, like aster and yarrow. Patches of fireweed nearby affirm that summer is indeed waning, for their leaves are shades of violet and crimson and their seeds are beginning to take flight. We set up camp, cook supper, and settle in for the evening around the campfire. The conversation ranges widely and includes many of the things one would expect to hear old friends discussing in the wilderness: jobs and families, the events of the day, what tomorrow will bring. Darkness comes a little early with the clouds, so we turn in around nine o'clock.

As I wait for sleep to come, my thoughts turn to the events that led us to this trip. Eighteen months ago, I began noticing subtle changes happening to my body: small muscles twitching endlessly, slurred speech when I was tired, an enhanced tendency to cry, and weakness in a hand and a leg. Searching for the cause, I went to my doctor and from there to a neurologist, neither of whom could figure it out (the neurologist because he dismissed my concerns as anxiety). I finally ended up at Stanford University Hospital in California, where concerned neurologists put me through a battery of tests and gave me a diagnosis befitting the delivery date—Friday the thirteenth (of September 2013, no less!): Amyotrophic Lateral Sclerosis (or ALS). More commonly known as Lou Gehrig's disease, the disease causes the sheath insulating the connections between one's neurons to gradually break down, preventing the brain's electrical impulses from reaching the muscles. Without such stimulation, the muscles progressively weaken and become paralyzed. Only the voluntary muscles are affected; involuntary ones like the heart are not, and the senses and brain also remain healthy. There is neither cure nor effective treatment for this disease. Uniformly fatal, 80 percent die within five years of diagnosis.

Still fit and strong at the time and close to completing a major project at work, I stayed on at Yosemite National Park for the fall and winter. Knowing the progression of the disease, though, I requested a transfer back to Yellowstone, where I had lived most of my adult life and where I still had a house. Without a wife, girlfriend, or children holding me in California, I wanted to return to the landscape that had my heart. On the same note, I laid plans to return to the Thorofare on a ten-day hike with these good friends.

I got the transfer to Yellowstone, but as the winter progressed, the disease did too. Where in January I could hike fourteen miles in a day and climb 4,000 feet, that ability dwindled to ten miles and 2,000 feet in March, and then just a flat four miles in April. When I arrived back in Yellowstone in May, two miles was the most I could do. I knew I would not be doing that hike to the Thorofare, so I looked into doing the trip on horseback. I contracted with an outfitter willing to do the trip with horses and mules, but then saw that plan, too, get tossed when a two-hour practice ride on one of his horses ended with the muscles in my neck too weak to support my head. One day—let alone ten days—on the back of a horse would not be possible.

Then the idea of the trip by boat entered the picture. A canoe on a lake is subject to little of the rough bumping and jostling of riding a horse. My friends were game for the different mode of transportation, so with little more than two weeks remaining before our time off began, we made plans to paddle. They did all the coordinating, shopping, and packing beforehand, and for the next week, they will paddle, set up the tents, cook the meals, clean the dishes, hang our food out of reach of bears, pump lake water through purifying filters, and do innumerable other camp chores. Because my fingers have weakened to the point where I cannot turn a key in a car's ignition, they will also pack my bags and help me dress, undress, and bathe. They will all do this without complaint or hesitation, because each of them has known me for fifteen years, has suffered through many wilderness privations with me, and is a solid friend. We are Emerson's masterpiece, comrades in life and, for the next week, in the Thorofare wilderness.

DAY 2 Into the Wild

Garbed in snow from top to bottom, they presented the most wonderful spectacle of mountain that I have ever seen. . . . I shall never forget the hour on Big Game Ridge, nor shall I forget the thrill that I experienced when I realized that I was standing in the midst of more wild country than exists anywhere else in the United States.
—Superintendent Horace Albright, 1920

Clouds greet us as we emerge from the tents, wet with rain that fell overnight. Rain is not falling right now, though, and as we break camp the sun emerges. Glittering off the lake, it warms our bodies and our spirits. We all know that today's weather forecast is for more rain and high temperatures only in the forties, so the warmth and sunshine seem like a special gift from the weather gods. We take advantage of it, enjoying a leisurely breakfast of egg burritos and drying the tents.

It is after ten o'clock before we finally have all the gear down by the two boats. Already, my three canoeing partners are working together so well that I can just sit and enjoy the view. Which I do, but not without feeling guilty that I am not contributing, even though I know my disabilities make that impossible. The three of them tell me that I contribute in other ways, such as by walking them through preparation of the backcountry meals that they have learned from me. True enough, but I am still reminded of how dependent on them I am. Certainly, almost all wilderness travelers depend on their trip partners for one thing or another, whether something as mundane as helping carry the group gear or as extraordinary as coming to the aid of a stricken companion, but in this case, I would be instant grizzly bear food without them.

With continued sunshine and the promise of a day of wilderness exploration ahead of us, spirits remain high as we stash our gear in the boats. That puzzle complete, my friends help me into the canoe, and we push off for a day of paddling. I am in the middle of the boat, propped up on assorted drybags containing our gear. Should the rain return or—perish the thought—we capsize, our gear will stay dry in these rubberized plastic bags. As we set to paddling, we begin encountering the host of landscape features that collectively create the wildness of this place. Some are the actual sights and sounds we experience as we paddle, while others are recollections from my earlier journeys through this area, triggered by something we see. The day will end up being both a welcome to the Thorofare and also a survey of the attributes that make a landscape wild.

Before we begin, it is worth taking a moment to look beyond the wilderness literature for other clues as to what constitutes wildness in a landscape context. Standard reference materials (mainly dictionaries) and law (mainly the Wilderness Act) contain important insights. Both *Webster's New World College Dictionary* and dictionary.com, for example, provide similar definitions, including wildness as a cognate of wild. The online source defines "wild" as (1) "living in a state of nature; not tamed or domesticated"; (2) "growing or produced without cultivation or the care of humans"; and (3) "uncultivated, uninhabited, or waste." I am not sure whether wildness in a landscape has anything to do with waste, but the dictionaries agree that it is the state of being natural, outside of human control and habitation. This is helpful, but insofar as we are concerned, overly broad and lacking precision. For example, weeds growing through the cracks in a parking lot could meet this definition of wild, even though few would think of a parking lot as a wild landscape.[1]

The Wilderness Act offers more precision and is probably the most relevant authority, since all of the Thorofare is either protected as wilderness under the act or recommended for such protection. Furthermore, almost all wilderness historians and critics ground their work in the act and its definition of wilderness. Like the dictionaries, the act does not define wildness (or wild), but the oft-quoted definition of wilderness has several hints of what it might mean for a landscape to be wild. That is not surprising, for the architects of the act (especially its primary author, Howard Zahniser) took great pains to define wilderness carefully, revising the bill sixty-six times before it finally became law in 1964. Here is the key passage from the act:

> A wilderness, in contrast with those areas where man and his own works dominate the landscape, is hereby recognized as an area where the earth and its community of life are untrammeled by man, where man himself is a visitor who does not remain. An area of wilderness is further defined to mean in this Act an area of undeveloped Federal land retaining its primeval character and influence, without permanent improvements or human habitation, which is protected and managed so as to preserve its natural conditions and which (1) generally appears to have been affected primarily by the forces of nature, with the imprint of man's work substantially unnoticeable; (2) has outstanding opportunities for solitude or a primitive and unconfined type of recreation; (3) has at least five thousand acres of land or is of sufficient size as to make practicable its preservation and use in an unimpaired condition; and (4) may also contain ecological, geological, or other features of scientific, educational, scenic, or historical value.[2]

One of the more lyrical passages in American environmental law, the first sentence has been widely quoted to define wilderness, by both friends and critics of wilderness. Almost none of them—especially the critics—have examined the full passage, wherein Zahniser (and Congress, which passed the bill) provided considerably more nuance. For instance, the first sentence establishes the fact that wilderness is fundamentally a place in and of nature, dominated by natural forces. The more detailed definition, though, includes the following key phrase: "generally appears to have been affected primarily by the forces of nature, with the imprint of man's work substantially unnoticeable." Note the three adverbs in this clause, all indicating that Zahniser and his colleagues were well aware that wilderness could include human impacts, both historic and prehistoric. This fact is often overlooked by those who dismiss wilderness as a valid concept because, in their view, no landscape is free of human impact, especially from Native Americans.[3] For Zahniser and the act, the bottom line was that wilderness should look, act, and feel like something of the natural world, not the built or farmed environments, and irrespective of past human influence.

In still more detail, the full definition indicates that wilderness has at least five critical attributes, with naturalness being the first of these. Wilderness is also undeveloped, lacking buildings, roads, and other human improvements: "without permanent improvement or human habitation." Its landscape and natural processes should show minimal human manipulation (while recognizing the human role in shaping some wilderness landscapes): "an area where the earth and its community of life are untrammeled by man." It should be of decent size: "at least five thousand acres of land," or, if less (such as an island), be a manageable unit. It should be suitable as a venue for certain traditional uses: "has outstanding opportunities for solitude or a primitive and unconfined type of recreation." And finally, it may have other attributes that further its wildness: "may also contain ecological, geological, or other features of scientific, educational, scenic, or historical value."[4] These are the things that define wilderness; all wilderness areas have these five attributes to varying degrees. They demarcate wilderness as a *place* apart, wherein the primary forces are not our own. Collectively, they are wildness, the fundamental *character* of wilderness. Wilderness is the *place*; wildness its most essential *character*. In sum, as indicated in the Wilderness Act, wildness in a landscape is the product of its being in and of nature, without significant human manipulation or development, all on a scale big enough to get lost in, with other unique features possibly adding to the feel. As we will see in the landscape itself today, the Thorofare suggests a very similar definition of landscape wildness. It grounds the Wilderness Act in reality—the wild reality we will immerse ourselves within as we paddle our way south.

((

For Eric and me, paddling the lakeshore is familiar terrain, for we circumnavigated the lake's non-roaded shoreline eleven years ago (there are roads on about a third of the lake's 110 miles of shoreline). Canoeing in the hot summer of 2003, we passed an enjoyable week paddling in the mornings, hiking in the afternoons, swimming in the lake when the hike was done, and then enjoying quiet (if occasionally buggy) evenings.

This time, though, two things have changed for the better. The mosquitoes are mostly gone, it being the golden time of late August when most of them have been killed either by frost or by annoyed wilderness travelers. And the forest on the shore has burned, either in the Promontory Fire of 2004 or in the Alder Fire last year (figure 2.1). Together, these two lightning-caused fires burned almost all of the Promontory forest. Greeting us now is a forest of gray and black standing dead trees with a rich understory of seedling trees, grasses, and forbs in various shades of green and gold.

It is hard to think of a natural force more obvious to the senses than wildfire—and more challenging to our concepts of beauty. Yet fire is about as fundamental an influence in creating the scene before us as any, and the same could be said even if the trees were green, tall, and alive. That was a lesson taught to all of us who were here in 1988, when the warmest and driest summer weather in Yellowstone's recorded history stoked and blew fires across 36 percent of the park, almost eight hundred thousand acres. That was my third summer in the park, and I

2.1. Canoeing past burned forest on the Promontory, 2014. Photo by Eric Compas. Used with permission.

joined everyone else here in watching the fires trounce the firefighting efforts of the most powerful government in the world. Up to ten thousand men and women were fighting the fires at any one point that summer, and while they did an admirable job protecting the buildings and structures in the park (none of significance were lost), nature held the upper hand in the forests and meadows away from the roads and tourist villages. Under conditions like those of 1988, fires are a force as raw and uncontrollable as hurricanes and tornadoes.

In the years after that hot and smoky summer, new words entered our lexicon, words like "serotinous" and "mosaic," which together hint at the pyrogenic character of these forests. "Serotinous" describes some of the cones borne by lodgepole pines (*Pinus contorta*), by far the most common tree in Yellowstone. Such cones are the primary fire adaptation of the tree; they do not open without fire. Like a life insurance policy bearing dividends when the bearer dies, the cones open after the tree burns, releasing their seeds onto the seedbed (bare mineral soil) left behind by the fire. The new forest is born. The latter word, "mosaic," describes the pattern of burning left behind by the fires. Patches of forest, burned and unburned, large and small, burned hotly or lightly singed, with meadows, ponds, and lakes scattered about. Then and now, such mosaics diversify the scenery and the wildlife habitat.

Along with such words came new ways of looking at Yellowstone's forests, especially as the years became decades. Serotinous seedlings greened the blackened forest floor, eventually becoming saplings. Patches of trees all the same age dotted the landscape, some dating to 1988 and others to years, decades, even centuries earlier, when other fires burned. As the 1988 seedlings passed the quarter-century mark, some became tall enough to crowd the view and thick enough to make walking through the sapling forests difficult or impossible. With no sunlight reaching the forest floor, these "dog-hair" thickets zeroed out the wildlife habitat value. In other areas, a lack of post-fire seedlings led eventually to open forest or meadow, the diversity of plants there sustaining deer and elk and those that prey on them. And as the forests in front of us attest, new fires and their mosaics have occurred, set within the larger mosaic. It is a whole tapestry of plant and animal life—the

Wilderness Act's "community of life"—responding to the shifting patterns of fire, moisture, soil types, herbivory, and time.

And to people, for we have been playing with fire since we arrived in this landscape ten thousand years ago. Whether Native Americans, scouts of the US Army (administrators of Yellowstone before Congress created the NPS in 1916), or NPS rangers, we have tried to shape the landscape with fire by burning or fighting it, accidentally or intentionally. The tapestry we have before us today certainly reflects some human influence, but the amount of that contribution is probably minor. Fires in lodgepole pine forests are climate-limited rather than fuel-limited, meaning that no matter how much fuel is on the forest floor, fire will not burn much until the necessary warm and dry conditions for it occur. On the cool, moist Yellowstone Plateau, only one or two years per century bring such a drought, so no matter how many people are out there igniting fires, they will not burn much until nature is ready. (In contrast, fuel-limited forests such as the Ponderosa pine forests of the Southwest see weather conducive to fire most or all years, so fires can burn as soon as adequate fuel accumulates, which can be as few as two years in those forests. In such forests, humans can readily ignite forest fires.) Furthermore, lodgepole pine forests generally lack sufficient fuel to sustain a fire until about 150 years have passed since the last fire, making them all the more impervious to fire, even in drought years. For now, looking at the scene in front of us, we know that no large fire had burned the Promontory forests since the 1800s or earlier, so they were primed to burn. NPS fire managers may have set some limits to where they would allow the lightning-caused Promontory and Alder fires to move, but the fires otherwise spread according to the whims of nature. And finally, no matter what our limits might be, fire is like a tiger in a cage, always prowling, watching for a chance to escape. As the fires of 1988 attest, given the right weather conditions, we cannot build a cage strong enough for this restless beast; so, the forest we canoe past is as much a reflection of natural forces as anything we will see today.[5]

The net result is what we have before us today, a forest responding to a disturbance. New seedlings take root amid a sea of grasses and flowers stimulated by the now abundant sunshine. Those pioneers, and the trees and plants that the fire missed, cast their seeds onto the new seedbed, enriching the diversity and helping stabilize the soil. Trees killed by the fire rattle and whistle in the wind, eventually falling to decompose and fertilize the new forest. Life, in other words, moves on, a natural rhythm it has followed here for millennia.

(

And we paddle on, passing two other parties of canoeists, one a party of two people and the other a solo paddler. The soloist passes us by without speaking (not surprising for someone probably seeking solitude), while the couple says hello and chitchats. These are the only other humans we will see at all for the next two days. In fact, we will talk with only two other groups—one of them a pair of rangers on patrol—for the rest of the trip. The Southeast Arm seems empty, and the solitude, exquisite.

Having spent several years in California's Sierra Nevada, I know that not all wildernesses are so empty. I was not surprised to find that in the country's most populous state, people crowd Sierra wildernesses. One of the most crowded areas is the John Muir Trail corridor linking Yosemite with Sequoia and Kings Canyon National Parks. On a Labor Day weekend hike on a part of that trail in Kings Canyon four years ago, I passed another party of hikers every five or ten minutes for the better part of two days. In open terrain, the trail was easy to discern in the distance, moving hikers catching the eye. Not only was solitude hard to find, but silence was too; if there was no creek nearby or breeze blowing to mask the noise, one could often hear people talking, some nearby, others far away.

What did surprise me is that Californians, most of whom live in large cities, often bring their comfort with crowds into the backcountry. For some, it is more a need to have other people around; in extreme cases, it is a fear of being alone, without others to shield them from a wilderness they view as dangerous but which is, in reality, fairly gentle. On that same trip, for example, my friends and I camped at Wanda Lake, a large lake above timberline. An hour after we set up camp, I watched in amazement as a party of three hikers, with dozens of suitable places available nearby—all well away from others—set up camp not fifty yards from us. Adding insult to injury, the three also exemplified the paradoxical anonymity that comes from living in a crowd, for they never acknowledged our existence.

By contrast, even if every campsite were taken here on the Southeast Arm, we would probably not have such experiences on this canoe trip. On the roughly thirty miles of shoreline we will paddle, there are only thirteen campsites, almost all out of view of each other. Because all paddlers must stay in one of those sites (so that all have easy access to food storage poles to hang their food out of the reach of bears), we know that the maximum density of people will not even be one party every two miles (a far cry from my experiences in the Sierra Nevada). While the requirement to stay in designated sites somewhat constrains our ability to travel freely, for us the trade-off is worth it. Not only can we store our food safely and easily, we know that we will see few other people. As we pass other campsites, moreover, we find almost all of them empty. Solitude and natural quiet are ours to enjoy.

☾

And vastness. Although the clouds have begun to gather and lower, we can still see that patch of snow on the Trident. As I indicated yesterday, that alpine plateau bounds the Yellowstone River, which emanates from the slopes of 12,156-foot Younts Peak about twenty miles southeast of the park boundary. That entire headwaters is protected as designated wilderness (the Teton Wilderness) pursuant to the Wilderness Act of 1964. Such designation precludes road and building construction, along with the use of motorized or mechanized equipment, except when they are the minimum necessary to protect the area's wilderness character. Although grazing and hunting are allowed, designated wildernesses effectively have more protections than most national park lands (the exception being wilderness in national parks). Designated wilderness sprawls away from the Yellowstone River drainage as well, encompassing large portions of the headwaters of the Snake (also in the Teton Wilderness), Wind, Greybull, Wood, and Shoshone River headwaters to the south and east (all in the Washakie Wilderness). Here in the park, almost all of the backcountry is "recommended" wilderness, meaning the secretary of the interior has recommended to Congress that such acreage be designated as wilderness, but Congress has never acted on that recommendation. Wilderness designation would preclude motorboat use on the lake's South and Southeast Arms, so Congress, unwilling to antagonize a powerful constituency, has not designated wilderness here. Despite Congress's failure to act, the NPS manages most recommended wilderness as designated wilderness, so we can add the lands—but not the waters—of Yellowstone's southeast corner to those of the Teton and Washakie Wildernesses to produce one giant area of contiguous, roadless land protected as one form or another of wilderness. All told, that is over twenty-six hundred square miles of land, one of the four largest blocks of wilderness in America outside Alaska, and an area of land a little larger than the state of Delaware.[6]

Such designations and statistics are one way of describing the size of an area. Another way is to consider the points most distant from a road in the wilderness complexes of the contiguous forty-eight states.[7] There are only fifteen points more than ten miles from a road in those states, with only two occurring east of the Rockies (in the Florida Everglades, 12.1 miles, and Minnesota's Boundary Waters Canoe Area Wilderness, 10.5 miles). The Thorofare contains the most remote point, with the exact distance varying between 18.8 and 20.2 miles depending on how the geographer handles the arms of Yellowstone Lake. If the geographer treats them as motorized non-wilderness, the lower mileage is the result, with the higher mileage the result if they are treated as wilderness. The exact point of remoteness moves around as well, from near the Thorofare Ranger Station in Yellowstone to the west end of the Thorofare Plateau, a few miles away (figure 2.2; figure 2.3). Interestingly, three others of the fifteen most remote points are also in the Yellowstone area: the Upper Lamar/North Absaroka (13.1 miles, and separated from the Thorofare wilderness by only a narrow strip of asphalt, the East Entrance Road), the Bechler (10.3 miles, and also just a thin strip of asphalt away, across the South Entrance Road), and the Absaroka/Beartooth (10.2 miles, and separated from the Upper Lamar/North Absaroka area by a third thin strip of asphalt, the Northeast Entrance Road/US 212). The Thorofare is

2.2. The vicinity of the most remote point, 1993. In this view from atop the Trident, the Yellowstone River flows from the left down the linear meadow above Bridger Lake, while Two Ocean Pass—and the rest of the fur trapper's thoroughfare—can just be seen center left. Bounding the land of the remotest point are the Two Ocean Plateau (just below the Teton Range punctuating the distant horizon), the Thorofare Ranger Station (just out of view, right of the lake) and the Thorofare Plateau (out of view to the left). Author photo.

clearly in good company: the middle of nowhere amid a whole collection of large blank spots on the map.[8]

A third way to describe the Thorofare's vastness is to think about the length of time one would need to thoroughly explore it by, say, hiking most or all of its trails. Consider, for example, my own experience. My first hike into the area was in October 1993, when my friend Linda Campbell[9] and I spent eight days on a ninety-three-mile hike through the Yellowstone side of the Thorofare. Our appetite whetted, that became the first of six weeklong (or longer) expeditions she and I took through the Thorofare. The hikes averaged ninety-one miles, and we quickly branched out to include the Teton and Washakie Wildernesses in our itineraries. Our longest trip was in 1995, when we backpacked to the Yellowstone River's headwaters from the park's south entrance. After climbing Younts Peak, we continued on across the Continental Divide, eventually coming out near Togwotee Pass, eleven days and 110

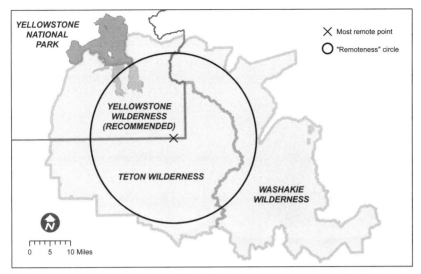

2.3. *The most remote point in the Thorofare. The point is computed by inscribing the largest circle within the wilderness complex (as defined by the three nearest points on its boundary) and mapping the center point. Shown is the point if the arms of Yellowstone Lake are treated as wilderness (with a radius of 20.2 miles—this is the point shown on the map in the front of the book); if instead they are treated as motorized non-wilderness (their current condition), the point shifts a few miles southeast (and the radius declines to 18.8 miles). Map by Eric Compas.*

miles later. After Linda married, I continued exploring the Thorofare with other friends, including all three of my current paddling partners. For fifteen years I took near-annual trips here, eventually hiking all of the major approaches into the heart of the Thorofare (the vicinity of the most remote point) and many—but not all—of the far-flung corners of this wilderness kingdom. All told, I racked up over two thousand miles traveled here, with only about a third of that being stretches of trail I repeated. In other words, I have hiked over thirteen hundred miles in the Thorofare wilderness (about 80 percent of the total trail mileage, plus significant mileage off-trail), but still have many trails left to leave boot tracks on (figure 2.4). Superintendent Albright said it well; the Thorofare is as big as its name, large enough for a lifetime of exploration.

☾

On all those trips as well as this canoe trip, we saw abundant sign of the native four-legged or feathered residents, or the critters themselves.

2.4: The author at the north end of the Two Ocean Plateau trail, 2001. Hiking this trail meant I had hiked all 1,200 miles of trail in Yellowstone National Park—a rite of passage for some. I came close to doing the same in the Teton and Washakie Wildernesses. Author photo.

Today we have already seen a bald eagle perched in a lakeshore tree, watching us, or fish, or both. Eagles are common enough on the lakeshore that it is a rare day when we do not see one. A rarer resident, the peregrine falcon, gave Eric and me a sighting when we were on the Promontory in 2003. We saw it in flight—flying fast enough, but not doing the two-hundred-mile-per-hour dives the bird can do. Other birds we will see most days on this trip include osprey, American white pelicans, assorted ducks, and a cormorant or two. We often see the pelicans in flight, winging their way to or from the Molly Islands. This afternoon we will pass the Mollies, keeping a respectful distance because the two tiny islands host the only nesting colony of pelicans in Wyoming. The somewhat ungainly birds are surprisingly graceful in flight, reminding us that beauty takes many forms in a wilderness setting.

On land, elk and grizzly bears dominate my Thorofare wildlife memories. On that hike to the Yellowstone's headwaters, for example, Linda and I did an off-trail side trip up onto the Two Ocean Plateau. Up there at 10,000 feet, we saw a gang (herd) of two hundred elk that took flight as soon as they saw us, even though we were a good mile away. Clearly, we did not meet their definition of good habitat, but everything else about that plateau does: an abundance of grassy meadows, enough water for drinking but not so much that mosquitoes are a nuisance, scattered patches of forest to bed down in, and protection from at least one of their main predators (us, in the form of hunters). It is such good habitat that elk migrate to it from all directions—some from dozens of miles away—to spend the summer in its breezy meadows.[10] Keeping them company, but in lower numbers and in somewhat different habitats, are mule deer, moose, and a few bighorn sheep.

Also at home throughout the Thorofare are the bruins that are constantly on our minds when we hike. Tracks on the trail with occasional piles of scat are something I have seen in abundance every time I journeyed through the area, evidence that this bruin home is well-populated. Sightings—some closer than desired—are common too. For example, Sean and I, with our friend Mike, had a close brush with one when we hiked by the Southeast Arm in 2002. I was well in the lead and looked up to see a bear ambling toward me about a hundred yards away. From the bear's vantage, I was alone, almost the most dangerous situation for a hiker (surprising a sow with cubs would be worse). So, I stopped, pulled out my bear spray and removed the safety, and began slowly backing toward the relative security of my hiking partners. Just a few seconds later—but what seemed like several minutes—they caught up to me, saw my bear spray unholstered and then the bear, and hollered to catch its attention. Realizing there were more humans present than it wanted to contend with, the bear diverted from the trail and away from us. After making sure it was gone and reestablishing our composure, we continued hiking, always alert for other bears (grizzly or black) or the large canines and felines that also call this area home. Then as now, we reveled in the fact that the full suite of native fauna is still present here, even the large predators. Outside Alaska, the only other wilderness for which that is true is the Crown of the Continent Ecosystem in Montana, consisting of the Bob Marshall Wilderness Complex and Glacier National Park. The Thorofare and the Crown, then, are twin wilderness wildlife kingdoms in the northern Rockies.

The presence of abundant wildlife is just the surface manifestation of the rich network of connections and interrelationships between and among the Thorofare's animal, plant, insect, soil, and microbial life. An uncountable number of relationships and functional bonds exist between predator and prey, animal and plant, flower and insect, microbe and soil, bedrock and water chemistry, precipitation and fire, disturbance and wildlife abundance. In wild places like the Thorofare, such relationships between all inhabitants are free to form, grow, and diversify—much as they do among wilderness travelers like us. It is, again, the community of life, complex beyond our imagination, endlessly enriching to humanity, and something to enfold ourselves within as we explore the Thorofare.

☾

The clouds continue to gather as we paddle on, but for now the sun still shines, so we stop at a vacant campsite for a snack. Enjoying the warmth, we relax and examine our surroundings. We are in a lakeside meadow with some live trees nearby and here and there a Columbia monkshood or harebell still in flower. The grasses are various hues of green and gold, hinting that summer is waning. With the lake nearby, it is one of many beautiful settings we will enjoy. While it is not that remarkable in this land of superlatives, it is definitely notable when one considers what might be found in a similar place—even designated wilderness. For example, in the Rattlesnake Wilderness near Missoula, Montana, one would be hard-pressed to escape spotted knapweed, an exotic plant that has spread throughout the entire basin in which Missoula sits. Native to the steppes of eastern Europe and Asia, knapweed was inadvertently brought here decades ago, but without whatever insects or fungi were keeping the plant in check there. Now the hillsides around Missoula, including those of the Rattlesnake, turn pink when knapweed blooms. Knapweed and many other exotic plants do occur in Yellowstone, but most are within sight of a road (cars are one of the main vectors of dispersal for exotic plants). Here, distance protects the meadow; only native flora graces it.

Another form of human disturbance is absent here but, again, present in the Rattlesnake: logging. The Rattlesnake is unusual in western wilderness areas in that parts of it were logged before it was protected as wilderness, but it would be in good company east of the Rockies, where almost all forests were cut over (but are now in various stages of regrowth). Thanks to Yellowstone's early establishment as a national park, there was never any logging here. Similarly, the US Forest Service (USFS), administrator of the Teton and Washakie Wildernesses, recognized their exceptional nature early on and protected them from

2.5. Enjoying good air quality on the Southeast Arm, 2014. Photo by Eric Compas. Used with permission.

logging. While those lands, and those through which we travel now, are hardly free from human disturbance (wolf eradication in the 1920s is perhaps the best example of such disturbance), the Rattlesnake illustrates the relative absence of disturbance here.

The same can be said about the air quality here: better than other wilderness areas, but not pristine. Remote as the Thorofare may be, it is still downwind of cities and farms. While visibility is pretty good here and improving (figure 2.5), ammonium deposition is on the increase. The prevailing southwest winds transport the ammonium, derived from nitrogen fertilizer, from farms in southern Idaho. Once deposited here, the ammonium can overenrich both aquatic and terrestrial plant communities, especially at or above our current elevation. Adapted to low levels of nitrogen, native plants can give way to exotics that thrive on fertilized soils. Wind also brings some mercury in from coal-burning power plants. Overall levels of these two pollutants remain low, along with sulfur and ozone, especially compared with their levels in other wilderness areas like those in the Sierra Nevada. Downwind of one of the richest agricultural areas in the world (the San Joaquin Valley) and the millions of people and cars both there and in the San Francisco Bay Area, the Sierra Nevada suffers from alarming levels of almost all these pollutants, especially in the southern part of the range. Visibility in Sequoia National Park, for example, is more often degraded than not, and sensitive trees in the park show adverse effects in the form of yellowed needles.[11] While the relatively good air here is refreshing, the pollution that does exist is a reminder that no wilderness is immune from our ill effects. Certainly, climate change makes the same worrisome point.

Desirable campsites like this one often appeal across cultures and generations, so a closer look around here would probably turn up signs of the Thorofare's previous inhabitants, the Sheep Eater Indians. At this elevation, the Sheep Eaters were mostly summer residents, the winters too cold and snowy; the surrounding low elevation basins were their winter abode. In summer, though, the lakeshore environment was a land of riches for them. Their namesake food source, bighorn sheep, was available in the nearby Absaroka Range, and in early summer cutthroat trout moving up the lake's tributary streams to spawn were easy prey. Dried in the summer sun, the meat from both would sustain them for months longer. Vegetable foods complemented the abundant protein sources. Tender greens like glacier lilies and spring beauties and the roots of both, along with other edible roots like yampa and biscuitroot, provided vitamins, fiber, and carbohydrates. As summer progressed, strawberries, gooseberries, raspberries, and other berries sweetened their larder, with pine nuts from whitebark and limber pines adding valuable fat some years (the trees do not always bear cones). Moving around the region, the Sheep Eaters established the fur trappers' thoroughfare and many of the other paths that became our modern-day trails and roads. Other tribes, including the Crow, Shoshone, Bannock, Blackfoot, and Flathead, followed these and other trails they (not the Sheep Eaters) made on their travels to and through the region. Far from being unknown, then, the Thorofare was a homeland and storehouse for many. However, the Native American hand on the land was relatively light here, especially compared with other areas like California, where a mild climate and abundance of year-round food sources allowed much denser and more permanent human habitation, along with the associated landscape-shaping effects. Hunting and gathering activities certainly had some effect on the landscape here, but compared to those of agriculture and, where possible, fire, such effects were small. The Sheep Eaters and other tribes, then, probably looked out on a landscape much like that greeting us today, a wilderness shaped by both human and natural forces, but dominated by the latter.[12]

In many ways, then, the Thorofare is a fairly untrammeled landscape. The Native American touch was gentle, as has been our impact. Exotic plants, logging, and air pollution are all, for the most part, absent or minimal, as are any lingering effects from Sheep Eater hunting and gathering. Moreover, some natural processes that are often prohibited elsewhere (even in wilderness areas), like burning from lightning-caused fires and predation by large carnivores, occur in the Thorofare, with minimal human manipulation. Certainly, the area is not completely untrammeled—few wildernesses are—but relative to most other wilderness areas, humans have done little to disturb nature and its processes here. Even if that were not the case, if the signature of humanity were heavier, the many qualifiers in the Wilderness Act definition of wilderness mean this land could still be considered wilderness. In short, the Thorofare is wild wilderness, about as untrammeled as may be found in the forty-eight contiguous states.

(

Mountains can be shrouded by something more benign and natural than pollution—clouds—as a look to the west reveals to us paddlers. Shortly, our sun disappears, so we throw extra layers of clothing on and shove off. Or rather, Sean and Josh help me shrug my way into an additional layer (my raincoat) because my arms and shoulders are too weak to do it myself, and then all three help me walk to the canoe, step over the gunwale, and sit down on the contrived seat. Then they pack drybags in around me (to serve as armrests), buckle on their life jackets, and push the boats in.

We are now at the south end of the arm, which widens out to about five miles across. As we paddle in and out of its bays, we notice dead trees at water's edge. Gray and weathered, some of them are practically in the water, a place ordinarily too wet for these trees. When they germinated, they were on dry ground, but Yellowstone's restless geology has submerged them enough to drown them. Under the lake's north end lies the Sour Creek Dome, one of two resurgent domes in Yellowstone, measuring several miles across. Over time, that dome has swollen with magma moving in below, pushing the ground surface up two or three feet in the last half century. With the lake's outlet right there, the uplifting dome has had the effect of tilting the lake southward, inundating and killing these trees.[13] They are mute sentinels of rapid geologic change, a unique attribute of this wilderness. Rarely is such dynamism so visible; it seems to enhance the wildness here.

☾

Dynamism is also becoming evident in our weather today, as the clouds have lowered and closed in around us, with sheets of rain falling in all directions (figure 2.6). Our liquid trail of glitter and blue has become a slate of gray, mirror to the blanket above. The temperature dropping, rain soon envelops us in its cold embrace. A fine mist turns into drizzle, the droplets lightly tinkling on the lake surface. We hunker down and paddle on, expecting it to last awhile, given the buildup we have been watching and the weather forecast. Yet, barely five minutes after it began, it tapers off. Our rain gear is barely wet, and the reprieve continues for the rest of the afternoon.

Such was not my fortune in 1993, when I first hiked through the Thorofare with Linda. Unable to get off work until October, we decided to gamble on good weather—snow is a virtual certainty if precipitation falls that time of the year—and took off on that long-sought hike. To reduce the risk of being caught out in a winter storm, I borrowed an NPS radio from work and lugged it along, tuning in to the weather forecast each evening. We enjoyed five cloudless days of glorious Indian summer weather, and then heard a chance of snow creep into the forecast for two days hence. The next day we hiked to the Southeast Arm amid a mix of

2.6: *Dark clouds threaten a chilling rain, 2014. Photo by Eric Compas. Used with permission.*

sun and clouds. Tuning in to the weather forecast that evening, we were mortified to hear that the chance of snow had become a winter storm warning with a prediction of eight to twelve inches of snow, starting the next day. Taking out the map, we saw that our intended route would take us above 9,000 feet and surely into the higher end of the expected snowfall amount. Eight inches of the white stuff would make hiking difficult enough; a foot, a life-threatening challenge. Casting about for other routes out, we saw that the lowest route still meant we had a tough two-day hike to the nearest road. Waiting out the storm here was an idea we quickly eliminated because more unsettled weather was predicted after this storm, so that left us little choice but to hurry out the two-day route. We prepared ourselves for an early and potentially snowy departure.

The next day dawned dry and cool but with a thick overcast. Not sure what to make of that, we hit the trail as quickly as possible. After an hour, we began to feel moisture in the air: a fine mist, perhaps the precursor to a wet, early season snow. After another hour, we passed the South Arm, where we paused for a quick snack. By then the mist had turned into a light rain—not snow, which was a mixed blessing, for rain would not obscure the trail, but it could penetrate even the best rain gear more readily than snow. That would not happen if, like most rain events in the Rockies, it tapered off after an hour or so. But if it persisted, a soaking could heighten the risk of hypothermia, especially at the temperatures we were looking at today, in the low forties.

Donning our rain gear and shouldering our packs, we resumed our westward trek, our goal being Heart Lake, about halfway out. We slogged onward, stopping after another hour of hiking at a dry spot under a subalpine fir to inhale a cold but much-needed lunch. Everything inside our packs was dry, but our legs below the knees were not, repetitively soaked by plants leaning over the trail, heavy with the rain loading. Our body cores, though, were still dry, and with the exertion of hiking, we were still warm. So, after finishing our bagels and gorp, we continued on, and so did the rain. Mile after mile that afternoon, we slipped and slid our way to Heart Lake, the trail now a muddy mess in the steady rain. We arrived at the lake around four o'clock soaked to the skin. Hypothermia now a real danger, we decided to mush on to the Heart Lake patrol cabin, another five miles around the lake. If the cabin were occupied, we would beg permission to dry out and warm up; if it were vacant, we would pull out my key and let ourselves in to do the same, gambling that any rangers who did arrive would take pity on their off-duty coworkers and let us share the refuge with them (off-duty rangers needed permission from the district ranger to use the patrol cabins, something that the exigencies of the day had precluded for us). As it turns out, no one was there, nor was anyone likely to come given the sodden conditions. We let ourselves in, kindled a fire in the woodstove, and opened our packs to pull out dry clothes. But almost all the contents were wet! The rain had persisted all afternoon, soaking into our packs, our rain gear, and (it seemed) our minds. Still, we each had some partially dry clothing, and the woodstove was warming the place up, so we would be OK. The forced march was over.

Overnight, the rain turned to snow, but only two inches had fallen by dawn. Putting on our now dry clothing and packs, we hiked out, three days early and with snow falling lightly the whole way. It continued to fall, off and on, for the next two weeks, switching over to rain at times. Indian summer had ended, along with our crash course in the risks of wilderness travel. Knowing what those risks were, we had prepared well; when one of those risks presented itself, we deployed our preparations and survived without mishap. Learning from that experience (and hiking more outside the park, where the radio and cabin key would not be useful), we took our next hike through the Thorofare in the summer, when all-day rains are rare. We had some thunderstorms on that hike, but the rain gear successfully mitigated the risk of getting too wet and cold.

Risk is inherent in wilderness travel, to varying degrees depending on one's activity, the particular wilderness area, and other factors. Involuntary risks—those that come with travel through a particular wilderness area, no matter one's activities—help define the character of a wilderness.[14] In the Thorofare, the higher probability of a summer thunderstorm compared with the Sierra Nevada means not only that

2.7. *Summer thunderstorms in the Absarokas: an element of wildness and source of beauty, 1998. Author photo.*

wilderness travelers here need to be prepared for rain (hiking without rain gear and a tent, as is common in the Sierra, is not advisable in the Rockies), but also that they are more likely to experience the natural power of thunder and lightning, not to mention the beauty of rainbows, thunderheads with the sun gilding their edges, and dramatic skies (figure 2.7). Such storms illustrate that forces more powerful than humans are at play here. They, and the risks they pose to our personal safety, add to the wildness of this area. They force us to prepare in advance, be observant as we travel, and recognize that we are not always in control.

☽

For now, the passing shower and ongoing threat of more rain remind me of the soaking wet day two decades ago, just as they remind my paddling partners of the risks we are taking today. The risks we are taking on this canoe trip are especially evident when we stop for lunch. Even though I am dry and have all but one of my layers on, I shiver occasionally, not having had the boost to my circulation that my partners have had from wielding the paddles (figure 2.8). I stay warm enough, but the near guarantee of more rain and chill makes our decision unanimous: tonight and tomorrow we will avail ourselves of the Trail Creek Cabin, adjacent to the campsite we had reserved for the next two nights. This time, we do not need to worry about being discovered, for Sean, concerned about the weather forecast, had called ahead and received permission to use it if we needed it. We will be glad he made that call.

After a final hour of paddling, we round a point and see the cabin nestled in a cove ahead of us. This cabin is one of ten backcountry "patrol cabins" or fire lookouts in the Yellowstone side of the Thorofare. The USFS has about the same number (including one owned by the Wyoming Game and Fish Department), spread much more thinly in the Teton and Washakie Wildernesses. The purpose of the fire lookouts (two in the Thorofare, on Mount Sheridan in Yellowstone and Huckleberry Mountain in the Teton Wilderness) is self-evident; the other cabins shelter rangers on patrol and work crews on assignment clearing and maintaining the sprawling trail network. Many of the cabins, including the one at Trail Creek, date from the early 1900s, and many of them

2.8. Josh, Sean, and the author enjoying a cold but welcome lunch, 2014. Photo by Eric Compas. Used with permission.

have a stable and/or horse corral nearby. They are located strategically, like this one at the jumping-off point for the Thorofare (Yellowstone rangers often travel by boat to it, trading paddles for boots at the cabin), and are usually a day's travel apart (by foot or horse). Today, both agencies depend heavily on them to administer the Thorofare, so they maintain them as the minimum tool necessary for that imposing job. Along with one stock bridge over the Yellowstone River in the Teton Wilderness, these cabins are the extent of significant human development in the Thorofare. There are minor trail improvements (like water bars to slow erosion) and a few research and monitoring stations (like remote weather stations), but otherwise the wilderness traveler will encounter less than one node of "development" per hundred square miles here, and those developments are entirely rustic architecture such as log cabins or A-frames that comport with their wilderness setting. As with most wilderness areas, then, the Thorofare is an undeveloped landscape, with nature the primary architect and engineer.

Letting ourselves into the cabin, we open the shutters and fire up the woodstove (figure 2.9). Soon its welcome heat dissipates the chill. We settle in for the evening, and an hour later, so does the rain. It is a chill rain, reminiscent of that October day many years ago, and like that rain, this one persists through the rest of the day. Despite the rain, though, our spirits are up. Being warm and dry certainly helps, but so does the knowledge that we have arrived at the edge of the Thorofare, this huge fastness so wild. As we saw on our journey today, the landscape itself suggested the elements necessary for wildness to be present. Natural forces like fire, herbivory, and predation dominate, doing more to shape the landscape than people do or have done. A rich and largely unaltered community of life is present, with the full complement of native flora and fauna and the countless interrelationships among them. Yellowstone's restless geology adds still another distinctive force. Human manipulations here have been modest at most, making the Thorofare largely untrammeled. Similarly, human development is so sparse it would fit on just five or ten of the area's sprawling 1.7 million acres. With over a thousand miles of trail and seventy-five miles of Yellowstone Lake shoreline, opportunities for traditional recreation—including solidifying our bonds with each other and with nature—are abundant, but human use is light, making solitude near universal. Finally, the fickle northern Rockies weather adds an element of risk that demands preparation and constant vigilance. The sum total of these attributes is wildness, the knowledge that we are just visitors here, the feeling that there are forces more powerful than our own at work in this place. As the authors of the Wilderness Act recognized and inscribed therein, all wilderness areas have such characteristics of wildness, such primal forces, to one degree or another (plus involuntary risk, which is not explicit in the Wilderness Act definition of wilderness). But here they do not just come alive, they veritably overwhelm the senses in a feast of wildness. Indeed, if one were to scale America's wilderness areas along a tame-to-wild continuum, the Thorofare would be far on the wild end, one of the wildest such areas in the forty-eight contiguous states. For that reason

2.9. *The Trail Creek Cabin, with its barn in the background, 2014. Affixed to the pole in front of the cabin is a solar panel for interior lighting. Photo by Eric Compas. Used with permission.*

and many more, wildness is the Thorofare's most precious resource, so much so that, to many who know the Thorofare, it is synonymous with the very word.

((

Wildness on a landscape scale like this is exceedingly rare in America today, with the great majority of our land given over to our works and working lands. Here, though, some Americans recognized early on that our works would only denigrate the landscape's most essential attribute. That understanding was by no means common to all of us, so much of the Thorofare story consists of struggles by those who managed it to safeguard the wildness they found here. Those efforts begin on the ground, in the day-to-day activities of the men and women assigned to patrol the Thorofare. Due at least in part (perhaps large part) to their actions, the area has been kept wild. Now that my paddling partners and I are ourselves using one of their tools—this cabin—it seems fitting to take a side trip through their protective efforts, tomorrow.

DAY 3 Keepers of the Thorofare

There are many wilderness patrol cabins in Yellowstone National Park, . . . but none of the[m] has quite the overwhelming power of the wilderness [as] around Thoroughfare where natural plant and animal life in such abundance reigns supreme with very little disturbance by the minor and temporary presence of man. —Curtis K. Skinner, n.d.

Familiar skies greet us as we awaken—overcast and gray. Last night's rain has moistened our world, but with no rain falling right now, the storm may be spent. Today is a layover day, ours to make of what we will. Over a breakfast of hot cereal, we decide to hang out here for a while, and if the rain holds off, to paddle over to the campsite we had reserved and enjoy the view from there in the afternoon.

Looking around the cabin, I see the collection of furniture and supplies typical for Yellowstone's patrol cabins and fire lookouts: two sets of bunk beds, a woodstove for cooking and another for heating, a small rustic table with even more rustic folding chairs, and some cabinets with canned food and cooking implements (figure 3.1). The familiar cabin smells are also present: firewood, wood smoke, wood stain—in other words, all things wood, a reflection of the cabin's connection to the surrounding forest. Many of the cabins also contain items of comfort, such as more supportive chairs, or other functional additions, such as the solar-powered lights in this one. Evoking the feelings that its users have for this cabin and its surroundings, it also has two stained glass windows high on either end. Designed by former Thorofare ranger Bob Jackson, each features a lesser-known but charismatic area resident: a cutthroat trout and a loon.

3.1. The author enjoying the warmth of the Trail Creek Cabin woodstove, 2014. Photo by Eric Compas. Used with permission.

The cabins remain tools of the wilderness management trade, as evidenced by the logbook for this cabin, which I spend the morning absorbed in. Everyone using the cabins is required to record their visit in the logbook, along with salient details about their travels and activities. Many also add wildlife sightings and personal stories and reflections. The logbook, then, becomes both a way to communicate to the next rangers using the cabin and also a history of the vicinity, a collection of stories about the cabin, its environs, and its users. Most of the entries are mundane, but there are often some memorable gems.

Reading this cabin's logbook, I see my own entry from 1993, the night before the epic walk in the rain. We had just come from the Thorofare Ranger Station and a breakfast of cheese crepes with Bob Jackson (exotic fare for two backpackers already tired of their oatmeal). About twelve miles by trail from this cabin, the Thorofare Ranger Station is the center of ranger activity in its namesake region, because it is staffed full time when the ground is not snow-covered (it is not, therefore, just a "patrol cabin"). A journey through its logbooks, along with some other first-person narratives (all held at the park's library and archives in Gardiner, Montana) gives us a window into the lives of the people working there and their efforts to protect the Thorofare. Stories are best told first-person (without being reworded), so the side trip that follows here is made up partly of unaltered stories from the logbooks and other first-person accounts. More than just a diversion, though, the trip also provides some insight into the motivations of those who guard the area, as well as evidence indicating that wildness is easily threatened, necessitating ongoing stewardship efforts.

☾

The first Thorofare cabin was probably built by army scouts in 1903 a mile or two west of its current location, between the Yellowstone River and its largest wilderness tributary, Thorofare Creek. That cabin lasted about ten years, after which scouts replaced it with a new one at the base of the Trident (its current location). That cabin stood for only about a year, destroyed by a bear between fall 1914 and spring 1915. It was quickly rebuilt, but in 1920 rangers converted it to a barn when they built the larger cabin still in use today next door (figures 3.2 and 3.3). About the larger cabin, the park's first NPS superintendent, Horace Albright, wrote: "A new cabin was built recently on Thoroughfare Creek in the southeast corner, designed to house two rangers who will be stationed there all winter. This cabin is built near the old cabin, which can be utilized as a stable, and is 16 x 30 feet in size, with two rooms." It was reconditioned in 1937, after a structural fire damaged much of the cabin's interior, and other times since.[1]

3.2. The Thorofare Ranger Station, with the Trident in the background, 2003. Author photo.

3.3. Rangers Mark Marschall, Gary Pollock, and Mike Pflaum clearing snow from the roof of the Thorofare Ranger Station, 1983. Rangers on winter patrol do this to prevent heavy snow loads from collapsing the roof. Photo by Jean Neutzel, courtesy of Mark Marschall. Used with permission.

Curtis Skinner was one of the rangers stationed at the Thorofare Ranger Station in that era. In addition to the lovely description of its setting (above), an essay he later wrote about the ranger station also provided a description of the cabin itself. It was an organic part of its surroundings—more than a casual glance suggested:

It was made almost entirely of logs and poles obtained from the nearby forest. It was approximately twenty five feet in length and fourteen in width with a partial partition to divide the cooking and living area from the bunk room. The roof was made of poles and a thick layer of meadow earth sod from which grasses and flowers and even young trees grew. Originally, the structure had only an earth floor, but eventually lodgepoles, hewed more or less flat on top, were installed over parts of the floor area. This improvement was never pursued to completion so that, at last account, a strip in the bedroom section some three or four feet wide remained hard-packed raw earth. This required frequent sprinkling of water to lay the dust. Eventually the pole and earth roof was removed and replaced with lumber covered with asphalt sheeting.

The structure had small windows all around. . . . A pit cellar was under the kitchen floor. Entry was through a trap door and down a vertical ladder.

The old building was equipped with wood-burning stove[s], which, as they rusted, were replaced with somewhat imporved [*sic*] designs. There was a small cupboard for dishes and most of the cooking utensils were hung alongside the stove from nails and spikes driven into the logs. Water was obtained from a nearby little mountain brook. Candles

in the early days provided night-time lighting. An outhouse and garbage pit in the nearby woods completed the living facilities.[2]

The NPS stationed rangers at the cabin most years, and as required,
those men and women (who entered the Thorofare workforce in the
1980s) filled the logbooks with their accomplishments and observa-
tions. For example, hardly a week passed without at least one mention
of time spent working on the corral fence. Were one to assume a direct
correlation between the number of times a task was mentioned in the
logbook and how much time was actually spent on it, repairing that
fence would easily have been their most frequent job. In reality, though,
they spent most of their time patrolling and clearing trails in the area
(figure 3.4), contacting visitors, and performing necessary upkeep on
the cabin itself.

Patrolling for poachers was probably the most serious of their re-
sponsibilities, and often their sole focus in the fall, when hunting season

*3.4. Ranger Mark Marschall on patrol in the Thorofare, 2010. Bridges are
uncommon here, so wilderness travelers must be prepared to ford rivers and
streams, as Marschall is about to do on the Yellowstone River. Even with horses,
fording in spring, when streams are murky and swollen with snowmelt, may
be the most dangerous part of a Thorofare ranger's job. Photo courtesy of Mark
Marschall. Used with permission.*

brought ardent trophy baggers to the national forests abutting the park. Here, in another essay about patrolling the Thorofare in winter, Skinner explains that poaching was a consistent problem:

By the 1930's many of the trappers and hunters engaged in these illegal practices had become too old to endure the hardships, and their sons, as they reached maturity, turned to less arduous, less risky and more profitable pursuits. Still, in the 1930's and 1940's, a few sure-enough poachers were apprehended within the park or pursued to their base outside and arrested there under authority of the "hot pursuit" clause. To mention only a few specific cases: Ranger Harry Trischman and others arrested a number of elk poachers along the north park boundary; Ranger John Jay tracked down and arrested an old time poacher who was trapping marten and other fur bearing animals in the Crags area of the West Yellowstone district; Ranger Jay and I tracked down and arrested elk hunters in the Mammoth district; and Rangers David Condon and Clyde Gilbert pursued two trappers from the remote Thoroughfare wilderness to their base near Moran, Wyoming, where they arrested them. These occasional arrests of trappers and hunters, together with the well known fact that rangers regularly patrolled the boundaries and interior sections, had an important deterring effect upon those trappers and hunters based outside the park.

Skinner went on to note that some of these poachers set up shop in the park, even building themselves small cabins or dugout man-caves to pursue their illegal activity.[3]

As Skinner suggests, poaching was nothing new. Indeed, it was a constant threat to the Thorofare's integrity, both in the park and in the neighboring national forest, as evidenced in a 1906 letter from the Teton National Forest Supervisor Robert Miller to Yellowstone's US Army Superintendent Major Pitcher:

I have reasons to believe that there will be poachers on the head waters of the Yellowstone, during the spring months, and would like to send a forest ranger in there, at intervals, on snow-shoes and want to ask if your cabin near the Park line is equiped [sic] for the ranger when in that locality, as it is very difficult to take supplies on snow-shoes to make the tour of the locality. I fully intended to build a cabin for this purpose during the past season but for lack of men and time, failed.[4]

Whether Miller got permission to use the cabin is not clear, but it is likely that he did, for a year later two men were brought to trial on charges of poaching in the park's side of the Thorofare, and it was a Forest Service ranger who gave the key testimony. A reporter for the *Pocatello Tribune* describes both Ranger Rudolph Rosencrans and the trial:

> He was brought to Pocatello to testify, reluctantly, not because he felt any sympathy for the accused men whom he had tracked relentlessly, but because he didn't want to leave his beloved Jackson Hole country for even a short time. . . . A remarkable character is Rudolph Rosencrans— he had trailed through the cloud-kissed Tetons, ever on the lookout for forest fires and poachers, extinguishing the one and arresting the others. No more efficient ranger ever threw a diamond hitch and a handier man on webs or skis with legs like a Hercules, clad in khakis, wide of shoulder, deep of chest, bearded like a bard because men do not shave who live in the Tetons—such is the man who tracked Purdy and Binkley [the two poachers]. For three years Rosencrans has dedicated his life to the breaking up of this gang of law breakers. The arrest and conviction marks the beginning of the end of a great work in this direction. Such is the man who tracked Binkley and Purdy in the Park and discovered evidence that landed them in a Federal prison.

Rosencrans was the manly superhero and the bad guys got their due but, down among the mere mortals, poaching continued, so the Forest Service soon built its own cabin in the Thorofare at Hawk's Rest, about three miles south of the Thorofare Ranger Station. Just as NPS rangers did in the Yellowstone side of the Thorofare, USFS rangers used the Hawk's Rest cabin (and a few others) as their base for patrolling and protecting the Teton Wilderness, while their colleagues did the same for the Washakie Wilderness (but without the benefit of a centrally located cabin there).[5]

Poaching remains a problem today. Every fall, the NPS attempts to staff the ranger station full time in September and October and sometimes into November. Some years like 1955 prove uneventful, but other years like 1958 prove the worth of having rangers on patrol in the Thorofare. That October, Thorofare ranger Bert McLaren spent five days following up on a tip that an outfitter had left bait on the boundary line to lure elk out of the park for his clients. McLaren not only found the bait station, but also three dead elk, all actually inside the park (as much as three-quarters of a mile in; if an animal is shot outside the park but moves into the park and dies there, the hunter may not retrieve it without poaching). McLaren soon identified and cited the responsible hunter and guide.[6]

Working in this wild place came with definite risks, from poachers, from the native fauna, and from many other things, like weather. In the cabin logbook, Ranger Dave Phillips writes about a 1975 nighttime visit from one of the area's most fearsome large residents:

Early entry—

04:30—Awakened by the screen door swinging and the top being ripped, followed by the front door creaking (hinges, latch, bolt, et al.) as if something was leaning and/or pushing on it (something *big*)—activity then ceased at door and began at southeast (east kitchen) window. It was smashed in, screen and all—

During commotion, I was reaching for flashlight, then gun, and yelling (shouting, cursing) in ever-increasing volume—the smashing window sounded as if something had landed in on the kitchen floor—

Ten minutes later a mouse sprang one of the mouse traps—that mouse trap probably had the most startling effect of any mouse trap in history!

In *broad* daylight, checked for tracks—found tracks . . . coming in from creek, but couldn't tell from which direction it had come—then found several clear tracks in corral . . . grizzly, measuring 10" from tip of toe pad to back of heel. (emphasis original).[7]

Phillips went on to note that he slept poorly the next night, but the bear did not make a repeat visit. That was indeed a large bear, and while bears are often seen in the Thorofare, nighttime visits from them are unusual. Many patrol cabins bear grizzly claw marks, indicating that bears have tried to get into them, but Phillips is one of the few who were present when one tried.

The Thorofare Ranger Station has had many other visitors of the bipedal variety, among them Bob Marshall, who signed the logbook when he visited the area in August 1939. Marshall, for whom the large wilderness area in Montana is named, was a legendary hiker, often putting thirty or forty miles on his feet in one day. One of the founders of The Wilderness Society, he was influential in the movement to protect roadless, wild areas of federal land as wilderness. Twenty-five years after his premature death by heart attack at age thirty-eight (which struck him just three months after his Thorofare visit), the movement he helped start culminated in the passage of the Wilderness Act, in 1964. Both the Washakie and Teton Wildernesses were included in the 1964 act, making them some of the first established in the country, a recognition of their exceptional character. Bob Marshall's legacy looms large at the Thorofare Ranger Station, in its wilderness neighbors, and in "the Bob" in Montana (the Bob Marshall Wilderness).[8]

Another Thorofare visitor was a man of less renown, an outlaw given the mysterious moniker "Tarzan of the Teton." The fall before Marshall visited, this shadowy fellow stole a saddle, blanket, chaps, and a few other things that ranger Frank Kowski had left on the cabin porch one day. In their place was a note saying that the perpetrator could not be tracked because he covered his soles with fabric. Looking around anyway, Kowski found the saddle and the remains of a tiny campfire near the cabin. Evidently, the same thief had also stolen some food from the Cabin Creek Cabin (a day's hike to the north and about midway between the Thorofare and Trail Creek cabins), where he had left a half pot of coffee. Shortly thereafter, a Wyoming man sought by the Cody police for murder was reported walking near Pahaska Tepee, near the park's East Entrance. Newspaper stories dubbed him Tarzan of the Teton, and he remained at large for a while. He eventually was shot down attempting to rob a Wyoming bank.[9]

Not all visitors were so mysterious, although they might have been equally rare, at least until gender roles loosened: women. Alone for long periods, Thorofare rangers generally mentioned any visitors in the logbook, but women merited special attention. This amusing account of a surprise encounter between Rangers Lee Shrum and Ralph Kirby and two women in 1940 comes to us from the ranger station logbook:

> After coming off the Trident we met the Elk Horn ranch outfit on Bridger Lake. In leaving the guide and starting on the trail home, Kirby and I saw a most *spectacular* sight. Two Dude gals were down on the Lake bathing. We rode right on to them before we saw them and I am afraid we were [none] too modest in our laughing. In fact it was fortunate that I carried a lariat as I just caught Kirby by the hind leg as he reached the shore. The girls gave off the usual modest screams and scrambled for articles of clothing. After controlling Kirby we rode back

on home. However Kirby bellowed and pawed all the way. No doubt he has been here too long. (emphasis original).

Assignments to the Thorofare could be weeks or even months in duration—too long for some, as suggested by Shrum's biped coworker.[10]

At least three women were more than just visitors. In his essay about the ranger station, Curtis Skinner writes about a ranger who brought his wife there for the summer:

> One summer in the 1930's, a new ranger recruit David Condon was assigned to the Thoroughfare wilderness. He was equipped with saddle and pack horses and his young bride Lorna, who I believe to have been the first and last lady to keep house for a summer at this wilderness station. If you happened to ride up that way in July or August you would come out of the forest and see this old mountain cabin with its silvery asphalt roof, green and uncluttered yard and glistening glass windows adorned with bright pressed burlap drapes. Upon inquiry, you would learn that the drapes were fresh hand made from burlap grain sacks. Veteran old-time ranger Harry Trischman, upon learning of the window drapery and sparkling glass windows, commented: "Leave a lady

3.5. Rangers Colette Daigle Berg and Barb Pflaum embarking on a winter patrol of the Thorofare, March, 1983. As is typical of such trips, they left from the Lake Ranger Station, skiing across Yellowstone Lake (shown here, with Stevenson Island in the background) to the lake's eastern shore and then by trail to the Thorofare Ranger Station, staying in patrol cabins along the way. (On such ski trips, they were not required to wear the NPS uniform.) Photo by Mike Pflaum, courtesy of Mark Marschall. Used with permission.

in one of these old cabins for a summer and in no time it won't look like it did."

And that, perhaps, was a good thing. By the 1980s and 1990s, it was no longer unusual to see women in the Thorofare sporting a National Park Service badge, uniform, and sidearm (figure 3.5).[11]

The second woman also spent the summer assisting her husband, in the southwestern corner of what is now the Teton Wilderness. She was Margaret "Mardy" Murie, and her husband was Olaus Murie, a wildlife biologist working on a study of elk in the Jackson Hole area. For the entire summer of 1929, she tended their camp on Whetstone Creek while Olaus and two teenage boys spending the summer with them did the necessary fieldwork.[12] Along with Olaus's mother (the third woman), Mardy did the cooking and washing and looked after the couple's two young children, Martin and Joanne. Mardy reveled in her job and the place, eventually including a chapter about that summer in a memoir of their time in Jackson Hole. The pleasures of that summer in the Thorofare wilderness come alive in these passages from her writing:

> My memory of the summer is studded with such items as 17 pounds of peanut butter, rice pudding cooked over the campfire in a small-size dishpan, and the two boys tossing a coin to see who got the last remaining piece of cake with chocolate sauce on it, which was a very special treat, the cake being baked with watchful care in our Yukon stove in the tent.
>
> But the memory is also bright with the unfailing good nature and willingness and curiosity of those boys, their real interest in the children, their whistling about camp and singing about the campfire, their eagerness to hear all of Olaus's stories about animals and adventure, and to help him in his work. . . .
>
> I stood a moment looking across the meadow [in which they were camped] to the low hills on the opposite side, beyond Whetsone [sic] Creek. Above the ranks of dark evergreen and lighter aspen, one flat-topped ridge dropped steeply to the forest in a bold scree of naked gravel, warm brown in color, and on this the setting sun behind our camp was casting its brilliant light, turning the brown into gold. Olaus and the boys (hungry, I knew!) were walking back through the tall green meadow grasses and bright flowers. Time to wash up, to gather about the fire for food and talk. It was a quiet golden moment. We had arrived safely. Martin came running: "Look, Mommy, here's a rock that's all red!" . . .

This was the pattern of our days on Whetstone Creek; this was the kind of adventure that punctuated the pattern. Most of them were happy episodes. I remember Martin and Joanne squealing with delight as Olaus stood them in the shallow part of the little creek, where the water was warmed by the hot mountain sunshine, and soaped them and scrubbed them and rinsed them—a hilarious game. I remember hot days of July when we sought the shade of the trees or the tents and many camp chores were left to the cool of the long evenings, and when the wild strawberries ripened and Grandma and the children went happily stooping and crawling through the grass out in the meadow to gather them. Then I would bake some biscuit, we would mash the berries through a little sieve, since they were too tiny to hull, and that evening we would have strawberry shortcake.

An idyllic time it was indeed.[13]

Both the Muries went on to become leaders in the multi-decade effort to pass the Wilderness Act. Mardy, in fact, was present when President Lyndon Johnson signed the bill into law (Olaus died in 1963). In 1998, at the age of ninety-six, Mardy shook the hand of another American president, Bill Clinton, when he awarded her the Presidential Medal of Freedom, the country's highest civilian honor. She deserved it; by then the national wilderness preservation system that she had helped foster had grown to over one hundred million acres. All of us who enjoy our own idyllic time in wilderness—or merely take delight in knowing that there is still a place in the contiguous states some twenty miles from a road—owe her, her husband Olaus, Bob Marshall, and many other wilderness preservationists a huge debt of gratitude.[14]

Dedication to the protection of the Thorofare is a common theme in the writings, male or female, NPS or USFS, about time spent in this place. This, despite low pay (or none at all), long hours, risks to personal safety, and the discomforts of sunburn, heat, cold, biting insects, flimsy mattresses, and many other privations. Through it all, many writers and rangers managed to keep a sense of humor; consider this Thorofare logbook entry by Ranger Terry Small:

Despite mosquitoes Terry Small and Joe Maxson made it most of the way to Thorofare without mention of trouble. It was not until we were within .5 of a mile from the Ranger Station that we did have trouble. Because mother nature had decided to reroute Escarpment Creek from the lovely creekbed to the man-made trail, we suddenly found ourselves embedded in a world of mud. All the animals (Brownie, Erwin, Ellie, Punkin and Kip) were stomach deep in it with no dry ground in sight (ironically most of it looked dry but was oozy bog two inches below the surface). All animals were down. We unsaddled all but Brownie and Erwin, since they were the strongest [and they] fought their way to dry ground. Finally, after unpacking the mules and unsaddling Kip we managed to move the[m] to a more substantial location. Then leading them one at a time to the cabin, where we found help from Keith Neal and his trail crew.

We managed to survive the mud bath. And through all that only two of 36 eggs were broken.

The crew later diverted the creek back within its streambed, drying up the trail. For them, this was all in a day's work, and the Thorofare and its users are the better for it.[15]

☾

Back at Trail Creek, by late morning it seems the détente in the weather is going to hold, for rather than seeing rain return, we have actually seen a few fleeting peeks of the sun. We gather our lunch and a few extra layers and head out to relax at the campsite we had reserved for these two nights. Only a quarter mile from the cabin, the campsite looks south to the Thorofare, where the cabin looks north and up the Southeast Arm. Additionally, the campsite is on a small rise, providing a more commanding view than that from the cabin. It is a view I have enjoyed several times, most recently with Eric, on our circumnavigation of the lake eleven years ago.

We end up soaking up that view all afternoon (figure 3.6). Across the bay at the south end of the Southeast Arm stretch the willow-studded flatlands of the Yellowstone River delta. After that river tumbles off Younts Peak and flows into the park (not far from the Thorofare Ranger Station), it becomes alluvial, meandering back and forth across its three-mile-wide valley before becoming part of Yellowstone Lake. Rising above the river and its delta are the Absaroka peaks, marching off to the south in a progression of taller peaks and loftier plateaus, giant stepping-stones in the sky leading to the remotest point. They are mostly out of the clouds now, although the overcast above them persists

3.6. Sean and the author enjoying a view of fresh snow on the Absaroka Mountains, August 2014. Photo by Eric Compas. Used with permission.

all afternoon. An occasional shaft of sunlight breaks through, though, spotlighting a distant cliff or patch of forest and hinting at the weather to come.

With the overcast, the temperature hovers only in the upper forties, keeping us in down coats and wool caps. The cool air is still and dry, with occasional wafts of dampness and pine needles, a reminder of the wet night now history. Accentuating the cold air is the white on the peaks—snow that fell overnight, down to about 9,000 feet. Virtually at our doorstep, the snow is a very visible reminder that here on the Yellowstone Plateau, winter is never far away. Everyone who lives and works here knows that, and once they spend a winter here they see hints of it everywhere they look: in the treeless lines extending down from peaks and cliffs (avalanche scars), the preponderance of lodgepole pines, spruce, and fir (all adapted to snow by the foot and subzero cold), and the gangly legs of moose (for striding through all that snow).

Few of Yellowstone's veterans better understand winter's primacy here than the rangers who have spent time on skis or snowshoes in this winter wilderness: those who have passed through on patrol, and especially those hardy few who have overwintered at the Thorofare Ranger Station. Several of these men gave oral histories or wrote their own accounts of their experiences in a Thorofare made cold, snowy, and dark by its six-month-long winters. In those stories, some of which follow, the passion and grit of the winter rangers shine as bright as snow in the winter sunshine. So does the area's beauty and wildness.

Curtis Skinner, who himself spent many a winter night in the Thorofare, provides a nice introduction to winter here in his essay about winter in the Thorofare:

> Over the years two park rangers were sometimes assigned to this station as a winter patrol base. At other times, rangers based at Yellowstone Lake Ranger Station patrolled the Thoroughfare country. Some of the last rangers to winter at this isolated post were Frank Childs and John Jay during the winter of 1930–31; and Maynard Bafrows and George Walker for the winter of 1932–33. Ranger John Jay in a taped interview made in 1962 described the old Thoroughfare cabin in these words: "It had a huge log floor which lacked about three feet of reaching to the walls. We did not have time to chink it very well before winter came, and several times during the winter when it was real windy and blowing snow through the cracks we would pack snow between the logs and throw water on it. Then it would freeze suddenly. That would last several days until we would get warmer weather which would melt our chinking. Then we would have to do it over again."

Eventually the floor was completed, but the need to be resourceful at that remote duty station has remained as constant as the snows in January.[16]

Ranger John Jay and Frank Childs were the main characters in another story about being snowbound, this one by a writer for the *Union Pacific Magazine*. Here we learn one way that they coped with the winter isolation:

> They are wholly isolated from the rest of the world except that which comes in via the radio. To go from the Thoroughfare station to park headquarters means a two-hundred-mile round trip, which would take thirteen or fourteen days of hard skiing.
>
> In their cozy cabin hemmed in by the deep snow, John Jay and Frank Childs hobnob with all the latest news of the world that filters in through the peanut tubes of their radio set. While the flames roar in the heating stove and the cold crackles at sixty below outside, they sit after a long day's patrol and listen to an opera coming from New

York City. On snowy afternoons they hear a football game when their alma maters clash on the gridiron, for the two rangers hail from rival Colorado schools and many a lengthy argument shortens long winter evenings. . . .

Going out for the mail is one of the high spots of each month. Childs has a police dog called "Duke" which he has trained to pull a small sled carrying the outgoing mail and hauling in mail and radio batteries and the like.

In today's world, where we even have cell phone reception at Trail Creek, it is hard to imagine being out of touch for weeks on end. Indeed, Jay and Childs must surely have treasured the letters they received in their mail.[17] Interviewed many years later, Jay spoke more about dealing with cabin fever:

Where you live alone with one person all winter, little things bother you. You don't like the way he smokes his pipe; he doesn't like the way you do most anything. Frank and I had little touches of cabin fever but not too serious. You are dependent upon the other man to a large extent, so you can not go too far with this. You may not speak to him for a week or two, but generally the feeling is, after you get out of the isolation in the spring, the majority of men end up being the best of friends; and Frank Childs and I are the very best of friends to this day, after some 32 years ago.[18]

Jay also spoke about Childs's dog; reading this account, we see that the pet probably furthered the friendship that was already developing between the two rangers:

Frank did accept a dog that winter from the hunters outside, a large German police dog, that turned out to be a bit of a problem before the winter was over; meaning by that that the dog preferred to sleep on top of my bed, which he did all winter except for one morning I woke up with a mouthful of dog hairs, and I said, "Frank, that's your dog, and from now on you tell that dog to sleep on your bed." Well, Frank made an effort: he talked to Duke (the dog's name) that night. Frank had a canvas tarp on his bed and I had what we called a soft sugan on mine. The dog stayed on the bed until the light of the old Coleman lantern started to flicker out. I am watching the dog and he is actually watching my bed too, and about the time Frank is asleep he tip[toe]s or sneaks across the floor and back up on my bed, and he stayed with me the rest of the winter.

One can envision the smile on Jay's face as he related that story.[19]

Knowing they would be snowbound for the winter, the two provisioned the cabin for the winter by boating supplies into Trail Creek and then packing them by mule the rest of the way to the Thorofare cabin, where they filled up the cellar. Done before the snow flew, this system worked for dry and canned goods, but not for meat (all fruits and vegetables would have been canned). In that same interview, Jay explained how they solved this problem:

> The rangers were not allowed to hunt outside the park at that time and bring their meat in. Our nearest source of supply was 100 miles away either at Mammoth or West Yellowstone, and it would have been impossible to bring fresh meat in and keep it all winter. So they allowed us to accept meat from the hunters who did hunt outside, and they gave us . . . part of a moose, and some elk meat; no deer that winter, we were sorry we didn't get any deer given to us. And we put that in a box built out of screen wire, that Frank had hung up in a tree, and we lived on moose and elk all winter . . . just [in] an outside freezer; the temperature there predominantly cold, so that keeping it in the box outside it would keep all winter. We did run short on some other things, but we got by all right.

Still, it is a safe bet that their first meal once they returned to civilization featured whatever fresh foods were available.[20]

To go anywhere beyond the ranger station meant strapping on skis or snowshoes. In his winter essay, Curtis Skinner recalls that this was not an activity to be undertaken lightly:

> While nowadays skiing is widely regarded as an enjoyable sport, with millions invested in snow-packed slopes and trailways, the early patrolling in Yellowstone was, with few exceptions, a laborious undertaking. Winter snow, due primarily to sustained sub-zero temperatures and practically no thawing, just piles up day after day and week after week into a granulated fluff with little settlement until late March or April. Heaviest snowfall accumulates across the southern part of the park where the western wind-driven storms dump their snow loads. . . . Thus, where the northern portion of the park may have maximum snow depths of four or five feet, areas in the southern section will have ten feet or more.
>
> Because of prevailing deep loose snow, scouts back in the Army days of park protection devised and used a specially manufactured wide and long ski which was adopted by the early day park rangers. These skis

were manufactured by the Strand Company and usually measured a full four inches in width and eight or nine feet, sometimes longer, in length. But, even with these large weight-bearing surfaces, skis would sink ten or twelve inches in the unpacked snow and in extreme cases of continuous snowfall they would sink to a laborious depth of eighteen inches or more, or just below the kneecaps. Under these conditions, the skis would tend to go deeper and deeper. Snow from the sides of the trench would slide down on top of the skis and it would be necessary for the skier to back up a pace or two, incline the skis up front as much as possible, then go forward again for a disgustingly short distance. In extreme cases, this maneuver had to be repeated again and again, so that the speed of travel would sometimes be less than a mile per hour. . . .

In such loose snow, when two rangers traveled together, one would break trail for fifteen minutes or so, then step aside and the man from the rear would take his turn at the heavy work up front. We sometimes called this deep breaking stuff *wallowing the trail* and the man in the rear was *riding the buggy*. Until the snow finally settled, usually sometime in March, ski and snowshoe travel was extremely slow and laborious." (emphasis original).[21]

One suspects that "floundering" and "exhausting" were considered substitutes for the word "wallowing." Whatever the descriptor, there was no other way to patrol for poachers, and such was the reason the NPS stationed rangers there. Animal pelts were most valuable when the fur was long and luxurious, so poaching was most commonly pursued in the winter. Here is the writer for the *Union Pacific Magazine* again, describing such winter patrols:

Patrols take up the major portion of the rangers' time. On the patrols, which they make together, they are gone from their station from six to twelve days. They travel on skis with packs on their backs and spend the nights in shelter cabins or as they call them, "snowshoe cabins" which are located from ten to eighteen miles apart on the patrol. On these patrols the rangers note carefully the condition of animals wintering in their district, study the snowfall, and guard their district against poachers.

Blizzards, extreme cold of fifty to sixty degrees below zero, hard hills to climb, two feet of fresh snow to break trail through, a broken ski binder and blistered heels are all in the day's work when on patrol. Sometimes an unexpected bath in a river is the result of a wild ride. (figure 3.7).[22]

3.7. Rangers Mike Pflaum and Mark Marschall enjoy a view of the Trident while on winter ski patrol in the Thorofare, 1983. At their feet is the frozen Yellowstone River. Photo by Barb Pflaum, courtesy of Mark Marschall. Used with permission.

Providing a more detailed glimpse at the rigors involved in such patrols is Ranger Harry V. Reynolds Jr., who did a two-week patrol by ski through the Thorofare with fellow rangers Nathaniel Lacy and Delmar Peterson in 1956. Reporting on the trip afterward, Reynolds wrote that temperatures never got above freezing, varying from twenty-eight above to thirty-nine below zero. Snow fell every day but one: "Unprecedented depth of snow and new, blowing snow covered or obliterated most trail signs; therefore, the patrol traveled crosscountry without the advantages of a marked trail. Visibility varied from poor to zero, necessitating use of the compass during most of the ski travel." Snow depths varied from forty-two inches at Park Point (a day's journey north of Cabin Creek) to ninety-five inches at Fox Creek (a day's journey west of the Thorofare Ranger Station), with that at Thorofare rising from sixty-five inches when they arrived to eighty-two when they left. They skied a minimum of eight miles every day but one, with one day being sixteen miles and another eighteen. Their skiing pace perhaps provides the best indication of their traveling difficulty, for on only two days did they top out at two miles per hour (on dry ground, most people walk two to three miles per hour). Their average speed was only 1.3 miles per hour because the trek over Big Game Ridge slowed them down considerably; it took them twenty-six hours to ski the twenty-three miles up and over it.[23]

After presenting these details—which are impressive enough—Reynolds went on to include a lengthy narrative in his formal report of that trip. The challenges that he and his partners faced on that epic journey come alive in his account. Here it is in its entirety:

> Storms attaining blizzard proportions had haunted us from the first day of the ski patrol into Thorofare. Snow accompanied by high winds dogged our travel, often reducing visibility to zero and necessitating frequent use of the compass. Depth of snow was at an unprecedented level. In most instances, all sign of the trail was obliterated, so we found it more practical to select our own route rather than to waste time and effort in locating trail markers.
>
> On the morning of March 4, we were up and about the Thorofare Ranger Station at 4 a.m. We departed the cabin at dawn in a light snow, breaking about 10 inches of new, wet snow. We traveled the four miles across the open meadows of Thorofare Creek and Upper Yellowstone River on a computed compass bearing, before reaching the protection of the timber at the mouth of Lynx Creek.
>
> Winds by this time had attained gale proportions, and the snow had increased in intensity. At this inopportune moment, one of Nat's toe irons broke completely free from one ski. The heavy snow and force exerted while he was breaking trail had been too much for the binding. After field repair and delay of an hour, we continued the long, steady climb toward the Continental Divide at the head of Lynx Creek.
>
> As our route increased in elevation, the breaking depth of snow on our trail increased until it was above our knees; consequently, our pace diminished. Gusts of wind whipped the surrounding trees, so that the falling snow not only literally blinded us but pervaded every opening and seam in our clothing and body. However, we pressed doggedly onward. By three o'clock, we had climbed to 9,000 feet in elevation, but were at least six hours from our destination at Fox Creek. Realizing the foolhardiness of spending a night under the trees at that elevation, with our upper clothing wet to our skin, we reluctantly turned back toward Thorofare. We arrived at the cabin after dark, weary, but ready to try again the following morning.
>
> However, the storm continued throughout the night and into the following day, increasing the snow depth to 82 inches at the cabin. Impatient to continue on our travel schedule, we reconciled ourselves

to wait until another day for the storm to abate and the new snow to settle. While snowbound in the cabin, we rechecked our equipment and repaired Nat's broken binding with a door hinge.

Upon reaching the upper limits of Lynx Creek on the following day, we inadvertently took the main drainage rather than veering to the northwest. We crossed the Continental Divide at a higher elevation than the trail route, through an open pass assumed to be near the theoretical east-west line of the park boundary. This pass led into the upper drainage of the Snake River . . . , which we followed in a southwest direction to Fox Park, thence to the Fox Creek patrol cabin. It was a long, tough day, and we didn't arrive at the cabin until an hour after dark. The cabin was almost completely covered with snow, except for a narrow space at the ridge line on the front or windward side.

Although the Divide was behind us now, we realized that the real test of the trip lay ahead over Big Game Ridge. That night the skies cleared and the temperature dropped; someone later said it was minus 28 degrees at Snake River Ranger Station that night. We believed that this was a good omen, as we had hoped for better visibility. We had previously considered two alternate routes to Harebell in event the storm had continued; one south of the park line via Wolverine Creek, and the other along the Snake River. However, the improvement in weather conditions invited us to attempt the shorter but more difficult route along the park boundary.

We were on our way shortly after dawn, with the towering ramparts of Mt. Hancock and Big Game Ridge gleaming ahead in the sunlight. We hadn't traveled far when the first in a chain of misfortunes was encountered when Nat suffered a severe muscle cramp in his right thigh. We adjusted our pack loads and placed him in the rear of the ski track for observation, so that he would have the advantage of the broken trail until the cramp became relaxed. Naturally, we considered turning back to Fox Creek, but Nat was game and stoutly maintained that he could continue. Our progress was necessarily slow up the long, tortuous ascent of the eastern slopes, and it was two o'clock before we reached the eastern limits of Big Game Ridge.

From this point, it was only 1.5 miles straight-line distance to the western edge of the ridge and the downward slope into Harebell cabin.

Just at this time, we observed weather moving in rapidly from all directions. Not realizing the duration or intensity of this new storm, we started across the exposed ridge toward the security of the timber at the head of Harebell Creek. Within an hour we were in the midst of a full-fledged, howling blizzard. Approximating 10,000 feet in elevation, snow was no longer snow, but ice. Our pathway was continually obstructed by deep snow couloirs, oriented north-south, perpendicular to our route of travel. Some of these necessitated detours of half a mile or more, forming a veritable labyrinth of confusing passages. We used our climbers to maintain balance and a foothold on the ice. We even tried removing our skis and traveling on foot, but this did not prove practicable. Cornices were 25–30 feet in height; others faced abysses of several hundred feet on the north shoulders of Mt. Hancock. Deep holes measuring 10–25 feet in depth pitted the exposed areas, scoured out of the snow and ice by the high winds. Half blinded by the whipping ice crystals, numb with cold, and lacking perspective [*sic*] because of the flat light and blowing ground ice and snow, it became increasingly difficult to avoid these pitfalls. The mounting wind increased in velocity to 100 miles per hour, but by this time it was as safe to keep going as it would have been to turn back. Naturally, we were aware that even a trivial mishap under these conditions could have fatal consequences. Well clothed and equipped, yet we could not have survived more than a few hours if we had been delayed for an injury to one of our party. Finally, it grew dark, and we were still moving westward, picking our way slowly over the irregular terrain.

Approaching the western limits of the ridge, we were forced by the topography onto the north-facing cornices, overhanging concealed depths above the swirling mists. As darkness increased, our predicament became even more grave. We moved cautiously forward, testing the route ahead with an extended ski pole.

Losing hope of locating the drainage to Harebell in the darkness, our objective turned to reaching the protection of the timber. Traversing the western flank of Mt. Hancock, we eventually dropped over a combing ridge line into a steep drainage offering shelter and fuel for the night. There we located a small fir stand on a steep slope, and prepared ourselves for the long night. It was two hours after dark, more than six hours after starting across the ridge.

We dug a snow cave into the uphill slope under the trees, placing a fire on a floater of green logs. Busily occupied with these duties, it was 2 a.m. before we completed our bivouac and were able to stand back, enjoy the fire, and wait for a new day. Of course, we endured an uncomfortable night, but we were sheltered from the full force of the wind and snow. Each of us was supplied with emergency rations, including pemmican for sustenance.

It was still blowing and snowing vigorously at daylight. Without avail, we waited until 8 o'clock in hope the visibility would improve.

Considering it impractical to climb back to the top of the ridge to get on course, we descended into the bottom of the drainage, which appeared to be oriented in an east-west direction. We realized that the drainage wasn't Harebell Creek, but hoped it would prove to be an upper fork; at least, it must flow ultimately into the Snake River.

The terrain was so steep and avalanche conditions so severe that we literally had to pick our way down the 1,500-foot slope, taking over two hours to make the descent. At first, the V-drainage followed a western course, then gradually turned south. As expected, we came out of the wooded area two hours later into Wolverine Meadows.

Impeded by heavy snow and violent winds, and generally weakened by exposure, we did not reach the mouth of Harebell Creek until shortly before dark. Darkness overtook us before we had traveled halfway up the hill to the cabin. It was still snowing. As time passed, we each silently became resigned to spend another night under the trees because of the unlikelihood of locating the cabin under the existing conditions. However, we did find the cabin at 9:30 that night, by inadvertently stumbling across the top of the stovepipe. We had fully expected to see the eaves and some of the upper logwork of the cabin exposed, but found it completely covered with snow. No shelter ever looked better to three tired and hungry park rangers!

The remainder of our trek was anticlimax. We reached Snake River Ranger Station the following night after dark; then home two days later. A final inventory disclosed that none of us was the worse for wear, except for frostnipped fingers and toes.

So much for an interesting but harrowing experience.

An understatement indeed.[24]

Reynolds recorded part of that same trip in the Thorofare Ranger Station logbook. On the morning of March 4, as they left for their first attempt going up Lynx Creek and across the Two Ocean Plateau, he penned, "Here we go / in 75" of snow / Where we'll stop / we don't know." Two days later, as they departed for their second attempt, his ditty became, "Here we go again; / Return we know not when. / Temperature at 27 below. / Thorofare, goodbye; Snake River, hello!" Of course, the three of them were in for quite the adventure before they would be greeting the rangers at Snake River, but the lighthearted acceptance of truly challenging duties is again obvious.[25]

According to Curtis Skinner, because of their night out on Big Game Ridge, Reynolds and his two companions were inducted into a tongue-in-cheek organization known as the "Amalgamated Order of Mountain Men." Skinner explains in his winter essay,

> Anybody who was caught out on one of these trips and had to sleep without blankets or food was eligible for membership. Sometimes it was difficult for us to find out who did such things because they weren't about to admit that they got caught out overnight. Whenever we learned that somebody did sleep out overnight under these forced conditions, we enrolled him in the order, and there were quite a number of them. Recalling a few, besides myself, there were John W. Jay, Frank H. Anderson, Rudolph L. Grimm, Lee L. Coleman and, of course, veteran rangers Harry Trischman and Joe Douglas. There were others.

With its punishing means of induction, rangers were probably not standing in line to get in, but after their night out, Reynolds and company certainly earned their membership (figure 3.8).[26]

3.8: Ranger Barb Pflaum skis below Turret Peak, 1983. Pflaum, enjoying obviously better weather than Reynolds and his two companions did, took part in the NPS tradition of Thorofare ski patrols that continues to this day. Photo by Mike Pflaum, courtesy of Mark Marschall. Used with permission.

❨

Back at Trail Creek, the afternoon is waning and our stomachs are starting to growl, so we head back to the cabin. Enjoying its warmth, we feast on tortellini, and then notice it getting brighter outside, not darker. A quick look out the window revealed a sight Reynolds and his companions would have given dearly for: clearing skies. We finish our last few bites and scramble outside to watch the sunset (figure 3.9). So many clouds have parted that the setting sun highlights the peaks, turning the snow to shades of orange and pink, and the bare cliffs and escarpments of volcanic rock to hints of red. One by one, the peaks lose their illumination until our world is nothing but shadow.

The sunset was a fitting ending for a remarkable day. The afternoon at the campsite, gazing into the Thorofare's wild heart, shafts of sun occasionally spotlighting a cliff face or stand of trees, would end up becoming one of the three most memorable, relaxing experiences of the entire trip. Heading in for the night, I understood the feelings that Skinner wrote of the Thorofare cabin and its "power of wilderness". Years after he wrote those words, his colleague Bob Murphy expressed similar feelings when he visited Thorofare one last time in 1996, at the age of eighty-eight: "It's the same great expanse of real wilderness . . . still really the same cherished opportunity." Indeed—thanks to his own efforts and those of his fellow rangers, both NPS and USFS, over several generations, in protecting this marvelous place. And as we will soon learn, their efforts in the field were complemented by similar efforts, taken by other defenders of beauty and wildness, in the murky meeting rooms and smoky hallways of the nation's capital.[27]

3.9. Sunset and clearing skies on the Southeast Arm, 2014. Photo by Eric Compas. Used with permission.

DAY 4 Beauty and the Beet

As we were about departing on our homeward trip we ascended
the summit of a neighboring hill and took a final look at Yellowstone
Lake. Nestled among the forest-crowned hills which bounded our
vision, lay this inland sea, its crystal waves dancing and sparkling in the
sunlight as if laughing with joy for their wild freedom.
It is a scene of transcendent beauty.
—David E. Folsom, 1869

There is a beehive of activity around me this morning as we pack to leave and clean up the cabin. Our sojourn through the activities of rangers in the field is over, just as is our stay at Trail Creek. Also clearing out is the slow-moving weather system that has been our constant companion on this trip—the skies today are blue, with mist rising from the lake after a clear, cold night. To continue enjoying cabin privileges, we have to leave it in as good a condition as we found it (or better), with a fire laid in the woodstove and matches handy for the next rain-soaked or ski-weary ranger to light with one match. So, Sean, Josh, and Eric empty the ashes, lay a fire, clean all horizontal surfaces, haul more firewood in, enter our visit in the logbook, and sweep and mop the floor.

It is mid-morning by the time we launch, those chores having taken a while, and the mists have dissipated in the strengthening sun. Our route this morning takes us past the broad delta built up by the Yellowstone River over time. About five miles across, it is mostly covered in willows, the soils too moist for lodgepole pines or any other trees. We take our time paddling along it, exploring the shoreline's many ins and outs. There is a lot to savor, whether it is the snow glistening in the sun on the

Absaroka peaks, the possibility of seeing a moose browsing the willows, or the delicate tension between sediment deposition by the river and erosion by wave action, which collectively determine the shoreline. That same dance leaves much of the near-shore lake shallow and covered in ripple marks, miniature sand dunes in six-inch-deep water. Nature's beauty surrounds us here, in scales large and small.

This natural beauty might now be under twenty-five feet of water had things turned out differently in a major national park policy debate almost a century ago, for Yellowstone Lake's level would have been raised to nourish agricultural beauty downstream in Montana. The dam proposed for the lake's outlet was one of several proposed for the waters of Yellowstone National Park in the 1920s; it would have backed water several miles up the valley, well into the Thorofare. Not only would such a reservoir have killed all these willows, but its oscillating levels would have exposed the former delta at times—transformed into a smelly, unsightly mudflat. The willow flats and sand dunes would be gone, that delicate tension impossible to recreate with the widely varying reservoir levels. At the time, it was not at all clear whether such dams belonged in Yellowstone or whether they would be built. Fortunately for us, natural beauty would prevail, but not without some compromises. The story is a fitting one, both because we see and enjoy its outcome today and also because it further illuminates the motivations impelling people to protect this place. Thanks to those who acted on their convictions, the premise that some places should remain free of human alteration, first given expression in 1872 with the establishment of Yellowstone, became more deeply rooted. National parks would remain dam-free, and the Thorofare would remain as beautiful as it is wild.[1]

(

At its core, the dam controversy was about differing ideas of beauty and which of those should prevail in Yellowstone. Montana and Idaho irrigators saw beauty in vibrant fields of cash crops like sugar beets and the prosperous society those would support, while conservationists saw beauty in undeveloped and untrammeled nature. Reclamationist thought was rooted in the ideals of utilitarian conservation, the idea that society should strive for the "greatest good for the greatest number for the longest time." To reclamationists, "the greatest beauty in the world is the beauty of use."[2] Conservationists drew from a different line of thought, one that emphasized the preservation of nature in an intact condition. To them, as John Muir said, "All that the sun shines on is beautiful, so long as it is wild."[3] It was to be beauty versus the beet, and conservationists feared that if reclamationists triumphed here, all national parks would be vulnerable to commercial development.[4] But the odds of defeating the dam proposals seemed long indeed: the political climate favored reclamation, Congress had set a precedent when it passed the Raker Act in 1913 granting San Francisco permission to build a drinking water reservoir in Yosemite National Park's Hetch Hetchy Valley, and the NPS had been in existence barely four years.[5] The stage was set for controversy, and one side had to lose.

Geography challenges agriculture in much of Montana and Idaho. Areas that receive adequate precipitation are often too high and cold to support farming while warm areas do not generally receive sufficient rainfall. Farmers have typically solved this problem by irrigating their cropland with water from the moist mountains. In the early part of the twentieth century, natural river flows provided enough water for irrigation except during extreme droughts, when even large rivers such as the Snake were dewatered completely, irrigation canals ran dry, and crops failed. To solve such problems, in the early 1900s irrigators throughout the West began damming the region's rivers to store the spring runoff. In this way, they provided themselves with a form of insurance against inevitable dry periods. As the scope of reclamation projects grew larger, however, farmers increasingly needed the approval, and financial help, of the federal government.[6]

Toward that end, a Livingston, Montana, group called the Yellowstone Irrigation Association formed in December 1919 to promote the construction of a dam at Fishing Bridge, the outlet of Yellowstone Lake. Such a dam would have raised the level of the lake, turning it into a reservoir of irrigation water for the lower Yellowstone Valley. Although the proposed dam was modest by today's standards (less than thirty feet tall), the huge size of Yellowstone Lake and the inundation of extensive flat areas in the Thorofare and Pelican Valley promised enough irrigation water for up to a million acres. The group envisioned a better society in the Yellowstone Valley, for the dam would both reduce the damaging floods wrought by the Yellowstone River and provide an "enormous volume of water [that now] runs to waste" for irrigation. Such protection and agricultural development would, in turn, stimulate growth of the region's cities; the population of Livingston, for example, was forecast to reach fifty thousand.[7] Senator Thomas Walsh of Montana formalized the proposal with a bill he introduced on December 7, 1920.[8]

The Yellowstone Lake project was only one of three substantial reclamation proposals that surfaced in 1920. The second arose from farmers in eastern Idaho's Fremont and Madison Counties, who formed the North Fork Reservoir Company in 1915. Seeking its own reservoir, the group homed in on a site on the Falls River in Yellowstone's Bechler region (the remote area just west of the Thorofare) that could store enough water to irrigate up to one hundred thousand acres.[9] After a severe drought in summer 1919 resulted in $10 million in crop damage, the Idaho farmers approached Secretary of the Interior Franklin K. Lane for permission to build two dams, one at the Falls River site and a second on Mountain Ash Creek, a Falls River tributary. They also persuaded Senator John Nugent and Representative Addison Smith of Idaho to introduce dam bills into Congress in early 1920 for the same purpose. The congressmen favored making constructive use of this "flat, low section . . . which has no scenic value," where "the mosquitoes are so ferocious that any one who has the courage to enter that section must protect himself with netting."[10] Nugent's bill flew through the Senate with little opposition, passing on April 6, 1920, but the House version soon stalled amid a storm of protests from national conservation organizations and demands for hearings on both the Idaho and Montana bills.[11]

The third proposal broadened the Yellowstone reclamation threats to all national parks and federal lands. On June 10, 1920, Congress passed the Water Power Act creating the Federal Water Power Commission, which was to promote water power development and navigation improvement by leasing public waters to private citizens or corporations. National parks were not exempted from the commission's purview, and it had blanket authority to impound waters without congressional approval, so the act posed a wider threat to national park integrity than the other two more specific proposals.[12]

By the end of 1920, then, Yellowstone was facing a three-pronged attack. Should any of the dam proposals pass or the Federal Water Power Commission authorize a dam in the park, Yellowstone would be opened to commercial resource development. And if development were allowed in Yellowstone, the national park system's crown jewel, all national parks would be vulnerable; Hetch Hetchy would become the rule, not the exception (figure 4.1). The Thorofare and Bechler regions would be wild areas no more, transformed into aquatic tools of industrial agriculture.

With Lane as secretary of the interior, the threat to park integrity was the more acute, for he had lobbied for the Hetch Hetchy project six years earlier. Indeed, in July 1919 he ordered NPS director Stephen Mather not only to allow a reclamation survey of Yellowstone but also to follow that with a report *favoring* the project. Mather, sensing the

4.1. O'Shaughnessy Dam and Hetch Hetchy Reservoir, Yosemite National Park, 2009. In 1913, Congress passed legislation allowing San Francisco to flood this scenic valley, a precedent conservationists hoped not to repeat in Yellowstone. Author photo.

potential disaster for the park—not to mention his fledgling agency—but under direct orders to promote that very calamity, was in an impossible position. Initially, he dragged his feet on the report, lost the order directing him to do it, and decided to resign if forced to write such a document.[13] Abandoning caution, he finally submitted in early 1920 a report vigorously opposing reclamation: "I can not submit at this time anything but an adverse report on this project. . . . Should I take any other view, as I see it, I would be violating the obligations imposed upon me as Director of the National Park Service, which is to so administer Yellowstone Park that it be preserved in its natural state unimpaired for future generations."[14]

Undeterred by Mather's protestations, Lane next directed him to allow Mr. I. B. Perrine of Twin Falls, Idaho, to make a preliminary reclamation survey of the Falls River Basin and Yellowstone Lake, along with the park's three other large lakes (Shoshone, Lewis, and Heart). Hoping to complete the survey before winter, Perrine wasted no time traveling to Yellowstone. Upon his arrival there, however, Superintendent Horace Albright informed him that the horses and boats he needed to fully survey the park were, unfortunately, not available, having already been sent to winter pasture or storage. Albright had been tipped off (via encoded telegram from Mather's office) that Perrine was soon to arrive for his survey, so, desperate to stymie the surveyor, he resorted to such guerilla bureaucracy tactics. In spite of them, Perrine was still able to survey the Falls River Basin and Yellowstone Lake, and to Albright's and Mather's dismay, he recommended both sites. Albright wrote dejectedly that "any or all of these projects will ruin absolutely Yellowstone Park for public use. [The] Hetch Hetchy project in Yosemite [is] insignificant in comparison."[15]

Fearing just such a threat to national parks, Mather and others had formed the National Parks Association (NPA) in 1919 to do what the NPS itself could not: lobby the public and their elected officials on behalf of the parks.[16] The young organization, led by Mather's publicist, Robert Sterling Yard, quickly jumped into the fray. Realizing that his nascent membership was too small for the challenge ahead, Yard quickly tapped into Mather's extensive social network to assemble a more effective defense for the parks.[17] Within a few months, he had a coalition of more than twelve thousand conservation-minded groups throughout the United States, with a combined membership of almost four million people, that included "chambers of commerce, teachers' clubs and federations, shooting and fishing clubs, manufacturers' associations, patriotic leagues, automobile associations, travel and outing clubs, universities, bar associations, nature study clubs, political clubs and all the greater scientific associations in the land."[18] This impressive and diverse network also included women's professional and civic organizations, who took bold stances against the dams.[19]

Yard found some of his strongest allies in the conservation community and in the popular press. He counted George Bird Grinnell, Emerson Hough, Horace McFarland, and other leading conservationists of the day among his friends, and he succeeded in soliciting donations for a National Parks Defense Fund by uniting virtually all conservation organizations against the dams, including the Sierra Club, Boone and Crockett Club, and National Geographic Society. The Appalachian Mountain Club, Sierra Club, Mazamas, and Mountaineers assisted him in setting up regional organizations to address the issue in Boston, Chicago, San Francisco, Portland, and Seattle. The Audubon Societies of America sent out twenty-five thousand circulars that called for letters expressing opposition. Of all the groups, though, the NPA was most consistent in its defense of Yellowstone and was the leader of the conservationist forces. In the popular press, Lyman Abbott, the editor of the *Outlook,* played a similar role. Throughout 1920 and 1921, Abbott used his popular magazine, similar in style to the *Nation* or the *Independent,* to publicize dam plans and congressional progress on the issue. Together, conservationists and the popular press mounted an increasingly impressive defense.[20]

Supporters and opponents sparred over many issues, but four recur in the voluminous literature generated by the controversy: differing ideas of beauty, the precedent such reclamation would create, dam functionality, and populism. First, because this contest was fundamentally about whether agroindustrial or natural beauty was to prevail in Yellowstone, the contestants made frequent reference to their preferred version. Not surprisingly, conservationists were on firm ground here, for Yellowstone National Park had been set aside to "provide for the preservation, from injury or spoliation, of all timber, mineral deposits, natural curiosities, or wonders within said park, and their retention in their natural condition."[21] Yellowstone Lake's beauty was particularly well known, so conservationists began by describing how it would be tarnished by a dam. The Thorofare and Pelican Creek areas floated right to the top of the list of affected resources, with about nine thousand acres in the two low-lying areas to be inundated. Of the two, conservationists were more concerned about the Thorofare, for a few hundred moose inhabited the Yellowstone delta, and even the modest dam being proposed would flood several thousand acres of that moose paradise. *Field and Stream* magazine darkly warned that if that were allowed to happen, "Congress will sign the death warrant of one of America's noblest wild animals . . . the famous Yellowstone moose." The white pelican rookery on the Molly Islands would suffer the same fate, as would the geothermal features at West Thumb. Also, the altered flows typical of dam-controlled rivers could affect downstream resources such as the Upper and Lower Falls of the Yellowstone River, which could be reduced or dried up when the reservoir was being filled each year.[22] Conservationists did the same for the threatened resources of the Bechler area, though they found themselves scrambling to determine just what its virtues were. Without the road access that the north shore of Yellowstone Lake had, the Bechler area's topography was still not well known. To address this weakness, William C. Gregg, a New Jersey member of the NPA, explored the area in 1920 and again in 1921. Publishing his findings in the *Saturday Evening Post* and in the *Outlook*, Gregg wrote glowingly of "divine beauties of which the men who fixed the limits of the park had no knowledge whatever. . . . [I] found more falls and cascades than in all the known parts of the park put together."[23]

The flip side of this coin was to point out the not-so-beautiful aspects of reservoirs, and here again conservationists had the advantage. The Jackson Lake Reservoir, just south of the park, provided a ready example of what irrigation impoundments could do to Yellowstone's natural beauty. The United States Reclamation Service had raised the level of the natural lake there with a dam in 1907, just as proposed for Yellowstone Lake. The agency had not bothered to clear the shoreline trees that would be inundated, so there was a ring of dead trees around the lake, right at the base of the imposing Teton mountain range (figure 4.2). Moreover, as irrigators gradually drained the lake to its natural level every summer, a bathtub ring of mud appeared to complement the dead trees. Conservationists found this deplorable—and the imagery powerful. For example, American Civic Association president Horace McFarland wrote that the "gradual drawing down of [Yellowstone Lake's] water . . . will almost certainly leave those shores slimy, marshy, and depressing, just as the same process has utterly ruined the once notable beauty of Jackson Lake."[24]

Reclamationists struggled to effectively counter the conservationist vision of beauty; they were on ground as soft as that of Jackson Lake's exposed mud flats. Idaho's commissioner of reclamation Warren G. Swendsen, for example, argued that the Bechler dams would enhance, not destroy, park resources: the Bechler dam "will result in replacing

4.2. Dead trees around Jackson Lake Reservoir, 1921. Conservationists found this image of destruction to be an effective tool in their campaign to keep reclamation projects out of Yellowstone. Photographer unknown; courtesy of NPS, Yellowstone National Park (YELL 44090, #18).

what is now mostly an unattractive swamp with a mountain lake." The swamp had "no value or scenic beauty, but [was] infested with flies and mosquitoes during the summer months." Similarly, knowing its dam would struggle to improve on Yellowstone Lake's already abundant natural beauty, the Yellowstone Irrigation Association focused instead on Fishing Bridge, which spanned the lake's outlet. The group argued that "a permanent, artistic bridge" atop its proposed dam there would improve the park by replacing a "rickety old pile structure."[25] Forced to acknowledge that drawn-down reservoirs often exposed ugly expanses of bare mud, Swendsen tried to downplay the impact: "Upon certain years of extreme drouth, [reservoir water] will be drawn out for irrigation uses, or partly so, at least during the period of perhaps two or three months." When these defenses failed, Swendsen played the irrigators' trump card, extolling agroindustrial beauty: "Beauty is only skin deep; but usefulness combined with beauty is a wonderful combination and a blessing to those who have this, and a joy to all." As the irrigators would come to find out, though, the conservationists held a more powerful trump card, for their idea of beauty harmonized better with national parks.[26]

The second issue was that the dams would set a dangerous precedent, opening all national parks to commercial exploitation. Many in the conservationist camp shared this fear, such as McFarland, who wrote in a May 1920 article in the *Independent* that Smith's bill was "the entering wedge of commercialism." Yard soon picked up on this fear: "One thing we certainly know, and that is that *the granting of even one irrigation privilege in any national park will mark the beginning of a swift end; within five years thereafter all our national parks will be controlled by local irrigationists, and complete commercialization inevitably will follow*" (emphasis original). Clearly, he felt that this was a nationally significant threat and that the Walsh bill "constitutes the most insidious and dangerous blow ever aimed at American Conservation."[27] With the recent loss at Yosemite's Hetch Hetchy, Yard's pronouncements were more than mere rhetoric. If Yellowstone were also impounded, then the country's two premier national parks would be industrialized; the remainder would be easy prey. Reclamationists had no easy answer to this claim, suggesting they agreed with it—or even welcomed it.[28]

Third, proponents and opponents grappled over the proposed dams' functionality. One would have thought the reclamationists, being more familiar with their proposals, would have won this debate, but conservationists again outmaneuvered them. In addition to the agricultural utopias made possible by their reservoirs, proponents felt that both the Yellowstone Lake and Bechler sites were the best sites available, and that dams there would help control downstream flooding.[29] Conservationists found these claims easy to debunk, especially with the Yellowstone Lake dam. In addition to promoting the beauty inherent to Yellowstone Lake, they pointed out that a dam at Fishing Bridge would do little to control floods plaguing the lower Yellowstone Valley because many large and undammed tributaries joined the river between the lake and the affected communities. Also, another obvious dam site existed at Yankee Jim Canyon, downstream of the park. A dam there would provide more effective flood control without inundating park land.[30]

The last of the dominant issues, embraced by both reclamationists and conservationists, was populism. As noted earlier, irrigators promoted the dams as key to building a democratic society in the West. They tried to characterize their opposition as elite, anti-populist outsiders: "I am getting a little tired of having everything that the West tries to do opposed by those super-men of the East, who stand with their heads in the clouds, agitating against the constructive development of the West," said Major Fred Reed, managing director of the Idaho Reclamation Association.[31] In contrast, conservationists argued that few irrigators would profit at the expense of the many who owned Yellowstone (all Americans), an anti-populist intrusion on public property and public rights. That some dam proposals called for government financing was particularly galling. As Abbott summarized, "It is bad to have natural resources, which belong to the people, taken by private interests; it is worse to have these resources used for exploiting the people who really own them; it is unbearable to require the people to pay for building the plants to be used in the exploitation." Reclamationists would soon find that the conservationists were more in tune with populist thought than they were.[32]

Most of this debate unfolded throughout 1920, and the new year brought confirmation that conservationists' advocacy had indeed been more persuasive. Smith's bill died quietly in February when the House adjourned without voting on it, but not so the Walsh bill. The senator had hearings on the bill scheduled for the start of the session, but when five members of the Yellowstone Irrigation Association arrived in Washington, Walsh held a surprise hearing on Washington's birthday and did not invite any dam opponents. Walsh scheduled another hearing for them, but he tried to catch them off guard by holding the hearing earlier than planned, on February 28, 1921. However, this strategy had little obvious effect, for Yellowstone Superintendent Albright was already in Washington and had met four nights earlier with his conservationist allies to work on their testimony. At the hearing, they repeated many of the familiar themes: Albright mourned the potential destruction of valuable park resources, NPS chief engineer George Goodwin stressed the proposal's factual inaccuracies, and both McFarland and Yard argued that the dam would open all national parks to resource exploitation. Stealing the show, though, was the new secretary of the interior, John B. Payne, who was more a park defender than his predecessor had been, stating, "When once you establish the principle that you can encroach on a national park for irrigation or water power, you commence a process which will end only in the entire commercialization of them all." Payne and the conservationists succeeded in killing the bill, which did not report out of committee. Although Walsh reintroduced his bill in 1922, it got caught up in election-year politics and failed to pass. Conservationists had defeated both dam proposals, at least for the time being.[33]

Only the Water Power Act remained. In 1920, upon learning that Congress had given the Federal Water Power Commission reclamation authority in the national parks, Mather had protested to Payne, who, in turn, protested to President Woodrow Wilson. Wilson felt compelled to sign the act or risk losing western states' support in the upcoming election, but he did get the act's sponsors to agree to amend it in the next congressional session. Knowing that the congressmen might forget that handshake agreement, Yard galvanized his allies nationwide to hold their representatives' feet to the fire. Perhaps thanks to that pressure,

Congress made good on its promise, amending the act on March 3, 1921, to exclude national parks from the commission's jurisdiction. With the passage of this amendment, conservationists rebuffed the last of the major Yellowstone reclamation threats; all three victories came within two months of each other.[34]

With these three successes, national park defenders conclusively demonstrated that natural beauty reigns supreme in the national parks, not agroindustrial beauty. The Hetch Hetchy precedent was ousted, and Yellowstone's waters would continue to ebb and flow by the whims of nature. By the time another two years had passed, the significance of the victories had become apparent. Delivering the opening address of the 1923 Yellowstone summer season, Dr. John Wesley Hill, speaking for President Warren G. Harding, said, "It is at last the established policy of the Government that our national parks must and shall forever be maintained in absolute, unimpaired form, not only for the present, but for all time to come." Hill's speech was more important than it might seem to us today, for it was carried by the Associated Press and reprinted widely. More significantly, it would stand the test of time, as events here in Yellowstone would soon illustrate.[35]

☾

Here on Yellowstone Lake, we have now paddled about halfway across the delta, putting us somewhere near the mouth of the Yellowstone River. Though the river is the lake's largest tributary, its mouth is surprisingly hard to pick out from the delta's dense willows. Just as Eric and I discovered a decade ago, we find it only by observing several logs stuck in the shallows, evidence of a river's current slowing upon entering the lake and losing the energy to push them along. They are also evidence of the river's power in spring, when it is swollen with snowmelt, for most of these logs were whole trees. At the volume needed to float forty-foot logs—complete with root balls—the willows masking the river at late summer's lazy flows would be partly submerged, the mouth would be marked by a powerful current pushing well out into the lake, and canoeists would have to detour widely around it.

Not today, though; looking hard at the nearby shore, we see the likely channel hidden in the willows. Our languid morning continues, giving us time to contemplate what a dam at Fishing Bridge would have done to our idyllic setting. Nowhere would the reservoir's impact have been more obvious than here, at least on the shoreline we have seen on this trip (figure 4.3). The "transcendent beauty" described by David Folsom would be gone, the willows on our right drowned by the reservoir's higher waters. In their place would be a sea of mud several thousand acres in size by summer's end, when the reservoir waters were drained for irrigation, exposing the former delta. While those reservoir waters would have covered the mud for the first part of the summer, by July the demands of the summer growing season would have exposed the mud, which would have remained exposed all the way through the following May. Along with the willows, the moose and other animals that call the delta home would have disappeared; so too the pelicans and cormorants nesting on the Mollies. On all shores a bathtub ring of denuded rock and mud would have spread like an annual cancer of reclamation, an

4.3. *The Yellowstone River delta and the Southeast Arm, 2014. A dam at Fishing Bridge would have inundated all of the low-lying land to the left of the water. Photo by Eric Compas. Used with permission.*

omnipresent reminder that much of the lake's beauty had been sacrificed for the sake of industrial agriculture. Its wildness would have gone too, the lake's fluctuating level mastered by humans, not by the vicissitudes of nature. In short, the most essential qualities of this magnificent landscape would have been washed away, its wildness partly tamed, its beauty submerged, and its community of life seriously compromised.

((

Bad ideas sometimes die hard, resurfacing in unexpected places or with new twists. That would be the case with Yellowstone's reclamation saga, as irrigators remained hopeful despite their triple defeat in 1921. In fact, barely had the flood of controversy subsided before Representative Smith of Idaho was back at it, this time with a 1926 proposal for another dam in the Bechler area—with a twist. He knew a dam *in* the park would not gain congressional approval, so he proposed moving the park boundary, removing the would-be-inundated area from the park, and building the dam at the same site on the Falls River. To make this bitter pill palatable, he tried to sweeten the pot with an addition to the park about five times the size of the excision and in the same general area. Park defenders were not so easily duped; they still smelled a dangerous precedent and lobbied against the dam. The proposal was bundled with several other pending boundary revisions, most of which would have conformed the park boundary with natural topography (though one would have added the Yellowstone River headwaters to the park, as we will soon see). Congress established the Yellowstone National Park Boundary Commission in 1929 to investigate and make recommendations on all of them. The commission also smelled something rotten in the Bechler proposal, writing that "in the absence of a demonstrated public necessity, the commission finds that it is unnecessary and undesirable to break into the integrity of the Yellowstone National Park by the elimination of the Bechler River meadows from its boundaries."[36] Due in part to the strength of the policy established a few years earlier, this chapter in the reclamation saga was over, settled comparatively easily.

That would be the case again in the late 1930s when a new reclamation proposal emerged, with another new twist. In 1937, Congress approved the Colorado–Big Thompson Project, which would bring water from the moist western slope of the Colorado Rockies to the dry Front Range cities via a tunnel under Rocky Mountain National Park. This project may have inspired Idaho's irrigators to concoct a similar plan for their favorite park. By then they had (wisely) given up on building their reservoir in the Bechler area, so they (not so wisely) resurrected the idea of damming Yellowstone Lake and (even less wisely) proposed sending the stored water to Idaho via a tunnel to Heart Lake and the Heart River, a tributary to the Snake River. Idaho's senator James Pope and representative Compton I. White introduced bills toward this end into both houses of Congress in 1937.[37]

As it happened, President Franklin Delano Roosevelt visited Yellowstone that same summer with his wife Eleanor. Touring the park with Superintendent Edmund Rogers (figure 4.4), Roosevelt learned of the proposal and had an immediate reaction to it, as Rogers later related to his supervisor:

> As we were driving along the lake shore after lunch at Fishing Bridge en route to Lake Butte, there was a cold bitter wind off the lake but the President was obviously enjoying it immensely. After the President had expressed himself on the magnificence of the lake I made a remark that he was fortunate to have an opportunity to see it before the Idaho irrigation interests despoiled it. He asked me a few questions about the proposal as if he had never heard of it before but made no comment at that time.
>
> Just after I got back into the car, after a few minutes stop at Lake Butte [an overlook featuring a commanding view of the lake], during which the President scarcely took his eyes off the lake, the President turned to me and said, "You do not need to worry, Mr. Rogers, no one will ever be permitted to touch that lake." When we were on the lake shore again the President made some remark on the subject again. In the wind I did not hear it. He repeated it to me again but I still did not get it all. As I understood it he said something to the effect that if Idaho felt they needed more water they could find it elsewhere.[38]

If FDR's opposition were not enough to kill the proposal, the Wyoming State Planning Board, which would not gain anything from the replumbing of Yellowstone waters, soon added its own opposition. With public opposition also growing, both bills died ignominiously, failing to

4.4. Franklin D. and
Eleanor Roosevelt
touring Yellowstone
with Superintendent
Edmund Rogers,
1937. Photographer
unknown; courtesy
of NPS, Yellowstone
National Park (http://
www.nps.gov/
features/yell/slidefile/
index.htm, accessed
September 19, 2015).

advance to the House and Senate floors for debate in 1938. With them died the last serious proposal to dam Yellowstone's waters.[39]

Three times, the idea of altering Yellowstone's hydrology toward commercial ends swung against the public's pitch, connecting with nothing but air for a collective strike out. Clearly, the idea was not a good one, but the same cannot be said of the idea of supplementing rainfall with stored water to support western agriculture. As FDR intimated, the Idaho farmers looked for a reservoir site elsewhere, eventually finding one nearby, on Mountain Ash Creek just outside the park's southwest boundary (possibly the same site that was a part of the original proposal). They built the Grassy Lake Reservoir there; its waters first flow into Yellowstone before becoming part of the Falls River, which flows out of the park and into potato and beet country. The Montana irrigators succeeded as well with the Huntley irrigation project, although they never got a reservoir (water is taken directly from the Yellowstone River). The river remains free-flowing along all of its 670 miles, the country's longest free-flowing river outside Alaska. And along its course one can find all the natural beauty and agroindustrial beauty one wants; both forms emerged from the dam battles victorious in a way, although natural beauty clearly triumphed in the park. Yellowstone Lake remains undammed, thanks to the park's defenders and a friend in a high place.

Why did park defenders win at Yellowstone when they had lost just a generation earlier at Yosemite? For several obvious reasons, and one not so obvious. First, the Yellowstone defenders included an agency whose express purpose was to protect the national parks. The NPS was that agency, created three years after the Hetch Hetchy decision, arguably because that sad story illustrated so well that Yosemite was a victim of administrative neglect. Hetch Hetchy aided the cause at Yellowstone in another way, by providing visual evidence of what did not belong in a national park. Visual symbols can be quite motivating, and Yellowstone's defenders successfully drew on two of them (the other being Jackson Lake) to illustrate the destruction that industry could bring to a park. The last obvious reason is that the number of people who stood to benefit versus those who stood to lose from dams in the two parks was different. All residents of San Francisco stood to benefit from the Hetch Hetchy dam, while relatively few irrigators stood to benefit from the Yellowstone dams. Moreover, only a few people knew Hetch Hetchy well enough to sense the aesthetic loss that a dam there would entail; by contrast, most Yellowstone tourists had visited Yellowstone Lake.

Park defenders also prevailed for another reason, one that is not as obvious but that strongly motivated them. It is a feeling best revealed in their writings, in language such as Gregg's "divine beauties" in the Bechler region. Similarly, Emerson Hough, another conservationist defending Yellowstone from damnation, described it as an "heirloom," a place "sacred, never to be parted with." Yard used such imagery too, stating that "the essential quality distinguishing National Parks . . . is their condition of untouched Nature, their status as museums of the original American wilderness."[40] To them, Yellowstone's natural beauty was sublime, imbued with a sacredness that made the proposals to exploit it all the more offensive. The sacredness of nature for conservationists is widely documented and accepted; anyone who finds such meaning in a landscape will go to great lengths to defend it, as suggested by the events in this chapter.[41] The nature that they found so sacred and motivating has inspired generations of conservationists since. Such far-reaching and cross-generational inspirations are more than mere feelings; they are deeply held values and beliefs fundamental to a large segment of our society. Values are fundamental, subconscious parts of our personal identity; they comprise the highest goals toward which we want to move our existence, along with the modes of behavior we must exhibit to attain them. Sociologist Milton Rokeach identified thirty-six essential human values, with salvation, a world of beauty, broad-mindedness, and responsibility among them.[42] Values give rise first to subconscious beliefs and then to more conscious expressions of those beliefs: the passions and attitudes we avow. Ultimately, we take actions consistent with our passions and attitudes. The Yellowstone dam story, then, nicely illustrates this fundamental element of the human psyche: strong conservationist values like those mentioned above give rise to the belief that nature is sacred. Manifesting these values, and the associated belief, conservationists consciously avowed love of Yellowstone's wildness and natural beauty, and then acted to defend those passions from the reclamation threat. This chain of causation, this motivating impulse, is a fundamental part of the Thorofare story.[43]

We can be glad that many of today's land managers share the same values and beliefs, for threats to the Thorofare's integrity continue to surface. In 1991, the Clear Rock Resources Company of Sheridan, Wyoming, proposed still another dam at Fishing Bridge, an eleven-foot dam that would have raised the level of Yellowstone Lake by five feet. As reclamationists had done sixty years earlier, the company promoted the dam's benefits, suggesting that its low profile "will make [it] nearly invisible to traffic crossing Fishing Bridge" and that it "would have a stabilizing influence on lake levels with potential benefits for the lake shore environment." Thanks to the strong policy established earlier, the NPS was able to quash this threat with only one letter. Still, this surprising proposal bears witness to something Robert Sterling Yard wrote at the conclusion of the earlier Yellowstone dam struggle: "The threat has been staved off, [but] for as long as the waters of Yellowstone Lake are kept inviolate they will be a continual challenge to irrigationists. . . . The fight for Yellowstone will be a continuous affair." Indeed—barely a generation would pass after 1938 before conservationists found themselves in another battle over the lake's integrity. Again drawing on their core values and beliefs, they girded themselves for another policy battle. As we will learn, the outcome then was more mixed than it was in the dam battles.[44]

❨

We today are the happy recipients of the fruits of our predecessors' labors defending Yellowstone's integrity. Stopping for a snack at Terrace Point, just past the east end of the delta, I take my last look into the Thorofare, this landscape of life (figure 4.5). This is the north end of the fur trapper's thoroughfare, that wilderness highway bounded in the distance by the flat-topped Trident (still sporting a fresh coat of white on top), and across the way by the Two Ocean Plateau rising above the azure waters of the Southeast Arm. The beauty and wildness here are as palpable as the southern breeze warming our world and the warm sunshine highlighting the leafy greenery of the delta vegetation.

While we take our repast, though, the breeze starts to pick up. More and more whitecaps appear, so with three miles still to go, we stow our gear and shove off. The rough conditions we are soon paddling through are a fresh reminder of the risks inherent in wilderness travel. Eric and

4.5: *Last look into the Thorofare, at Terrace Point, 2014. Photo by Eric Compas. Used with permission.*

the kayak do fine, his craft more designed to weather adverse conditions with its closed top. Not so with the canoe, open to the air and carrying a heavy load. Each wave threatens to overtop the gunwales, slopping water into the boat and increasing the chance of a capsize; the biggest waves come within an inch of wetting us. We respond accordingly, staying within a few feet of the shore and quartering the waves (angling the canoe to hit them at a 45-degree angle). A direct hit would amplify the height of the wave, increasing the chance of taking on water and making for a rougher ride. The zigzag pattern that sometimes results from quartering means that occasionally we quarter the waves from behind, letting waves overtake us at an angle.

Under these conditions, we progress slowly up the shore, each wave provoking both thrill and fear. The canoe and its contents rock and roll but stay dry. The wind stays with us, neither abating nor increasing. After an hour of this aquatic roller coaster, we round a point into leeward conditions and coast into our campsite for the next two nights. Centered on a small clearing, we set up the tents on one side and make our kitchen on the other. As if to underscore the message that wilderness travel must be done on nature's terms, a thunderstorm overtakes us shortly after we arrive. We had seen it building, so we had thrown the tents up right away, eaten lunch, and hung our food out of ursine reach. When the storm was five minutes out, we retreated to our tents and listened to the waves build as the storm approached. They were easily large enough to have grounded us, had we still been paddling.

Snug in our tents and sleeping bags, we snooze to the sounds of nature's symphony. Wind in the pines, waves striking the shore, and the pitter-pat of rain on the tent roof complement each other like the wind and string sections of an orchestra, peals of thunder the percussion crescendo. Shortly, the storm moves on, though the rain continues for a while. Eventually it too pauses, only to return for an encore, then a short second one.

Afterward, we gather for dinner. I am the last to arrive, dependent as I am for help getting up from my cot. Sean pulls me up to a sitting position, slides my feet into the boots that no longer see a hike, and carefully helps me out of the tent. Eric and Josh, meanwhile, have dropped our food from the food pole and boiled water for our first freeze-dried supper. With me unable to paddle and therefore the third person in the canoe, we had to minimize our weight and bring food normally reserved for backpacking, where every ounce matters. Still, out here the food is delicious, as is our dessert of chocolate truffles.

The rest of the evening is cool and calm, with enough clouds lingering to color the sky red at sunset. A campfire warms and relaxes us in this water wilderness, its shorelines kept wild thanks to the passions of committed conservationists several generations ago (figure 4.6). Not so wild are the motorcraft we will begin to see on the lake as we paddle north—or the noise that comes with them. Because these craft are allowed here, most of the Southeast Arm (along with the South Arm) cannot be considered wilderness, even though these waters have been recommended for such protection. The story of why they are here, in what otherwise might be an aquatic northern branch of the Thorofare, is a tale for tomorrow.

4.6: Campfire on the Southeast Arm, 2014. Photo by Eric Compas. Used with permission.

DAY 5 To Drive or Not to Drive

*This is an ideal country for the trail traveler, and ought to be reserved
forever for people who desire to get a bit of wholly unsoiled nature.*
—Superintendent Horace Albright, 1920

There is fog on the far shore as we crawl out of our tents, an indication
that the night was clear and cold. Cold enough, in fact, to freeze a few of
the raindrops still clinging to our tents. Beads of frozen pearls, another
reminder that we stand on the cusp of autumn. We shiver as we break
our fast, trying to stay warm by following the shafts of sunlight as they
wend their way through the trees.

Today is another layover day, and with the promise of sunshine, a hike
is afoot for the three others. Eric and Josh soon take off for a climb of
Langford Cairn, a point to our south affording a sweeping view of the
upper Yellowstone River Valley and delta. It is as good a look into the
Thorofare as one can get. Sean will stay back in camp with me and putter
around until the hikers return, at which point he will stretch his legs. I
relax for the day, reading, enjoying the view, and luxuriating in nature's
silence.

Sean takes Eric's kayak out to familiarize himself with it. He is gone
about an hour, during which time I close my eyes and listen. The soundscape (everything that reaches one's ears in a particular place) with
which we Americans live is surprisingly motorized or automated, so
much so that true silence, or a completely nonhuman soundscape, is
hard to find.[1] Even in the national parks, where most of us would expect
the soundscape to be dominated by nature, noise from automobiles,
jet traffic, and motorcycles (especially Harley-Davidsons with altered

pipes) pervades, often even in backcountry areas. Searching for a nature-dominated soundscape in Yellowstone in 2014, for example, I did not have success, limited as I was to locations accessible by car or by foot with my walker (boardwalks and paved paths).

Today, though, is different, with only the sounds of nature for company. Seated at the edge of the small clearing, I first notice red squirrels chattering in long cadences to me, upset that I dare sit quietly in their front yard. They are low to the ground in the trees to my left; higher up chickadees murmur quietly, audible only when the squirrels take a breather. Behind me, gray jays take a different approach to communication, boisterously expressing their disappointment about the general lack of food dropped by these temporary campsite occupants. A chipmunk rustles the grasses on my right, standing on its hind legs to pull a seed head down and nibble. Done with that one, it turns its head in a movement too fast to see or hear, then scurries off to another grass stalk. In the background, puffs of wind sigh softly in the pines to the accompaniment of wavelet rhythm on the gravel beach I am facing. The infrequent fly buzz and mosquito whine in my ear are reminders that summer is hanging on, if barely (and that few soundscapes are perfect!). Only an occasional jet interrupts the reverie, the plane's noise drifting down from thirty thousand feet and unnoticeable if a squirrel has my attention. For once, I have found a predominantly natural soundscape, about as good as one can find in America today. I bask in it, trying to memorize the sumptuous experience. I bask as well in the warming sun, which gradually replaces the morning smells of damp grass with the spicier aroma of dried pine needles and resin. The strengthening sun also deepens the blue dominating my view, subtly transforming aquamarine into turquoise, the lake and sky racing each other to cobalt. My senses are full, the exuberant life around me hard to ignore.

Of all the sensory experiences of this trip, that hour immersed in the sounds of nature is perhaps the most vivid. It was to my ears as the views at Trail Creek were to my eyes: pure tranquility, peaceful silence that will last me far longer than that one hour. Along with Trail Creek and another experience yet to come, it becomes one of the three most sensual, powerful, and enduring times of the trip.

Such an experience is not only hard to find, but it is also a bit ironic that I found it here, for the NPS twice proposed building a road up the east shore of the lake, both times as part of a larger proposal to enlarge the park by adding the Yellowstone River headwaters to it. As it turned out, cars would never come here, but other motorized vehicles—boats—soon did. In a role reversal, the NPS later found itself fighting even harder to ban motorboats from this arm and the South Arm. Why the agency failed in these endeavors is the subject of my storytelling today, as is the effects of motorboats on the Thorofare. These policy contests helped to define the area, for better and for worse. The efforts demonstrate the agency's changing relationship to motorized vehicles—at one time considered a way to make nature's sacredness accessible to visitors, but later considered a disruption to it—and that, often, values more powerful than those of conservationists have to be reckoned with in park policymaking. Ultimately, a policy defeat for the NPS did not always mean the Thorofare wilderness was somehow diminished; but at the same time, actions intended to protect it did not always carry the day.

((

The road-building idea first surfaced in 1918, when the newly arrived NPS included it in a proposal to expand Yellowstone to the southeast to encompass the Yellowstone River headwaters. This was not the first time that this addition had been suggested; as early as 1882, General Philip Sheridan had suggested adding the Yellowstone Forest Reserve (the predecessor to the Shoshone National Forest, encompassing most of the Absaroka Range east and south of Yellowstone) to the park. His suggestion was not adopted, but the idea of protecting some of the grand scenery and abundant wildlife of the Absarokas continued to circulate. For example, in 1898, the Department of the Interior, acting on the suggestion of the US Army acting superintendent of Yellowstone, proposed adding the huge area extending from the Yellowstone River headwaters to the Teton Range, including the northern half of Jackson Hole, to the park. Had either of these proposals become law, Yellowstone would have doubled in size, but the 1898 proposal also withered away.[2]

The next time this idea was considered, in 1918, it almost did become law. The land to be added had shrunk considerably, to 1,265 square miles, but it still swept from the crest of the Absaroka Range to the crest of the Teton Range. To sweeten the pot, the road was now part of the package. To make the prospective addition accessible, the NPS proposed building a road from Jackson Hole onto the Yellowstone Plateau via Pacific Creek, Two Ocean Pass, Atlantic Creek, the Yellowstone River Valley (figure 5.1), and the east shore of the lake, finally connecting with the East Entrance Road. The agency could have called it the "Trapper's Thoroughfare," for this was the fur trappers' route that, simplified in spelling, is our region's namesake. However, enough opposition arose from Jackson Hole residents, concerned about possible restrictions on their activities in the proposed park addition, that the Senate never voted on it (the House had passed it).

The motivations to protect the Thorofare's scenery and wildlife remained, however, so just seven years later, the land proposal resurfaced again. This time, the proposed addition had shrunk again, to just the Yellowstone's headwaters (including Thorofare Creek), about 340 square

5.1: Josh pauses for a view of the Yellowstone River Valley, 2003. The Two Ocean Plateau rises 2,000 feet above the valley that would have had a road through it had a 1918 NPS proposal become reality. Author photo.

miles. Several boundary adjustments to the park were under consideration at the time, the others mainly intended to conform the boundary to natural topography. The prospective Thorofare addition was referred to that special committee, mentioned before, chartered to investigate the various land swaps. Both that committee and a similar one, created a few years later, recommended the Yellowstone headwaters be added to the park, but neither time did the addition become reality. By that time hunting big game in the Thorofare had become institutionalized, so members of the public joined with some Cody, Wyoming, representatives of the outfitting industry to protest the potential loss of a favorite hunting ground. The Wyoming Game and Fish Commission made the same complaint, so Congress left the Yellowstone headwaters under USFS control (while making most of the other boundary adjustments).

Interestingly, the Forest Service supported the headwaters addition, even though the agency stood to lose the land—but only on the condition that the road *not* be built. The agency recognized, perhaps earlier than its sister agency, the NPS, that the Thorofare's most special attribute was its wildness. As William B. Greeley, chief of the Forest Service, wrote, "In my belief, the area should always be preserved as a wilderness and game sanctuary accessible only by trails. I would be loath to see it added to the Park if that should mean the extension of main automobile roads, the construction of large hotels, and the other features now found in the highly developed and utilized portions of the Yellowstone Park." By 1929, when Greeley wrote those words, Horace Albright was the NPS director; his preference for preserving the "wholly unsoiled nature" of the area had not changed from 1920, so the road was not a part of this proposal. Nonetheless, opposition to a headwaters hunting prohibition remained strong, and allowing hunting in a national park remained anathema to NPS leaders, so the headwaters addition remained tabled.[3]

The headwaters area has remained under USFS control ever since, even though the NPS considered the addition one more time in the 1930s, with an even smaller land area of eighty-two square miles encapsulating only Bridger Lake, Hawk's Rest, and Two Ocean Pass (all in the vicinity of the Thorofare Ranger Station) (figure 5.2). The road reappeared, also reduced to just a loop staying within two miles of Yellowstone Lake. Evidently, the NPS never made this proposal public, fearing it would inflame the tense and concurrent discussions about adding Jackson Hole valley bottomlands to nearby Grand Teton National Park. Perceptions of a federal land grab were already threatening to derail that effort; resuming the push for the headwaters addition would likely have doomed both efforts. Wisely, the NPS demurred on it, focusing instead on the Teton expansion. Those efforts finally paid off in 1950, when most of Jackson Hole was incorporated into Grand Teton. One of the compromises struck to make that happen was to allow hunting in the part of the park east of the Snake River. There, hunters temporarily deputized as "rangers" could continue elk hunting, a novel solution not envisioned in the earlier Yellowstone headwaters debate.[4]

Since then, the USFS has continued to protect its side of the Thorofare as a roadless wilderness where hunting is permitted. As noted previously, that policy of protection became the law of that land with the passage of the Wilderness Act in 1964, with wilderness designation bestowed immediately on both the Teton and Washakie Wildernesses. In most

5.2: *Bridger Lake, 2003. This scenic jewel is now protected within the Teton Wilderness, although part of its south shore is severely trampled by packstock. Author photo.*

ways, then, the USFS side of the Thorofare ended up being protected better than if it had been transferred to the NPS, due to the Wilderness Act's prohibition on road building and its requirement that any permanent structures be the minimum necessary for the job. So, not only will the "Trapper's Thoroughfare" not be built, but the law also forbids most structures. NPS policy prescribes the same for its part of the Thorofare, but such administrative policy is not as strong as federal law.

It is significant that, almost a century ago, the scenery and wild character of the Thorofare so impressed those who were debating the area's fate at the time that virtually everyone involved, including the heads of both responsible land management agencies, could agree that it should be protected as wilderness. Even though the first round of the dam controversy had just affirmed that human developments should not mar national parks, it is still notable that the policy was broadened to exclude roads in the Thorofare, for the NPS continued to make its unsullied nature accessible to the public by building roads through the parks for many years to come. For example, the Going-to-the-Sun Road in Glacier National Park was completed in 1932, and Trail Ridge Road in Rocky Mountain National Park six years later. Perhaps nudged by its sister agency to recognize the merits of keeping the Thorofare wild (and with roads already leading to Yellowstone's major attractions), the NPS agreed to keep roads out of the area. Regardless, protecting the Thorofare's wildness was the most powerful motivation, as Albright and Greeley both expressed. Owing to their consequent actions, it is still roadless wilderness today, and we still have the opportunity to hike or ride its trails, to immerse ourselves within its natural soundscape (and community of life), and to let the area's grandeur develop the same passions in us.

((

Here on the Southeast Arm, the day is moving along. Spread out before me are the lake waters, approaching cobalt in the now-warm sunshine. Across the arm, Mount Sheridan and the Red Mountains rise above the Promontory's spine and, farther left, Mount Hancock peeks through a low point between the hills west of the Two Ocean Plateau. The only sign of humanity in this panorama is the fire lookout atop Mount Sheridan, visible (if I squint) as a tiny lump on the summit.

But, as I am soon rudely reminded, a more obvious sign of people is the occasional motorboat. My ears, now keenly tuned to the wilderness soundscape around me, pick right up on the distant throb of a boat motor. The noise gets progressively louder, and my eyes soon find the boat approaching from the north. Insult is soon added to this sensory injury as I realize the boat is traveling well over the five-mile-per-hour speed limit. Only when the boat's pilot sees me does he throttle down to the speed limit. One injury is not enough, however, for the fellow does not stop until he is fairly close to my beach, and then he fires up a generator and runs it for the next hour.

Had Yellowstone's managers been successful in another major policymaking effort that arose a generation after debate about additions to the park had died away, this experience would have been much more unlikely. Led by park superintendent Lemuel Garrison, the NPS tried to ban motorboats entirely from the South and Southeast Arms. Garrison saw the arms as places defined by wildness and beauty—but threatened by motorized vehicle access. That newer attitude against motorized vehicles, increasingly voiced by the leaders of the national wilderness preservation movement of the time, was slow to be embraced by NPS leaders. While many in the agency shared the conservationist reverence for nature, most saw nothing wrong with tourism by motorized vehicle, whether by automobile, RV, or boat.[5] Garrison felt the same way, but not when it came to Yellowstone Lake's arms, for which he would go to great lengths to restrict motorized boat access over the next few years. He became one of the earliest and most visible NPS administrators to advance the newer passion for a motor-free wilderness; he effectively reinterpreted the NPS's mission to place preservation above recreation. To him, places like the arms and the Thorofare were wilderness cathedrals more than they were human playgrounds.[6]

But as events would make clear, Garrison came up against powerful boating and business interests favoring the status quo (promoting recreation). Those interests found more meaning in two other American values—freedom and independence—and rose to defend the passions that those gave rise to, especially the freedom to move around, such as by motorboat.[7] Soon they found a powerful politician sympathetic to their cause, and with his support they stymied Garrison's proposal, forcing him to accept a weakened compromise.[8] In so doing, they demonstrated that conservationist passions, especially when they conflict with freedom-related passions, may not always prevail in national park policy contests.[9] For the Thorofare, that meant that it was not to have a water wilderness on the lake's arms. This story, then, is a tale of what the Thorofare could be, but is not. It is a long story, a fitting one for a long and lazy layover day.[10]

☾

"Lon" Garrison, as he was known to his employees, was a lifelong ranger, having begun his career in Sequoia National Park in California (figure 5.3) in 1932. Like many rangers, he moved around the national park system, ending up in Yellowstone in 1957. He loved wild places, and regularly got out in the park's backcountry.[11] Riding his horse into the Thorofare via the trail behind our present campsite one summer day in 1958, he had his mind full. Motorboat use on the lake had more than doubled in the past few years, in part be-cause inexpensive fiberglass, aluminum, and plywood hulls were making boats more affordable to Americans. The rising numbers of boaters were associated with errant behaviors such as speeding, wildlife chasing, and creating waves that swamped canoes, all of which threatened the lake's resources and wilderness values. Human waste had become an additional offensive problem because boaters were not at the time required to seal their heads. Garrison had attempted a year earlier to compel boaters to seal

5.3. Yellowstone superintendent Lemuel Garrison, circa 1960. Photographer unknown; courtesy of NPS, Yellowstone National Park (YELL 43349).

them, but even this minor action stirred a surprising amount of controversy. After only two months he had been forced to back off, leaving it and the other problems unaddressed.[12]

As he rode that day, Garrison contemplated a more sweeping solution to the boating problems: banning motorboats from the lake's remote arms.[13] While the arms constituted only 20 percent of the lake's surface, they contained the wildest portions of the lake and its best wildlife habitat, such as the Molly Islands. Garrison was excited about the idea's potential, but he knew that if an action as small as sealing motorboat heads caused controversy, such restrictive zoning would cause a near riot among boaters. Motorized boating on the lake was popular locally, especially among wealthy businessmen from nearby Billings, Montana, and Cody, Wyoming (figure 5.4). Some virtually lived in their boats on the lake in summer; others took regular outings with their staff and clients; and virtually all loved fishing for the lake's cutthroat trout. Consequently, boating clubs were a powerful interest group that zoning could antagonize.[14] As the park's superintendent, Garrison knew he would take the brunt of their wrath, and that zoning the lake in such a manner could cost him his job.

Continuing his ride, Garrison enjoyed views of the glittering lake and noticed an osprey following him. He later wrote that the osprey "would stoop gently to me, hover over me, wing ahead, drop back, circle, calling frequently." Contemplating the decision before him, he "discussed my problems that day with Omar," the name he gave the osprey. He felt it was calling to him, as it were, to protect its wilderness home. Sensing the import of that call, Garrison headed back to political reality, his mind made up. "Omar" that day gave him his answer: "I had a dream of upper Yellowstone Lake with limited access so that it became in truth a water wilderness again!"[15] Over the next five years, he would often recall this ride as he attempted to protect Yellowstone's water wilderness by banning motorboats from the lake's arms.

Contemplating the ride's significance, and finding support from an internal committee he had formed to examine the matter, Garrison wrote Regional Director Howard Baker seeking his approval for the partial boating ban in December 1958. Baker, a cautious man more removed

5.4. *Speeding motorboat on Yellowstone Lake, 1977. In the background is the Lake Yellowstone Hotel, where the concession boat operations were based at the time of the zoning controversy. NPS photo by J. Schmidt; courtesy of NPS, Yellowstone National Park (http://www.nps.gov/features/yell/slidefile/index.htm, accessed September 19, 2015).*

from the front lines of nature preservation in Yellowstone, instead wondered if a better solution lay in improved enforcement of existing regulations, which would curtail the errant boater behaviors. Accordingly, he suggested gathering more data in summer 1959 to determine whether zoning was truly necessary.[16] Sensing that such research could bolster his argument and that the summer's delay would also provide time to build support among regional conservationists, Garrison concurred and had his staff research boating's impacts. Park Ranger Naturalist Joseph Murphy found that nesting pelicans and cormorants on the Molly Islands moved off their nests when boaters approached within a hundred yards. Ranger Naturalist Paul Sebesta similarly found an inverse relationship between motorboat use and wildlife presence (for example, moose often moved away when powerboats arrived in the morning). Additionally, by paddling the lake's seventy-five-mile roadless shoreline, Chief Ranger Otto Brown, seventy-one-year-old Olaus Murie (Mardy's husband and director of The Wilderness Society), and several others demonstrated that canoe expeditions on the lake could be both safe and

5.5. Historic circumnavigation of Yellowstone Lake by canoe, 1959. Photo by John Montagne. Used with permission.

enjoyable, in contrast to the common knowledge of the time that windy conditions were too severe for such small craft (figure 5.5).[17] While none of this research was peer-reviewed, it did document the wildlife impacts and demonstrated that nonmotorized boating was feasible. Such findings made Garrison anxious to make his proposal public, but Baker continued to hold him back. Increasingly unable to contain his zeal for wilderness protection, Garrison bristled under his superior's hesitancy.

Meanwhile, and perhaps due to the delay, Garrison found that the local boating community had learned of his proposal. The probable source was park employees discussing the idea off-record with Sherman Jones, manager of the Yellowstone Park Company's Boat Division (the company was the primary hotel and service provider in the park). Jones offered guided fishing trips on Yellowstone Lake, garnering a little more than 10 percent of his division's business from trips to the lake's arms. Upon learning of the proposal, he not only authored a report summarizing his division's operations and the economic threat that the zoning proposal posed to them, but he also mentioned the proposal to Curtis Lees, commodore (director) of the Billings Boat Club. In so doing, Jones let the cat out of the bag, and put Garrison in precisely the defensive position he had hoped to avoid. Instead of a proactive campaign to zone the lake, Garrison would from this point forward be fighting a reactive battle.[18]

Lees, an elected state representative from the Billings area, oversaw a boating group with considerable power. While his club had only about 120 members, some had "virtually unlimited personal means," with significant boat investments.[19] Learning of Garrison's proposal, the club grew concerned it would lose access to its favorite haunts and commissioned the printing of two thousand oppositional brochures. In them, the club decried the impending loss of access to favorite boating areas and criticized Garrison's reasons for the proposal, which were the need to protect the lake's water wilderness, to protect wildlife along the shoreline, and to control the shoreline erosion caused by speeding motorboat wakes. The club felt instead that Yellowstone's Organic Act directives (that it be managed as a "pleasuring ground" for the "benefit and enjoyment of the people") indicated that personal access to remote portions of Yellowstone Lake was more important than what it perceived as minor wildlife disturbance. Regarding the shoreline erosion argument, the club, knowing that winds on the lake occasionally produced six-foot waves, stated, "The attempt to assign the natural consequences of the elements to motorboating on the lake is nothing short of ridiculous." Garrison would come to regret ever having made the erosion argument; as the reaction to the brochure illustrated, it became a red herring, distracting from his primary reason for promoting lake zoning, which was to preserve the water wilderness.[20] Indeed, the club used this weakness to its advantage as it distributed its brochure to boaters and congressmen throughout the region. Lees himself soon claimed the support of congressional delegations and/or governors of twenty-two states for his club's position.[21]

With his proposal increasingly drawing flak from the boating community and his studies complete, Garrison pushed Baker to implement the plan that September. As the autumn progressed, the two sparred via mail, with Baker now pushing improved enforcement and a four-mile-per-hour speed zone for boats in the arms. Garrison responded defensively, worrying that such a low speed limit would be difficult to enforce and then reiterating his concern about increasing motorboat numbers. He closed by complaining that "if we do not move positively during the next few months to restrict the use of power boats, we do not believe it will be possible to ever again do so. We will be outweighed by sheer numbers and could well lose the support of conservation groups which we now have. . . . We must act while we still have such support." Finding they could not reach agreement, Baker took Garrison's rebuttal into consideration and deferred to Director Wirth for guidance. Garrison had had Wirth's support from the beginning, so it was no surprise that he responded with a strong endorsement of the proposal in January 1960.[22]

Actually, Garrison knew Wirth from his previous assignment, chairing the steering committee for the National Park Service's "Mission 66" program in Washington. Mission 66 was Wirth's brainchild, a ten-year program of capital improvements that Wirth and Garrison believed was essential for the NPS to cope with the rising numbers of national park visitors following World War II. Neither Garrison nor Wirth evidently saw a contradiction between the increased motorized visitor use the program would facilitate and the preservation of a water wilderness. Instead, Garrison promoted the balance of uses on the lake that typified the NPS and Mission 66: protect wilderness in the arms through curtailed motorized use there, while simultaneously building two new marinas on the lake (both Mission 66 projects) that would better facilitate motorized boat use elsewhere on the lake. The lake was large enough to be zoned for both uses, allowing Garrison to remain a champion of water wilderness and at the same time to promote the agency's longstanding approach to nature preservation combined with motorized vehicle access. However, his nontraditional (for the NPS) stance on preserving wilderness in the lake's arms increasingly drew opposition from members of the public who placed more value on boating freedoms.[23]

While Garrison and his superiors were settling their internal divisions over the matter, public debate about the proposal continued to grow, thanks in part to the Billings Boat Club and its brochure. Boaters from Wyoming and Montana pressured their congressional representatives, many of whom in turn contacted the NPS about the proposal. Some conservationists, spurred to action by Garrison over the summer, also wrote their congressional representatives. The NPS's national office sent out dozens of responses to the representatives between March 1959 and January 1960. In the local states, several of the Utah congressmen appeared to support the proposal, while most from Wyoming and Montana were less supportive, perhaps reflecting the numbers of boaters among their constituents.[24] One of those politicians was Wyoming's junior senator Gale McGee, who, after investigating the matter during a visit to Yellowstone in summer 1959, announced he would be holding a hearing on it the following February, in Cody.[25]

Elected in Wyoming in 1958, McGee represented a unique state, large in geographic extent but with the country's smallest state population, only about 330,000. In such a place, it was easy for a citizen to get a senator's ear, which is probably why he chose Cody for the hearing venue: many of his constituents opposed to zoning lived in that area. It was (and still is) an isolated, conservative community, not especially easy to access in the winter (at least one person made this complaint in his testimony).[26] Because more regional conservationists lived in Bozeman, Montana, than in Cody, winter geography dictated that boaters would find travel to the hearing easier than conservationists. Sensing this potential weakness, the conservationists rallied, hoping to put in a strong showing. Although they did, verbal testimony at the hearing was still dominated by boaters opposed to the zoning proposal. Written statements were almost evenly split, however, between supporters and opponents, with a majority of Montana comments favoring Garrison's zoning and Wyoming comments almost evenly split.[27]

Records of the testimony at the hearing provide insight into the motives of both boaters and conservationists. Boaters generally believed that Americans should have the freedom, as expressed in boating, to explore their heritage; one boater, for example, wrote: "It seems to me that [zoning] would be a most shortsighted action that would deprive hundreds of American citizens from the inborn privelege [sic] of enjoying their native country."[28] By contrast, conservationists such as Garrison were more motivated by the belief that nature was sacred, and that the boating ban would preserve or restore an opportunity for spiritual experience. Many conservationists, in fact, quoted an article by Murie, one of the country's leading defenders of that belief and associated wilderness passions.[29]

Beyond such insights, the hearing's testimony records the arguments advanced by the two primary camps. The most common theme echoed by zoning opponents was criticism of Garrison's arguments, especially his shoreline erosion claim. Boaters also commonly criticized the agency's claim that boats harmed park wildlife, raising questions about the Sebesta study. Although Sebesta's research certainly suggested that boats frightened animals away, it was confounded by the fact that boats typically arrived at about the same time the mammals bedded down for the day. It was unclear whether the boats were frightening them away or whether they were just following their natural patterns of diurnal rest and crepuscular activity. Although it did not become the red herring of the erosion argument, this confusion further weakened Garrison's cause. Meanwhile, conservationists, including former Yellowstone superintendent and NPS director Horace Albright, argued at the hearing for the preservation of quiet and wilderness, protection of park wildlife, and the prevention of a motorboat racing atmosphere and litter.[30]

Senator McGee entered the hearing with the appearance of an open mind, objectively taking testimony, questioning speakers, protecting Garrison from hostility, and relieving the atmosphere with humor. However, he had been overheard a few months earlier stating that he felt Garrison's arguments were weak and that his staff was not familiar with the remote arms, suggesting sympathy with the boaters' position.[31] He may have been predisposed to a compromise, which he left the hearing definitely believing was possible. He specifically hinted that implementing a motorboat speed limit in the two arms, along with a boating ban around the sensitive Molly Islands, could satisfy him and the boating community. It is not known whether he got the speed limit idea from Baker, who had first suggested it months earlier.[32]

Garrison, manager of the country's oldest national park, had a more national constituency than McGee, which may have blinded him somewhat to the local concerns. Garrison left the hearing convinced that supporters had equaled opponents, and resolved to forge ahead with his zoning plan. He quickly recommended to Baker that the agency move forward with public review and eventual plan implementation. Baker, by now realizing the issue's prominence and his boss's support for zoning, concurred and rapidly forwarded the recommendations on to Wirth and Secretary of the Interior Fred Seaton. Two months later, Seaton published the proposed zoning plan (not the final decision) in the *Federal Register*, the publication that the government uses to advise Americans of proposed actions.[33]

Despite this support and rapid action, other players in Washington, DC, were not as supportive. At an early March meeting, Director Wirth found that McGee's opinion had crystallized into direct opposition, a view shared by the state's senior senator, Joseph O'Mahoney. Moreover, Wyoming representative Keith Thomson had asked for another hearing, believing that the February scheduling had made it too difficult for some to attend. Eventually, Idaho senator Henry Dworshak echoed Thomson's request, so Secretary Seaton agreed in May 1960 to hold further hearings (there would be three) the following August.[34]

Garrison, wanting these hearings to go better than the first one, had his staff prepare accordingly. Worried about the beating he was taking over the erosion claim, he had Chief Park Naturalist Robert McIntyre revisit the issue. McIntyre advanced a more nuanced claim, that only those birds nesting close to the shoreline were swamped by passing motorboat wakes (not an impact of erosion, but an unacceptable one nonetheless). Consequently, he felt that they should sharpen their focus on the arguments that misbehaving boaters harassed wildlife unacceptably and that the increase in boating endangered wilderness preservation. Garrison's staff continued their publicity efforts as well, explaining their proposal and its reasoning to several groups outside the park. They derived cost estimates for the increased lake patrol that seemed necessary to enforce the prospective zoning. Although they had begun such patrols the previous summer, their old, slow boats hampered the patrols' effectiveness, and funding this activity deprived other park programs of resources.[35] Finally, they conducted a thorough cleanup of trash left by boaters on the shores of Yellowstone Lake. Camping ethics of the era directed backcountry users to bury their trash after burning the combustibles. Not all campers complied, and bears often learned to dig up remaining food scraps. Escalating motorboat use exacerbated these problems, so Garrison's staff policed the lake's entire 110-mile shoreline. All told, in summer 1960 they removed over a thousand gunny sacks of garbage, weighing over thirty-five tons.[36]

Meanwhile, the issue was increasingly drawing national attention, thanks to the publicity efforts of zoning opponents and proponents alike. For example, the Outboard Boating Club (OBC), a boating equipment manufacturer's trade group, solicited support from its 375 affiliate clubs and their eighteen thousand members, encouraging them to attend the hearings or submit testimony rebutting the Park Service's wildlife protection and erosion arguments while emphasizing that "public recreation is supposed to be the paramount consideration."[37] On the proponent side, Olaus Murie published several more articles supporting the zoning proposal, including one that spring in *The Living Wilderness,* the magazine of The Wilderness Society. The Wyoming Izaak Walton League and Montana Wilderness Association (a two-year-old Montana-based group dedicated to wilderness preservation) were also on board.[38]

Garrison and Wirth knew this would not be enough national support, so they turned their attention to garnering more. Their challenge in that endeavor was that conservationists nationally had been preoccupied with passage of the Wilderness Act for the last several years. Pleading directly for support from the leaders of most national conservation organizations, the two men argued that "the outcome of this issue will establish a precedent for years to come for the highest use of wilderness waters throughout the United States." Sierra Club director David Brower responded with the opinion that getting Congress to pass the Wilderness Act should be their first priority because, once passed, conservationists could use it to protect Yellowstone Lake. Wirth, however, reemphasized that they should not be so focused on the Wilderness Act that they suffer the loss of existing wilderness, which was, to him, precisely the threat that increasing motorboat use posed to Yellowstone Lake. Repeatedly, NPS personnel made the case for Yellowstone with conservationists, arguing that saving the lake's wilderness atmosphere could not wait for the act's passage; the time to act was now.[39]

By the end of summer 1960, the NPS had successfully elevated the Yellowstone Lake zoning question to a national conservation issue. It did not displace the Wilderness Act debate, but rather grounded it in a specific, prominent place, at least for a time. Conservationists nationwide came to embrace Yellowstone Lake zoning as a model for wilderness preservation. For example, having been persuaded by Wirth, Brower directed his staff to solicit membership support for zoning and sent his editor, Bruce Kilgore, to Yellowstone to attend all the August hearings. Almost all national conservation groups came to support the motorboat ban, bringing the matter to their members' attention and providing regular updates through their publications.[40]

Murie was perhaps the most articulate writer on the conservationist side, with one of his articles at the time providing clear evidence of the sacredness he found in nature (figure 5.6). Writing about his canoe trip around Yellowstone Lake, he discussed an important experience he had enjoyed. He had fallen asleep in a meadow near the shore and when he awoke, he recalled,

> I turned my head, and there a few inches from my eyes was a mass of sedge leaves standing out against the blue sky. Just a bunch of sedge leaves, but at that moment they affected me strangely. Suddenly I felt a kinship, a strong friendliness with those blades before my face. . . . I wondered: was this a realization of a kinship with all life on this planet, represented so humbly by those sedge leaves? . . . To me, wilderness is synonymous with values.

Clearly, Murie saw sacredness in wilderness and therefore wanted it preserved, as did many of his supporters.[41]

Viewed retrospectively, Murie's belief, shared to a large extent by Garrison, was unfamiliar to many boating supporters, especially those in the political world. Motorized boat access had existed in the arms for some time, becoming institutionalized, along with the meanings boaters associated with their activity. Freedom and independence were the values at stake for them: these widely held American values manifested in the belief that personal freedoms are paramount and,

5.6. *Olaus Murie sketching a duck, 1959. Photo by John Montagne. Used with permission.*

ultimately, in a passion for motorboating and in actions to defend that in the Yellowstone Lake arms. These values and this belief were being challenged by the values and beliefs the conservationists held dear, and neither side could fully relate to the other. Just as Murie and Garrison failed to appreciate the freedom of boating, motorboaters and Wyoming politicians could not understand the kinship of sedge leaves or conversations with osprey. This difficulty was evident to some in the NPS camp, including Mr. L. F. Cook, chief of NPS Ranger Activities in Washington, who wrote Director Wirth that Senators McGee and O'Mahoney did not understand the motivations of those promoting wilderness preservation. Some in Yellowstone perceived the same problem, but Garrison instead attempted to educate the public on the need to protect wilderness, evidently believing he could instill his values and beliefs in just one summer. With motorboat use rapidly rising, he had little choice but to do what he could to protect Omar the osprey's wilderness home. Still, he would find the twin values of freedom and independence, and the motorboat fans who embraced them, difficult to overcome.[42]

As the August hearings approached, Garrison encouraged his NPS colleagues to support the proposal cohesively. Having been frustrated by Baker's earlier delays, he wrote, "We must present a united front on the proposal from the Park through the Region Two and Washington offices. There is no room for further dissension within our own ranks." And none showed; rather, in a show of solidarity, Director Wirth traveled to Yellowstone in part to chair the hearings, and the agency suffered no further internal delays.[43]

The hearings, in addition to again highlighting the respective arguments of the two main camps, also provided good evidence that powerful interests were active on both sides of the controversy. The first hearing, held in Cody on August 23, was again dominated by boat club representatives, with only three zoning supporters speaking. In fact, four of the sixteen boating supporters present identified themselves as members of the Billings Boat Club. Former Wyoming governor Milward Simpson spoke against the proposal, as did former assistant secretary of the interior Robert Rose of Casper, Wyoming (by then a lawyer counseling boaters). Additionally, S. J. Gardner of Cody's Husky Oil Company provided a who's who list of guests he had taken out on the lake in his company's boat: "two Secretaries of the Interior, Governors of a number of States, Senators, Congressmen, executives of large oil companies and industrial and commercial firms, such people from the entertainment world as Arthur Godfrey and Esther Williams, [and] Admirals Nimitz, Radford, and Byrd." Although some motorboaters sympathized with nonmotorized users, the boating fraternity was fairly well organized, enjoyed powerful backing, and believed that public access superseded nature preservation.[44]

The second hearing convened at Yellowstone's Lake Hotel the next day and, in contrast to the Cody session, was dominated by zoning supporters. Conservationists who spoke included Olaus and Mardy Murie for The Wilderness Society and National Parks Association, F. Howard Brady and Charlie Piersall for the Wyoming Izaak Walton League, Frank Craighead for the Outdoor Recreation Institute, Kenneth Baldwin for the Montana Wilderness Association, and Bruce Kilgore for the Sierra Club. Additionally, over a hundred people signed petitions in favor of zoning, while seventy Yellowstone Park Company/Lake Hotel employees submitted a petition against it (Sherman Jones's boating operation was based at the hotel, which may have accounted for the opposing petition).[45]

The final hearing was held at Idaho Falls two days later, and produced mixed testimony. For the three hearings collectively, forty-one people spoke in support of zoning, and thirty-one in opposition. However, written testimony, which the secretary of the interior accepted through the end of September, strongly favored zoning, with about 85 percent of over eleven hundred letters (a significant number for the day) written in support. Garrison and Wirth were buoyed by the large majority, and Wirth rapidly proceeded to urge Secretary Seaton to approve the zoning plan. Garrison thought he would make a decision on the matter sometime after the fall election, as he was busy traveling with Vice President Nixon on the presidential election campaign trail.[46]

Senator McGee, not Seaton, took the next step, just after the election. Writing Seaton twice, he articulated his feeling that Garrison was promoting zoning to solve three problems: shoreline erosion, motorboat abuse of park regulations (such as speeding), and wildlife harassment. Addressing these, McGee felt that erosion had been dismissed as a concern. Further, he had been successful in early 1960 in convincing Congress to appropriate funds to Yellowstone for the purchase of new police boats. These new, faster boats enabled park rangers to enforce lake regulations adequately, thereby addressing the second concern. Finally, regarding the wildlife harassment concern, McGee suggested the compromise he had alluded to earlier: ban motorboats from the southernmost two miles of the South and Southeast Arms, where most of the sensitive aquatic birds nested. The remainder of Yellowstone Lake would remain open to motorboats. His proposal made no mention of a speed limit in the arms.[47]

Seaton, though, was not to be dissuaded from the NPS position. He was back from the campaign trail, was a lame duck because Americans had elected John F. Kennedy to be president, and did not fear political retribution if he approved zoning. Moreover, Kennedy and his interior secretary nominee Stewart Udall were both Democrats, sharing party

5.7. Canoeist on the Southeast Arm, 1959. In late 1960, the NPS succeeded in restricting the arms of Yellowstone Lake to nonmotorized boats such as canoes. The policy victory, however, was to be on paper only. Photo by John Montagne. Used with permission.

affiliations with McGee, which made their support for Garrison's proposed zoning unlikely. So, Seaton approved Garrison's zoning plan on December 29, 1960.[48] Garrison and the conservationists rejoiced at this "great conservation and wilderness victory, one with more than local meaning." (figure 5.7). To prepare for future canoeists, he had his staff prepare a canoe manual for the visitors he expected to come seeking out such trips on the lake.[49]

But, strange things can happen in Washington when the White House changes party affiliations. As winter turned into spring, it became clear that Garrison's canoe manual might have been premature. Rumors abounded that McGee was working to overturn zoning, and the rumors were true. In his correspondence with his constituents through June 1961, McGee detailed dogged efforts to overturn the recently approved boating ban. He was "very greatly" disturbed by the matter, and shortly after Seaton announced the zoning regulations, he determined to "press for a realistic regulation governing the use of power boats on

Yellowstone Lake." Before Kennedy even took office on January 20, McGee had already spoken with Stewart Udall about the matter. Udall promised to look into the issue as soon as he assumed office. In his first week there, in fact, he had another conference with McGee, who discussed "at length" the zoning issue. The two also met independently with NPS director Wirth.[50]

In March, McGee gave his compromise proposal to Udall, and then discussed it with him on an all-day plane trip to Wyoming the following month to dedicate a dam. On June 9, McGee wrote a constituent, "By the time you receive this letter, the Department of the Interior will have announced the revised regulations concerning boating on Yellowstone Lake. . . . With the boating season starting June 15, everything should be in order." McGee also wrote another constituent, "Believe me, it was an effort to get the Interior Department to reverse its position regarding the closure of the south and southeast arms." The Department of the Interior announced revised boating regulations that same day. The areas closed to motorboats were reduced to the southernmost two miles of the South and Southeast Arms (recall that this was McGee's compromise proposal), while motorboats would be allowed in the remainder of those two arms at five miles per hour or slower (the source of the speed limit is unclear, although it certainly echoed Baker's suggestion from two years earlier).[51] Certainly, McGee felt so strongly about the issue that he went to great lengths that winter and spring to retain motorboat access to the arms. Wilderness preservation was not the primary issue to him; retaining motorized access was.

Indeed, absent from McGee's letters was any acknowledgment of Garrison's desire to protect the wilderness experience. Instead, he focused exclusively on those things that could be proved (wildlife harassment and motorboat speeding) or disproved (the erosion claim). Although he did acknowledge that the agency wanted to protect portions of the lake "in their natural state," he essentially disregarded the humanistic motivation to preserve the wilderness experience. Instead, as his correspondence illustrates, he favored the boaters' concerns, cooperated closely with them, and knew them on a first-name basis (Wyoming's small population makes this easily possible). In fact, he knew them so well that they had made possible a fish fry that he hosted for his fellow Senate Appropriations Committee members in summer 1960. Stationing their craft on Yellowstone Lake that summer, five boat owners amassed a collection of 160 large Yellowstone cutthroat trout. When McGee gave the word, they flew them to Washington for his fish fry, at which he pitched the case for the special patrol boat allocation ($25,000). The committee took the bait, enabling McGee to push his compromise more successfully (figure 5.8). Simply put, for McGee, who by now was the most powerful character in this story, freedom and independence were values stronger than those put forward by the conservationists. The rest of the story suggests that the same values of freedom and independence prevailed for Americans in general—as they still do.[52]

Just as McGee and his boating constituents had done when Seaton approved zoning, conservationists reacted vigorously when they learned of Interior's action rescinding it. Promptly, Howard Zahniser, author of the Wilderness Bill, and Anthony Wayne Smith, executive secretary of the National Parks Association, requested a repeal of Udall's decision

5.8. Motorboats on Yellowstone Lake, c. 1940. Although this photo dates from before the zoning controversy, it illustrates a problem (boaters speeding, and ranger inability to catch the perpetrators with outdated, slow boats) that Garrison and Senator McGee sought to address in different ways: Garrison, by banning motorboats from the lake's more remote and sensitive arms, and McGee, by securing faster boats for improved law enforcement. Photographer unknown; courtesy of NPS, Yellowstone National Park (YELL 29061).

and yet another public hearing on the matter. Assistant Secretary of the Interior John A. Carver Jr. consented, scheduling the hearing in Salt Lake City for July 17, 1961 (this would be the fifth, and final, hearing).[53] Throughout June and July, letters contesting Udall's decision poured into his office, and conservationists once again rallied their members to attend or send statements to the Salt Lake City hearing. Even the *New York Times* weighed in, encouraging a return to the motorboat ban.[54]

Interior solicitor Frank J. Barry presided over the July hearing as examiner. About ten persons spoke to contest Udall's decision, and six persons supported it. Boaters claimed that boats, unlike cars, left no trace of their passage. They desired use of the whole lake and requested a twenty-mile-per-hour speed limit in the arms instead of five miles per hour (saying such a low speed would be hard to maintain). Conservationists viewed Udall's decision as a capitulation to boating interests, Senator McGee, and seven of his constituents (who were not specifically named). William Riaski of the Izaak Walton League particularly deplored the fact that Udall's and McGee's actions stripped the NPS of "its entire power to regulate national parks." Barry also accepted written testimony through the end of September, receiving more than 450 letters by August 1.[55]

Garrison attended the hearing and gave a comprehensive history of events. He touched on the erosion issue, but noted that it was only a concern at the Molly Islands, where boaters' wakes—from as much as a half-mile distant—inundated sensitive shoreline nests (clearly, he downplayed the red herring and emphasized the valid concern). Of more concern to him now was enforcement of the five-mile-per-hour speed limit. At that time, such a slow speed, over water instead of land, was basically impossible to measure. Land-based radar would not work over water, and inquiries around the country were unsuccessful at finding any effective over-water speed measuring devices. Already he had been frustrated in court, his staff unable to give a judge exact speeds of violating boaters. Certainly one could expect some reluctance from the agency to embrace watered-down regulations forced upon it, but it was clear that the five-mile-per-hour speed limit was essentially unenforceable. By the time another three months had passed, Garrison emphatically told Director Wirth that Udall's regulations were a failure: "Our experience failed to show that the new regulations achieved the wilderness use objective we had hoped they would have. . . . The present regulations do not achieve the preservation of wilderness, they do not satisfy the boating fraternity, and they are extremely difficult to enforce."[56]

The rest of 1961 passed without further action by Barry, Udall, or McGee. A "deathly silence" reigned on the matter; Udall's office made no announcements one way or another about it. Solicitor Barry took the time to contemplate the hearing testimony, Garrison's letter, the science of the day, and some experiences he had had in Yellowstone just before the hearing. With Garrison, he had traveled to Yellowstone Lake's arms, camping off the shore of Frank Island, the lake's largest. The next day, the two men landed and walked ashore, where they enjoyed (in Garrison's words), "a completely hushed and primitive environment. There was nothing to indicate that man had ever stood here before—no ax marks, no footprints, just a quiet, deep spongy moss on the forest floor. We sat on a moss-draped log and conversed in whispers . . . . It was humbling. We could hear the silence."[57]

The two men returned to their boat, where their wilderness experience continued with an osprey flying overhead from its nearby nest. The bird caught a fish, then fought off both an eagle and a raven attempting to steal its catch. This "raw wilderness battle," however, abruptly ended, when (as Garrison wrote):

> a fast-planing cruiser rounded the west end of Frank Island. It suddenly began to circle wildly and criss-cross its own wake. Our binoculars revealed that the boat operator was using a $25,000, twenty-five-foot cruiser with a heavy motor to pursue a pod of molting and flightless ducks. We could not observe his results, but we could easily see his boat number. As our own cruiser began its journey to the lake dock, I could not help reflecting on the tragedy of this hapless boatman. We had his number, and Solicitor Barry had a new view of the problem.[58]

Indeed he did; the two experiences amply illustrated what Garrison was trying to protect—and protect against. After his Yellowstone visit, and given the testimony from the hearing, it was probably no surprise that the following spring Barry recommended returning to the motorboat ban in the arms. He also denied that the NPS was in any way obligated to allow motorboat use in the park. By zoning the lake as Garrison desired, "those willing to expend the effort will still be able to visit the area in its natural state. The wilderness will be preserved."[59]

Assistant Secretary of the Interior Carver concurred with Barry, and urged Udall to "face the music as early as possible" by briefing the congressional delegations of the four most affected states. Udall's staff then drafted a press release announcing that only hand-propelled craft would be allowed in Yellowstone Lake's arms.[60] But the press release was never issued. Rather, McGee, once again disagreeing with the restriction on motorboat use, played his last hand: he took the matter to President Kennedy for relief. The historic record is silent on Kennedy's response, but it is clear that Udall backed off on reinstating the boating ban.[61] Although he initially assured conservationists who complained about his earlier retreat from the boating ban that it was "quite likely that some changes will be made" to the park's boating regulations, by fall 1962 he was no longer predicting any change. When asked several months later what he was going to do about the matter, Udall said he would do nothing, because boaters would "kill him if he tried." Udall lived, and although several persons called for investigations into McGee's actions, none were ever performed. McGee, backed by the president himself, was still the most powerful character in the story; indeed, he—and the values he espoused—was the undisputed victor.[62]

The matter of wilderness designation on the arms came up again in the late 1960s and early 1970s, when Yellowstone authorities developed their formal wilderness proposal pursuant to the Wilderness Act. Although they did not at first include the Yellowstone Lake arms in the proposal, they changed their minds after the formal hearings on the proposal in 1972, at which members of the public expressed widespread support for such inclusion. The agency then revised and forwarded the wilderness recommendation on to the secretary of the interior, the president, and Congress, all in 1972. There it has sat ever since, never receiving congressional consideration. Although the reason for this lapse is unclear, including the arms in the proposal probably doomed it. To pass a wilderness designation, proponents must have support from their state's congressional delegation. Senator McGee was in office until 1977, most likely killing support for the proposal then and thereafter.[63]

Garrison left Yellowstone in 1964. In boldly promoting a motor-free love of wildness during his tenure there, he brought to the surface a conflict that would likely reappear were the NPS to revive the long-dormant wilderness recommendation. He and his conservationist allies promoted a vision of sacred nature temples where motorized vehicles were not welcome, while motorboat groups defended a form of access imbued for them with meanings of freedom and independence. Overall, the latter meanings were more familiar to Americans than nature's sacredness, so the eventual compromise preserved some motorboat access.[64] Trying to ban motorboats from the arms today would likely be no more successful than it was for Garrison fifty years ago, for freedom remains stronger as a majority value than nature's sacredness. In fact, twice since the zoning controversy Yellowstone managers have tangled with Wyoming interests over forms of motorized access symbolizing freedom and independence to their adherents, and both times park managers lost.[65] No matter how passionately conservationists might endeavor to protect the Thorofare's wildness, Wyoming politicians (especially those from Cody) have repeatedly demonstrated that, when it comes to policymaking in the park, they hold the upper hand. The Thorofare is the winner and the loser, roadless yet motorized. Were it possible to make these arms motor-free, the Thorofare would be even more remote than it already is, and it would also feature a sizeable chunk of water wilderness. For the foreseeable future, though, freedom and independence reign for visitors to the arms.

Ten years after he left Yellowstone, Garrison wrote a postscript to the controversy. He couched it within a fishing trip on Yellowstone Lake, regaling in its splendors. With the passage of time, his opinion of the compromise had changed; his bitterness had softened. By 1974, he felt that the five-mile-per-hour compromise was an "85% victory on zoning and a compromise with which the park has been able to operate harmoniously." Certainly the compromise preserved some motorized access and protected most wildlife in the area, and the agency learned to live with it (in part because boater behavior improved).[66] However, as my experience earlier today illustrates, Garrison's assessment may not be entirely accurate. After an hour, that motorboat with the generator left, obediently adhering to the five-mile-per-hour limit as it traveled north, out of sight and sound. Motorboats were absent for the rest of the day, leaving me with a natural soundscape for about 85 percent of the day. That figure might, as Garrison wrote, seem to suggest that a wilderness experience on the South or Southeast Arms is largely assured. Yet, as anyone who has been jolted out of a natural reverie knows (like Frank Barry), one experience like that can color, mar, or even ruin a whole trip.[67] That is true for me, for as quickly as I now recall the tranquility of my hour with only the sounds of nature for company, I also remember how it ended. We are all the loser when compromises leave room for such disharmony.

((

Eric and Josh return from their hike mid-afternoon, happy and a little sunburnt. Looking at their photos of the Thorofare from

5.9. Looking into the heart of the Thorofare: the view from Langford Cairn, 2014. In this view, the horizon is delineated by (right to left) the Two Ocean Plateau, the Thorofare Plateau, and the Trident (with patches of snow on it). Photo by Eric Compas. Used with permission.

5.10. A common sight in the Thorofare: a grizzly bear track, 2014. Photo by Eric Compas. Used with permission.

Langford Cairn, it is easy to see why trappers found it such an inviting thoroughfare, for the Yellowstone River Valley dominates the view. Three miles wide and flat as a pancake, the valley curves out of view into the distance (figure 5.9). Just within view is the Thorofare Plateau, the vicinity of the remotest point. This view, then, encapsulates the heart of the Thorofare, a wild place with few equals outside of Alaska. As if to emphasize that point, Eric and Josh show me more photos from their hike: grizzly bear tracks in the mud from yesterday's rain (figure 5.10).

Langford Cairn also provides a sweeping view of the Southeast Arm. Across the arm in their photos is the Promontory, with Mounts Sheridan and Hancock rising above its rumpled spine. In the distance to the north, the arm's waters expand to the main body of the lake where the Promontory ends. Our drop-off beach is out of sight, but plainly visible is the entire route we paddled from there, as well as that we will traverse tomorrow. No boats are visible, giving one the illusion that it is wilderness. It is a deceptively comforting illusion, belied, of course, by my morning visitor and the outcome of a controversy a half century ago.

Sean takes off for a stroll, and the rest of us take advantage of the warm sunshine and rinse off in the lake—myself included, holding on to Eric and Josh. The water is shockingly cold, not much warmer than having a bucket of ice dumped on us. Sean takes a dip when he returns, despite our warnings—or perhaps, perceiving a neighborly challenge, because of them. The rest of the day passes peacefully and quietly, with tortellini for dinner again and camaraderie abounding. We enjoy another sunset reflected in the lake, this roadless yet motorized place, so near and yet so far, politically, from the Thorofare (figure 5.11).

As we will see, Garrison's successors continue to navigate managerial challenges to protect wildness and beauty in the Thorofare, though their challenges are not always as political as his was. They are, however, every bit as complex, with resolutions sometimes even more difficult to produce.

5.11. Sean and the author enjoy another sunset on the Southeast Arm, 2014. Mount Hancock is the small bump on the horizon above Sean, seated on the ground. Photo by Eric Compas. Used with permission.

DAY 6 On the Edge

A thing is right when it tends to preserve the integrity, stability, and beauty of the biotic community. It is wrong when it tends otherwise.
—Aldo Leopold, 1949

Another clear sky with patches of fog greets us as we emerge from the tents. We are up early, anxious to break camp and get to paddling while morning stillness keeps the lake calm. Eric and I know there is a mile or two of rock-bound shore to put behind us today. Regularly pounded by waves that build to six feet tall across one of the lake's longest fetches— about fifteen miles, aligned with the prevailing southwest wind—that shoreline has lost all easily eroded material and consequently offers no shelter to the unfortunate canoeist caught in high wind. When he and I paddled it eleven years ago, rough water forced us to wait a couple hours before attempting it. Feeling the wind diminish slightly, we hopped in and took off. That reduced wind still was strong enough to reduce our speed to a crawl, our most powerful strokes advancing the boat a mere six inches. That same wind kept the waves tall enough to splash occasional droplets of water on our load, despite our quartering moves. We were at the limit of what our boat and our bodies could do, with no room for error. Happily for us, the wind did not increase, so we made it through, pulling into our campsite an hour later, our arms and shoulders aching from the sustained effort.

Today we do not want to repeat that excitement, so my three companions busy themselves pulling down the tents (still wet and cold with a blend of dew and frost) while I plod my way through breakfast. ALS has weakened my tongue and the muscles in my throat, turning each meal

6.1. Another day of paddling begins, 2014.
Eric is in the bow, Josh in the stern, and the
author is along for the ride. Photo by Eric
Compas. Used with permission.

into an hour-long affair as I slowly chew my food and concentrate on swallowing safely. My epiglottis is slow to close (again due to ALS), so I am at constant risk of choking. The three of them understand this, so they regularly serve me first and then clean up while I finish eating. As well, they try not to engage me in much conversation while I am eating, knowing that it is both difficult and a little unsafe for me to talk with food in my mouth. In this way, a side effect of ALS is that meals lose some conviviality, compounding the isolation that slurred speech already forces on the disease's victims. My three friends compensate by discussing topics of interest to all four of us and by seating themselves around me, so I still feel an integral, if muted, part of the group.

Breakfast eaten and our bags packed, we are under way by nine o'clock (figure 6.1). Today we will paddle out of the Southeast Arm and onto the main body of the lake. In so doing, we will leave the Thorofare farther behind and enter a place where humans and their impacts are more evident. Much as the landscape itself prompted thoughts of wildness as we paddled into the Thorofare four days ago, paddling out of it today will provide signs of how easily wildness can be lost. Such evidence of contemporary human impacts reminds us that what we have in the Thorofare is something both special and fragile, necessitating ongoing efforts to protect. Today's land managers love wildness and beauty as much as yesterday's, so they carry on with efforts to pass the Thorofare on to our children and grandchildren in the same condition we enjoy today. Through such actions, the history of preserving this marvelous place continues into a second century.

☾

The first sign we see is a buoy with a small flag on it, marking a place where lake trout are abundant. There is, perhaps, no greater an intruder in the Greater Yellowstone Ecosystem than this fish. First confirmed in Yellowstone Lake in 1994, the fish were illegally brought here a decade or two earlier from nearby Lewis Lake, where they were stocked by the US Army in the late 1800s. Native to the Great Lakes, lake trout are well-adapted

6.2. *Yellowstone cutthroat trout migrating up a lake tributary to spawn (no date). NPS photo by Bob Gresswell; courtesy of NPS, Yellowstone National Park (http://www.nps.gov/features/ yell/slidefile/index.htm, accessed September 19, 2015).*

to deep, cold water. They prey on other fish and have dramatically altered local ecology when introduced to other western lakes. In those lakes, they eventually wiped out the resident cutthroat trout, which is precisely the threat they pose here in this lake, home to most of the remaining Yellowstone cutthroat trout.[1]

Rarely is one species an ecological substitute for another, and that is the case here. Yellowstone cutthroat trout inhabit the top of the water column, where they are prey for a suite of predators, including bald eagles, osprey, and pelicans. Moreover, they spawn in tributary streams, where they are potential food for many others, such as grizzly bears (figure 6.2). All told, over forty species of birds and mammals feed on them here, the fish sometimes making up a majority of their diets. At the peak of their spawning runs (one of which goes up the Yellowstone River, well into the Thorofare), for example, a well-positioned (and hungry) grizzly can pack away fifty cutthroats in a day. Not so with lake trout, which live and spawn down deep, safe from most predators and from becoming part of the food chain—except that of top predator.

Alarmed by the prospect of an ecological collapse, park managers immediately responded to the lake trout news by attempting to curtail their numbers (in a lake of this size, no technology exists to eradicate the pests). Using gill nets sized to target the intruders, and focusing on areas where lake trout are especially abundant, they have run a netting program ever since. When scientific reviews of that program in 2008 and 2011 found that it was not making a large enough dent in the lake trout population, park managers redoubled their efforts by adding a second netting boat, using more nets, employing new ways to home in on lake trout concentrations, and constantly searching for new ways to improve their success rate. As of late 2015, the program had removed over two million lake trout. They weigh up to thirty pounds (cutthroats top out at about five pounds), and when cut open, fisheries biologists find that many of them have small cutthroats in their stomachs (figure 6.3). Based on lake trout predation rates, each lake trout removed means forty-one cutthroats still living (per year).

Still, this may not be enough, for cutthroat numbers have taken a nose-dive. Perhaps the best measure of that decline is the number of spawning cutthroat annually swimming up Clear Creek, a Yellowstone Lake tributary we will pass on our last day. Park managers have monitored this number for over half a century; it peaked around seventy thousand in the late 1970s, but bottomed out at only 538 thirty years later—a 99 percent decline. Also contributing to the decline is whirling disease, caused by a microscopic parasite from Europe that makes a fish swim in circles, reducing their ability to forage and to escape predators. First identified in the lake in 1998, cutthroat trout in Pelican Creek (the second-largest lake tributary) have virtually disappeared due to the disease, compounding the threat from lake trout, which are immune to whirling disease. However, there are preliminary indications that the lake trout control effort may finally be paying off (whirling disease seems to be confined to the lake's northern margins). Beginning in 2012, the number of spawning cutthroat in Clear Creek began a modest increase, while

6.3. *Lake trout removed from Yellowstone Lake and dissected to reveal multiple cutthroat trout in their stomachs, 2007. NPS photo by Stacey Gunther; courtesy of NPS, Yellowstone National Park.*

the number of lake trout caught per net began to decline. It is too early to break out the champagne bottles, but these new numbers at last provide a small ray of hope.

All this—twenty years of effort—because some misinformed or ill-intentioned person or group of people thought it would be a good idea to introduce an alien fish here. There is hardly a better example of the fragility of natural ecosystems, or of the ease with which an element of wildness can be compromised or lost. For us and the Thorofare, the ecological loss is compounded by the intrusion of more motorboats and noise into the South and Southeast Arms, as the netting crews follow lake trout to the lake's far corners (indeed, the boat that ended my hour of natural quiet yesterday was one of the netting boats—going too fast, but otherwise doing its job). It would be next to impossible to do the netting from a nonmotorized boat, so for the foreseeable future the control program means we will have motorboats in the arms. In sad irony, this means that for now, Wyoming's bullying influence is moot.

"The foreseeable future," moreover, seems to understate the impact. The program will have to be continued *in perpetuity*, unless and until technology enables us to kill every last lake trout without also killing the native cutthroat trout. We are nowhere close to having such a tool now, and it is hard to conceive of any technique that would eliminate every last lake trout in a water body this big and deep (the lake's maximum depth is just over four hundred feet). The perpetual demand of the control program, then, is emblematic of the commitment required to protect this place, to hand a little wildness to the next generation. It is a responsibility bordering on forever, always assisting an ecosystem that, not so long ago, was thriving.

But, if our experience with another charismatic animal species—grizzly bears—is any indication, that assistance may some day drop to a level much reduced from today's efforts. In the 1970s, grizzly bear numbers plummeted to only about a hundred throughout the Greater Yellowstone Ecosystem, due to changes in NPS's waste management that brought bears into increased conflict with people. Seeking to restore more natural conditions to the park and its wildlife, park managers closed several open dumps at which many bears fed. Casting about for replacement food sources, some bears went back to wild foods while others went to nearby campgrounds, where they obtained food from careless or uninformed campers. Property damage and injuries to people rose as the bears pursued human foods. When that happens, the bears lose out, as park managers trap and remove them to protect humans and their property. Well over a hundred bears were removed at that time, a hit to the population that resulted in the bear being declared "threatened" and gaining Endangered Species Act protections in 1975.[2]

To restore bear numbers to safe and natural levels, land managers throughout the Yellowstone area adopted new policies, all intended to protect the bruins and prevent them from obtaining human food. They began educating visitors about proper food storage and enforcing associated regulations. They also installed bear-proof garbage cans throughout the park and closed certain backcountry areas (including large portions of the Thorofare) at times when bears frequent them. Finally, Wyoming and Montana terminated their hunting seasons for bears.

Slowly, the grizzly population responded, doubling their numbers by 1990 and then again by 2004. Three years later, the US Fish and

Wildlife Service felt they were doing so well that the agency removed them from the threatened and endangered species list. However, several environmental organizations contested that decision and the courts sided with them, putting the bear back on the list in 2009, where they remain. Meanwhile, despite the concurrent loss of cutthroat trout, one of the grizzly's richest food sources, bear numbers continued growing, to about six hundred in 2010. They have expanded their range to the south and east, reoccupying areas in the Absaroka, Wind River, and Teton mountain ranges where they had not been seen in decades. To accommodate this growth, Forest Service managers have extended their existing bear management policies to new areas and also begun working with the National Wildlife Federation (a well-respected national conservation organization) and willing ranchers to move cattle and sheep out of harm's way. In this voluntary program, the federation has purchased and retired grazing leases that had entitled ranchers to graze livestock on Forest Service lands. Targeting areas newly occupied by bears, which occasionally prey on cows and sheep, the federation and Forest Service have been able to eliminate grazing from over six hundred thousand acres, thereby enabling grizzlies to reoccupy those areas without becoming nuisances for area ranchers.[3]

In the 1970s, the idea that grizzly bears would be occupying such far-flung corners of the Yellowstone ecosystem just thirty years hence would have been greeted with amazement and possibly even derision. Bear numbers were so critically low, and their rate of reproduction so slow (only two or three cubs per female of reproductive age, every three years), that extinction from the area seemed more likely. Yet, given a helping hand (or several) and sufficient time, they prospered. Their management is no longer a crisis, more a part of everyday park and forest operations.

The situation is the same for two other species found in the Thorofare, wolves and bison (an occasional bull bison wanders south as far as the ranger station, though no herds do). Wolves were eliminated from the Greater Yellowstone Ecosystem in the 1920s, and bison were all but eliminated a little earlier, numbering only twenty-three at the turn of the century. As with grizzlies, however, both species are now abundant, owing to a twenty-year reintroduction effort for wolves and an equally long time period of careful stewardship and supplementation for bison. Their management remains contentious, but there is little concern for their welfare.[4] The same outcome for cutthroat trout is the hope. However, they are a different species, inhabiting a different environment and facing different threats, so management attention befitting a crisis will continue. For now, they are the most recent animal whose future in the Thorofare depends on the interventions of park managers and the animal's ability to respond.

The next such animal could be moose. As noted two days ago, moose were once very common in the Thorofare. References to sightings of forty or more moose in one day are common in the historic literature, and one traveler through the area in 1938 had a one-day total of seventy-six sightings! Researchers estimated there were a few hundred of them in the Thorofare in the 1920s and 1930s. Today, there are far fewer, in part because the 1988 fires burned a lot of their winter forage, the needles of subalpine fir and Engelmann spruce. Hunting outside the park and predation by wolves and bears are factors as well, as are the increased prevalence of a parasite that attaches to their carotid artery and low birth rates (mainly a low percentage of twins). Researchers suspect an additional, more systemic cause lurks behind some of these problems, such as global warming, but that connection is unconfirmed. Consequently, the prognosis for the Thorofare moose is unclear.[5]

The native residents of the Thorofare, then, reveal a recurring pattern of disturbance by people, protective intervention by the NPS, and recovery to healthy levels. In the past, relatively straightforward techniques of reintroduction, animal husbandry, and protection were sufficient for the task, and important contributors to the area's wild character were restored. With cutthroat trout and possibly moose, though, such techniques may not be enough, challenging the NPS to search for new technologies and methods to protect its charges. The threats are more complex now, and it remains to be seen whether we can successfully meet them. The fate of the cutthroat trout, moose, and other animals in the future, therefore, hangs in the balance, as does the all-too-easily-compromised characteristic of the Thorofare we call wildness.

In the boats today, though, our fate seems more secure, as the breeze remains light with waves just a couple inches in height. Soon even that breeze disappears, replaced by a calm that lasts the rest of today's journey. Under a blazing late summer sun, the temperature soars into the upper seventies. Our biggest risk today is sunburn, so we substitute sunscreen for our extra layers. Soon the gravelly beach gives way to boulders and then a twelve-foot wall of volcanic bedrock (figure 6.4). We have arrived at the stretch of shoreline with the long fetch, but today the only water movement is the trickle of sweat behind my ears. We soon pass the spot where Eric and I hauled out in 2003 to wait for calmer conditions. Today, we paddle on, loitering now and then to study the swirls and bands of color in the rock. This is andesite, deposited by volcanic activity fifty or sixty million years ago, with occasional streaks of sulfur and iron hinting at more recent thermal activity. Andesite weathers into fertile soils, though here, even above the reach of waves, it is thin. Trees are sparse above the naked bedrock and dominated by limber pines,

6.4. *A shore with no place to land, 2014. On windy days, waves the size of ocean swells erode all sand and gravel here, leaving nothing but volcanic bedrock. Photo by Eric Compas. Used with permission.*

which, like the grasses surrounding them, can cope with the frequently dry conditions that come with the thin soil.

Soon we notice something we have not seen in several days: another group of paddlers. There are seven of them, all in kayaks, and soon they pass us, southbound. Smiles grace their faces and their pace is relaxed, like ours. It is obvious that they are enjoying the day and the scenery as much as we are.

The image of relaxed kayakers taking in the scenery is not, however, one that a kayaking advocacy group known as American Whitewater has projected in its requests to open Yellowstone rivers to boating. In 1950, the NPS banned boating on the park's rivers to make enforcement of its fishing regulations easier. Except for the Lewis River providing boat access to Shoshone Lake, the prohibition remains in effect today. Twice in the last twenty-five years, American Whitewater has led campaigns to coax the NPS into lifting that ban, but neither time has the group succeeded. Both times, the group focused solely on rivers offering whitewater runs, leaving the mellower rivers, like the upper Yellowstone River through the Thorofare, out of the debate. In so doing, the group subtly, and perhaps unknowingly, perpetuated the image of kayaking as a thrill sport, an image readily observed in the group's magazine, which is filled with pictures of kayakers paddling through whitewater and even shooting out over the brink of eighty- or one-hundred-foot waterfalls. One can get an adrenaline rush just looking at them.[6]

That thrill sport image is at odds with the vision of parks as contemplative places where recreation is more reflective, a vision long advocated by national park observers, from landscape architect Frederick Law Olmsted Jr. in the late 1800s to twentieth-century legal scholar Joseph Sax and writer Edward Abbey (figure 6.5). Yellowstone's managers have continued to articulate that vision in denying the kayaking requests. In their reasoning, they also include resource concerns like the fact that boaters could disturb wildlife, but preserving a vignette of wild, unpeopled nature is at the core of their thinking. To them, recreation in the park should be a means to an end—that of absorbing the park's grandeur and considering its meaning—not an end in itself, as whitewater boating can be.[7]

6.5. Kayaking: a thrill sport or a form of contemplative recreation (2014)? The latter vision is suggested in this image (of Sean), while the former is often seen in images of kayakers on whitewater rivers. Photo by Eric Compas. Used with permission.

Of course, kayaking or rafting a river can be a means to that end, as anyone who has floated the Grand Canyon or paddled a kayak can attest. There is actually even a website making that point about touring the Thorofare by inflatable rafts or kayaks. Boating is allowed in the Teton and Washakie Wildernesses, and the sponsors of that website chronicle an extended trip through that part of the Thorofare. Included are many photographs and three videos of glorious scenery, some with members of the trip soaking it in while in their kayaks. For every such contemplative view, however, there is another showing the thrills that seem to be part and parcel of the sport. Some show the men shooting rapids while another shows one of them boldly, and with challenge in his voice, stating that the trip has been "f***ing awesome!" The website includes a link to a companion site that advocates that the ban on floating the Yellowstone through the park's side of the Thorofare be lifted.[8] For some viewers, it would be hard not to agree (particularly if such use were subject to the same backcountry camping rules and limits governing other wilderness users), but others would object (perhaps citing the overt testosterone or thrill-seeking).

As exemplified by that website, kayaking epitomizes the conundrum facing the Thorofare's managers when new forms of recreation or new evolutions of existing forms appear: Are they appropriate in the wilderness? The answer to that question is often not easy. Managers turn first to the direction provided by law and policy. Some forms of recreation that are explicitly thrill-seeking, such as BASE or bungee jumping, are either specifically banned or so obviously at odds with park and wilderness purposes that the decision is straightforward. As well, anything motorized or mechanical is forbidden by the Wilderness Act, so the decision on things like drones and personal hovercraft is already made. When those forms of guidance fail to provide a clear answer, managers examine the activity more closely, looking for potential impacts of the activity on natural or cultural resources. For example, many studies have shown that noise from recreationists can adversely affect wildlife. If there are any impacts that cannot be tolerated or mitigated, then the decision is again easy.[9]

For many activities like river boating, these sources of guidance do not provide a simple answer. When that is the case (and it often is), managers have to rely on more subjective criteria, such as whether the activity fosters or encourages an appreciation of the place, and whether it comports with the park or wilderness tradition.[10] Kayaking clearly can do the former, but whether it can do the latter is not so clear. As a nonmechanized means of travel, it certainly is in line with the modes of travel envisioned by the architects of the Wilderness Act, which provides guidance to both park and forest managers. This rationale is, at least in part, the reason the USFS allows it in the Teton and Washakie Wildernesses (also, the USFS has long been more accommodating toward recreation than the NPS, but, conversely, may have been unable to consider the use and its impacts before it became established). For park managers, though, the more salient point is that no form of river boating has historically occurred in the Thorofare, predisposing them against it. However, there are still more considerations.

Abuses with existing recreation are another factor for land managers to consider. In the Thorofare, the most widespread problems are associated with horsepacking. Horses and mules are heavy animals, easily capable of trampling vegetation if they are not carefully managed. For example, trails may have up to a dozen parallel tracks in meadows, where packstrings can spread out. Similarly, at unbridged stream crossings and wet areas, trails can turn into mud wallows. Wet weather conditions magnify this problem, turning entire reaches of trail into a slippery mess. I once had the misfortune of hiking a stretch of the Box Creek Trail in the Teton Wilderness that epitomized this problem, having been churned into an impassable thigh-deep mess of muddy water by a previous pack train. Linda and I had to bushwhack alongside the linear mudhole for two or three miles before conditions improved. Campsites can be equally affected, turned into wastelands of bare dirt with a liberal mixing of pounded horse and mule droppings. On the south shore of Bridger Lake (again in the Teton Wilderness), such mismanagement has made much of that shoreline—a mile of it—an eyesore unusable to anyone with working eyes and nose.[11]

Of course, proper trail construction and maintenance, responsible outfitter behavior, and adequate enforcement of regulations would fix or prevent all these problems. Budgets for both managing agencies have been hit hard in recent decades, though, so enforcement is suffering and much trail work is done by volunteers. The situation is worse for the Forest Service, but the NPS is not so flush with funding that it can easily handle another use. Kayaking would almost certainly create far fewer impacts than horsepacking does, but ranger staff would still have to be prepared for another form of rescue (swiftwater). Without sufficient funding to address existing training needs and resource problems, park managers may feel hard-pressed to welcome a new form of recreation.

They may also be concerned about the erosion of wilderness space that new and evolving forms of recreation can cause. Some of these incarnations, especially the "extreme" sports that challenge participants to achieve new records or extremes, encourage and enable people to cover more ground in a day of hiking, running, or paddling than ever before.

Distances that used to require several days of travel are now covered in just a day or two. In this way, more people travel farther into wilderness, and remoteness comes to mean less. Some wildness disappears when trails and streams turn into racetracks for extreme athletes and the country's remotest point becomes just a way station on a one- or two-day paddle.

Ultimately, in matters like this, park and wilderness managers are guided by an unwritten code of restraint. Such has long guided them; indeed, it is the reason we still have such a large chunk of wilderness. By saying no to most uses, we have the Thorofare. To be more permissive would have meant this area would be just another developed western landscape with roads, golf courses, ski areas, condominiums, and noise in place of meadows, forest, elk, grizzly bears, and natural tranquility. Even if the transformation had not been so complete, park managers know that, once established, a given park use is almost impossible to eliminate, as motorboat use on the arms of the lake illustrates. Also, they are sensitive to the wilderness experience and how easily it can be radically altered by people. My memory of the Cirque of the Towers in the Bridger Wilderness in Wyoming's Wind River Mountains, for example, will forever be colored by climbers on the towers shouting to each other. Having hiked for two days in 2004 to get to that spectacular place, my wilderness experience suddenly seemed more suburban than wild as I listened to their calls (and I never returned to the area). It does not take much imagination to hear the shouts coming from excited kayakers in the Thorofare. Restraint means saying no to most uses, even apparently benign ones like kayaking, but it also means preserving the remotest place intact.[12]

For these reasons, Yellowstone's rivers are, for now, off limits to boaters. Public debate about river boating in the park continues, though, with another interest group, the American Packrafting Association, persuading Wyoming's congressional delegation to introduce the "River Paddling Protection Act" into both houses of Congress in 2013 and 2014. The bill directed the NPS to open Yellowstone's rivers and streams to hand-propelled boating, rescinding the park's ban on such. In early 2014, the bill actually passed the House but stalled in the Senate amid concerns about congressional meddling into agency affairs and citizen opposition. Such high-level visibility indicates that the debate is far from resolved and that potential threats to the wild continue; indeed, Wyoming congresswoman Cynthia Lummis (R) reintroduced the bill early in 2015.[13]

Kayaking the park's rivers is the example used here, but there are and will be other forms of recreation with proponents equally ardent about their activity and its merits in the Thorofare. Park and wilderness managers are in the unenviable position of having to tell some disappointed enthusiasts no, that wilderness cannot be all things to all people without losing some of its fundamental wildness. A few kayakers could multiply or, when combined with some other new form of recreation, catapult human presence to a level that means solitude is rarely available or an especially sensitive animal moves on. If managers do not exercise restraint in their judgments, in other words, death by a thousand cuts may be the result. A once-wild landscape may be tamed.

☾

A better kind of tame envelops us today, as we continue paddling a lake whose greatest disturbance, at least for the moment, comes from our paddles. Soon we round the rocky headlands we have been enjoying and see that they will soon give way to cobblestone beaches. A mile or two distant is Park Point, its sloping grassy meadow the namesake for the point. Our campsite sits in a graceful curve of the shore between the point and us, where forest temporarily resumes its lakeside presence. A half hour later, we arrive and set up camp for the last time.

We eat lunch and then relax for the afternoon. It is a warm one, the warmest of the trip, so we seek shade. Looking around, I realize that, despite being in a forest, shade is not plentiful here, for many of the trees—half or more—are dead or dying. Fire has not burned here for many decades, so they are most likely victims of beetles, the spruce budworm in the spruces and the mountain pine beetle in the lodgepole and whitebark pines. Such beetles lay their eggs in the bark, and the larvae burrow into the cambium, eating and tunneling their way through that growing tissue. Eventually, they girdle the tree and it dies, while the larvae transform into beetles, exit the trees, and fly off to mate and lay their eggs on more trees. These beetles are native, and outbreaks of them are nothing new, having occurred several times here in the twentieth century. They seem to be linked to drought, such as the one that was gripping this area when Eric and I last paddled through here. Trees can ordinarily flood insect pests like these out with sap, but when stressed by drought that defense can fail. Usually, enough other trees survive to reseed the forest, or fires burn through, as happened in 1988 in much of the Thorofare, hard on the heels of the previous outbreak. Either way, the forest cycle carries on, as it has for millennia.[14]

However, global warming is warping that cycle, mainly by warming things up and giving the beetles more of an edge. Tens of millions of acres are now infested with them, with trees dying by the hundreds of millions from New Mexico to British Columbia. Here in Yellowstone, the situation is not that acute, largely because the fires of the last thirty years have produced a lot of young trees that are not as susceptible to beetle kill. The same cannot be said for the Washakie Wilderness, where global warming is magnifying the drier conditions already present there. Thousands of acres of trees are dead, especially in the more arid eastern sections. Of particular note is the whitebark pine, suffering precipitous losses there and throughout the Greater Yellowstone Ecosystem. In some whitebark stands, all or nearly all mature trees have succumbed. For example, above the desk at which I write hangs a photo of the upper meadow on the South Fork of the Yellowstone, with Younts Peak and Thorofare Mountain rising above it. The lowest slopes of the two peaks have a thin covering of the pines, over half of them gray, their needles gone. I took that picture in 2003; when I first camped there eight years earlier, there were few gray trees. Whitebarks are not only stressed by mountain pine beetles and drought, but also by a third stressor, again anthropogenic: white pine blister rust. This nonnative fungus has been present in the Yellowstone area for decades, but only recently has it caused substantial mortality—again, likely because whitebarks are drought-stressed. This triple whammy is killing whitebarks by the millions in the Greater Yellowstone Ecosystem (figure 6.6).

6.6. Dead whitebark pines in the Absaroka-Beartooth Wilderness north of the Thorofare, 2011. Eric's son Tom and the author pause in this rapidly dwindling forest type. Photo by Eric Compas. Used with permission.

The loss is more than just aesthetic, for a host of animals depend on the tree and its nuts, loaded with fat. Clark's nutcrackers cache them, sometimes forgetting to retrieve a few, which can then germinate into the next generation. Red squirrels pile the cones at the base of favorite trees, digging through winter snow to bring them up and eat the nuts. Known as middens, these storehouses are sought out and raided by grizzly bears fattening up for hibernation. In years of good cone production, nine out of ten grizzlies will feast in the whitebark pine groves, and pregnant females will have larger litters the following winter. Like the center stone in an arch, whitebark pines support many other species, so ecologists consider them a keystone species.

The Forest Service and the Park Service have responded to the whitebark's decline by initiating several monitoring programs, searching for trees that are resistant to the rust and cultivating such varieties in nurseries for eventual transplant back into the landscape. They have found an abundance of young trees alive and seemingly thriving in the landscape, as well as occasional adult trees apparently resistant to the rust. These are encouraging signs, but they are tempered by the fact that whitebarks do not bear cones until they are at least eighty years old, so it will be a long time before grizzlies feast on their nuts as they did a decade or two ago. Additionally, the tree ranges throughout the Greater Yellowstone Area—10 percent of ecosystem forests—so even an ambitious planting program would be hard-pressed to make a dent in the vast range from which they are disappearing. Finally, wilderness management policies strongly discourage broad-scale interventions on such lands, favoring a more hands-off approach. In sum, the ecological significance of the tree is at risk, the arch in danger of collapsing without its keystone.

The long-term consequences for grizzly bears are not clear. Certainly, they will have to find substitute foods, but ecologists differ on whether they will succeed in doing so. As omnivores, bears are flexible in their feeding habits. For example, when blister rust wiped out whitebarks from Glacier National Park in the 1960s and 1970s, grizzlies switched to eating berries and have prospered. Here, though, berries do not grow in such abundance, and cutthroat trout are also in trouble. For these reasons, the bear's future here is as uncertain as the whitebark's.

In reality, global warming is probably the ultimate wild card for the bear, the whitebark, and many other forms of life in the Thorofare. Already we are seeing clear signs of a warming climate, both globally and in the Thorofare. Temperatures are increasing, with the average temperature in the Thorofare climbing by 0.31° F per decade since 1948, or about two degrees warmer since then, and about twice the globe's average increase. Seemingly small changes like this can have big effects; as a result of the warming here, winters are a full month shorter, and snowpacks are declining in size and melting earlier. In fact, the snowpacks in the drought years of the early 2000s are tied with those from the Dust Bowl years in being the smallest in the last eight hundred years. The growing season is also longer, which might sound like welcome news for the chilly northern Rockies, but the typical fire season is also longer— a whopping seventy-eight days longer than the historic average here.

be melted off by then. Precipitation will increase somewhat in spring but remain about the same in summer, which means soils will be much drier because the higher temperatures will substantially increase the rate of evapotranspiration. Such conditions will be intolerable for the whitebark pine, so it will disappear from most of the ecosystem by the end of this century. Whitebarks will not be the only trees affected by a warming planet, for the fire regime on the Yellowstone Plateau will switch from being climate-limited to fuel-limited. Years like 1988 and 2003 will occur with such regularity by the end of this century that fires will only be limited by how much fuel has accumulated since the last fire. Such conditions, which favor frequent fire, will overwhelm the ability of lodgepole pine, subalpine fir, and Engelmann spruce (the three most common trees here) to persist in most areas they inhabit now. Species adapted to more frequent fire and drier climates, like Douglas-fir and Ponderosa pine (both of which produce bark thick enough to insulate the cambium from lower-intensity fires) and many grasses may take their place, with ripple effects throughout the ecosystem (as with trout, plant species rarely substitute for another ecologically). Fires will burn an average of six times as much acreage as they do now annually. Even Douglas-fir and Ponderosa pine may find this climate too hot and dry, and be replaced by sagebrush desert scrub in the hottest areas. Compounding all these changes will be the speed with which they will overtake us: within just one hundred to two hundred years. The Earth warmed by a similar amount when the glaciers melted off, but that warming took eight thousand years, an amount of time sufficient for plants and animals to accompany their moving habitats. The hyped-up speed of the changes in store for us will leave many species high and dry, searching for a habitat that has leap-frogged out of reach. In short, the Thorofare's climate, vegetation, and associated community of life will hardly be recognizable, never having been seen here before. Its landforms will be familiar, but we will otherwise be in uncharted terrain.[17]

Global warming and its effects on natural processes draw into question whether restoration actions are merited. If we know that climatic conditions may become so unsuitable throughout the area in seventy-five or a hundred years, should we even bother raising rust-resistant trees in nurseries? More broadly, given that we are causing global warming, should we be helping species move from once-favorable sites to places predicted to become so in the future? If so, should we apply such policies everywhere, or tailor them to the species in question and/or the particular protected area? Such questions are stirring robust debate, but we are far from agreeing on the answers. More and more, though, we do agree that we should be fostering resilience in plants, animals, and the design of our protected areas (to the extent possible), so that they can resist and readily respond to environmental change as it unfolds. In view of that understanding, the agencies are continuing to search out and grow resilient whitebark pines. Hope springs eternal, even in the face of this overwhelming threat.

((

In these ways and more, the Thorofare's managers continue to protect this amazing area, carrying on the legacy of their predecessors. As with the reclamation and lake zoning controversies, the threats usually originate outside the park and wildernesses, with a society that is crazed over personal freedoms or ignorant of the effects of its actions on nature (sometimes willfully), or both. The nature and pressure of contemporary threats increasingly require sophistication in technology and science to address them. Additionally, the solutions more and more involve lands, policies, and people outside the parks and wildernesses, demanding diplomacy, patience, and creativity from park and forest managers. Many of them share Lon Garrison's values and beliefs, so they are up to the task, but only time will tell if society is. For now, at least, the Thorofare remains a land of beauty and wildness.

Time for us this afternoon glides by, the sun blazing in its arc across an almost cloudless sky. Eric gloats in the warmth, his memory of our previous trip having lured him into a false sense of complacency about the clothing he would need for this one. Today is about the first day that the shorts he has worn since day one seem appropriate for the weather. Sean takes the kayak out again to practice some strokes, and Josh catches up in his journal. We all nap and read, enjoying an exquisite late summer day in the northern Rockies.

Knowing I will probably be disappointed, I nevertheless spend another hour listening for silence. Here on the main body of the lake, there is no speed limit for motorboats, and calm conditions like we have today can carry their noise across miles of water. Indeed, sustained natural quiet is not to be found until a light wind picks up later this afternoon, masking the low throb of boat motors. Even though there are only one or two motorboats in sight—and they are so far away that they are just specks—the open water easily propagates the throb, filling most of my hour. This part of the lake may look wild, but it does not always sound that way.

The good cell phone reception here makes the same point, that we have left the Thorofare. Since it is so good, I turn my iPhone on and check the webpage of the ALS Association (the main nonprofit sponsoring research toward a cure or effective treatment for the disease) to see what the tally is for the ice bucket challenge. This social phenomenon began a month ago; a person who has been so challenged must either dump a bucket of ice water on their head and challenge three others to do the same, or make a contribution to ALSA. Shortly before we left on this trip, the challenge went viral, and ALSA began to see donations rise sharply. The day before we left, the ice bucket challenge stood at $42 million, with the daily total eclipsing $5 million and rising. Today I see that it has surpassed the symbolic figure of $100 million. I was expecting to see this, but it still took my breath away. That figure was about sixty times what the group received in the same time period last year, a spectacular act of collective generosity.[18]

By the time the challenge fad ended a few weeks later, another $15 million had been added to ALSA's total, with still another $105 million given to related charities worldwide. Some friends, family, and colleagues took the challenge in my honor, and I know that others probably did so in response to an article in the *Bozeman Daily Chronicle* about this canoe trip. Eric's wife is a former newspaper reporter, and she tipped off the *Chronicle* about our trip. With the ice bucket challenge grabbing national headlines at the time, the *Chronicle* reporter thought it would be good press and got in touch with me. I agreed to be interviewed on the condition that the article include information on how readers could contribute. Two days after we left, "Once More into the Wild" appeared, the lead article for the day, taking up the entire front page above the fold. I suppose the story about the park ranger struck down by disease and escorted into the wilderness by his buddies must have made good copy, for the article was reprinted throughout Montana and by papers as far away as Florida. More important to me is that the disease and the ice bucket challenge got more attention, with more donations to ALSA. For, as I told the reporter, "ALS is worse than almost any cancer. No hope, no effective treatment, only imprisonment in one's own body. This is partly because there has not been much funding for research. Until now. This ice bucket thing is the biggest cause for hope that ALS sufferers have ever had."[19]

The evening is mild, with just a few clouds gracing the sunset. Meal preparation consists of merely boiling water to pour over freeze-dried beef stroganoff and then waiting ten minutes for the food to rehydrate (the wait is the hardest part of this meal) (figure 6.7). After dinner, we enjoy a freeze-dried treat: raspberry crisp for dessert. As twilight fades, we retire to the tents, my thoughts dominated by to-day's experiences. Thankful that our collective love of wildness and beauty has thus far preserved those qualities in the Thorofare, I lie awake for a while thinking of my own encounters with them there. Tomorrow, our last lay-over day, presents the opportunity to recall more of them and to consider their meaning. With that as the plan, I drift off to sleep.

6.7. Josh prepares the first course of our second-last supper, 2014. Photo by Eric Compas. Used with permission.

DAY 7   The Journey of a Lifetime

I am glad I shall never be young without wild country to be young in.
Of what avail are forty freedoms without a blank spot on the map?
—Aldo Leopold, 1949

The dawn is clear and cool, but without the frost that has greeted us the past few mornings. We sleep in for a while, but being in our forties and accustomed to rising early for work, that means only an extra thirty or sixty minutes. For me, no matter how much sleep I get, it is never enough. One of the symptoms of the disease is fatigue, as weakening muscles make all tasks more difficult (and eventually impossible). Some of the medications I take—to help deal with other symptoms, there being no treatment to control the disease—cause drowsiness, exacerbating the fatigue. So, I take naps when I can and try to budget nine hours for sleep, but still find myself yawning a lot.

Chores of daily living not only are more difficult, but they also take longer. Showering and dressing expand from twenty minutes to an hour; preparing a simple breakfast of yogurt and granola, from two minutes to ten; buckling a seatbelt, from almost nothing to a couple of laborious minutes. Add to this stretches and exercises intended to help me retain the use of my muscles as long as possible ("use it or lose it," for ALS sufferers, becomes "use it or lose it even faster"), and my day can become a series of energy-draining tasks, with little time to relax. Friends and visiting family take care of laundry, cooking, and cleaning for me, but they cannot eat my meals or take my showers. I have compensated by working shorter days and four-day workweeks, and by carving out time to sit and read at the start and end of each day. These have turned the forced-march nature of life with ALS into something more enjoyable, but having a full day of nothing to do but relax—my plan for today—is still a rare luxury.

For breakfast, Eric prepares a pot of "African porridge," which I first learned from my friend Dave Lee, who hiked through the Thorofare with me in fall 1998. It is a dish he learned while in the Peace Corps in West Africa, in which one stirs peanut butter into a bowl of cornmeal mush. With some sugar sprinkled on top and raisins mixed in (the latter being my addition), one has an easy backcountry breakfast that, unlike many other such breakfasts, is loaded with fat and protein. All three of my paddling partners like it so much that a wilderness trip with me would not be complete without it, they tell me.

Here on our last full day of the trip, it seems appropriate to take a retrospective look, not only at this trip but also at my three decades of experiences here, to see if we have indeed succeeded in preserving the Thorofare's wildness and beauty. In this case, such experiences are a relevant form of "data," for several reasons. Not only do my experiences encompass the great majority of trails in the Thorofare (along with a fair number of off-trail experiences), but they are from the time period in question, the modern era. More importantly, those data are uniquely appropriate for answering a question that is fundamentally experiential: Do the signs of wildness we encountered on our second day (from natural processes to vastness and a lack of development or disturbance to the ability to find solitude or partake in traditional wilderness activities) actually confer a feeling of wildness in the Thorofare? Why or why not, and what does it matter? Certainly, the experiences on this trip thus far suggest that wildness may be found in abundance in the Thorofare, along with natural beauty (figure 7.1). If my earlier experiences are any guide, they confirm that the area is very much defined by wildness and beauty—but they also reveal a surprise or two, and they contain threads of richer meaning.

((

For starters, thinking of Dave and his African Porridge reminds me of our first two nights on that trip, camped at Cabin Creek. Like every

7.1. Dunrud Peak, whitened by a two-hour hailstorm the night before, rises above Coldwell Creek, 2005. The Thorofare's wildness and beauty are evident in this view. Author photo.

campsite I have used in the Thorofare, this one had a nice view, out over the sprawling stands of willow covering the delta (figure 7.2). It was September, the peak of the rut for both elk and moose. Wolves were just beginning to colonize the Thorofare (we would actually see a loner a few days later), so elk and moose were both still abundant. As the setting sun dropped behind the Two Ocean Plateau across the valley, multiple bulls of both species serenaded their cows late into the night. For hours, the elk bugles joined the moose bellows in an unbroken symphony of ardor. Rising and falling in volume with the distance from the bull to us, the music lasted long after we turned in. For us, it was loud testimony of the abundance nature can produce when afforded some protection. Wolves have altered that abundance some since then, but now we are blessed with abundance of a different sort: the full suite of native preda-tors. Wolves, coyotes, red fox, black and grizzly bears, mountain lions, lynx, and bobcats are all present here, along with all native weasels and avian predators. The only other place in the forty-eight contiguous states able to make the same claim is the Crown of the Continent Ecosystem

7.2. Frosty mornings, golden light, bellowing moose, and bugling elk are the sights and sounds of fall in the Thorofare, 1998. Author photo.

in Montana (Glacier National Park and the Bob Marshall Wilderness Complex).

After climbing Colter Peak the next day and tuning in to nature's symphony a second night, Dave and I continued hiking south to the Thorofare Ranger Station. There, we turned west, climbing up over the Two Ocean Plateau and dropping down to the Snake River. Following it through its canyon, we enjoyed fireweed's second blaze, its crimson, violet, and orange palette of fall color. The canyon had burned in 1988, so it was still largely open; the tree seedlings there were just two or three feet tall and widely scattered. Fireweed and other forbs and grasses covered the ground, though; those that had already dried rattled in the warm autumn breeze. Nature's daytime movement had been considerably softer than her twilight ones the last two evenings.

Another day of solitary hiking brought us to another lovely campsite, perched on the river's bank and overlooking a grassy meadow. The gurgling river, here just the size of a large stream, was the day's final movement, save one. Late that night, my ears keyed in on an addition to the rhythm, which brought me out of sleep immediately. Something big—bigger than Dave or me—was walking in or across the river, its footfalls almost indistinguishable from the fluid background. I listened breathlessly, my pounding heart adding a drumbeat in my ears. Suddenly, a footfall in deep, still water, much like a rock being dropped in it, and then nothing. Silence, aside from the water, reigned for the rest of the night. What played that finale I will never know, but I sensed it was not ursine, and probably moose-ine.

Several years earlier, on my first visit to the Thorofare with another friend named Dave (Moser), we had a four-legged nighttime visitor whose identity we did come to know. In the autumn of 1990, he and I rendezvoused in Yellowstone to check out the changes resulting from the 1988 fires. He injured his knee on one of our hikes that fall, so with a week of time still left on our calendars, we found a canoe and set off for the Southeast Arm. It was mid-afternoon by the time we launched, and the lake was rough. We paddled for less than an hour before we were forced ashore. There we sat for the rest of the afternoon, the winds unrelenting, the waves almost the size of ocean swells. Gambling that the wind would subside after sunset, we cooked and ate our supper as the afternoon shadows grew long. Sure enough, the weakening sun began to calm the wind, and by the time the horizon hid the sun completely, the lake was once again safe to paddle. Supper gone, we pushed off for the second time that afternoon.

As we paddled, dusk became night, wind turned to calm, and waves stilled into black glass. Stars came out, first one at a time, then dozens, and finally hundreds and thousands. Even without the moon, navigation was simple, the trees on shore marking the way by their silhouettes of starless blackness. Evening chill became the cool of night, our bodies kept warm by propelling the boat forward. Sounds of waves striking rock muted into wavelets on gravel, then drips from paddles. After a couple hours of such sensual overload, the shore on our left subtly brightened. Trees had given way to meadow, and soon we picked out an angular shape at odds with what we had been seeing. It was a sign marking a campsite. We put in, happy to have found an unoccupied site.

Before too long, we had the food strung up and our home for the night ready to climb into. Dave fell into the deep sleep I so envied; my sleep when camped in bear country was always a state of partial wakefulness, as I listened for large quadrupeds. A few hours after we went to bed, my half sleep became complete alertness as I actually began to hear noises from one. Several hundred yards away, something was breaking branches. After listening to it for a few minutes, I nudged my tentmate awake, for by then it was clear that the animal was moving our way—and that, whatever it was, it was BIG. If the volume of the crashes and booms was any indication, the animal was breaking branches the size of a man's wrist. In whispers barely audible, Dave and I tried to guess what it was and what to do about it. We had answers to neither question, but in Yellowstone at that time of the night we both had only one animal in mind: a grizzly bear, and it was moving in the wrong direction. What the animal did next left little doubt in our minds as to its identity, and silenced even our muted whispers.

The crashing ended as the animal stepped out into the meadow. Slowly it approached our tent, its breathing, labored from its exertion, becoming louder and louder. Soon it was just inches away, so close we could smell its breath (which reeked). The only thing between us and a terrifying attack from a predatory grizzly was the thin wall of our tent—little more than a puff of air to a bear intent on a meal. Bear spray was still a thing of the future, so we had little choice but to lie there and await our fate. Not daring to breathe, we lay there petrified, each of us expecting the sound of ripping nylon and the terrifying and possibly—no, probably—deadly melee that would follow.

But instead, after assaulting our noses and equanimity for another eternity, the animal slowly moved away. We could still hear it moving around, but gradually becoming more distant. After gathering our composure and taking a few deep breaths, I summoned the courage to unzip the tent and find out what it was. Given the silence we had been maintaining, the zipper seemed loud, almost a dinner bell advertising what the bruin had left behind. Peering into the starlit meadow, I saw an animal with brown fur and a hump, two characteristics of grizzly bears. But, the bearer was not a griz; instead, grazing peacefully there was a bull bison, quiet and content in his native habitat.

In twenty-eight years of exploring the Yellowstone ecosystem, that bison incident is by far the most frightening nighttime experience with a large animal that I have had. Other animals have visited, but most were just passing through and none approached as closely as that bison. Only one was a bear—that I know of, for scientists say that up to 90 percent of the time, if a bear or a human sees the other, the biped is the one being watched. Who knows how many bears have padded silently by while I was sleeping or busy with some camp chore—and knowing this, I never did sleep too well in Yellowstone's backcountry. The one bear that I did see at night actually greeted me when I stepped out of the tent in the morning. That was in Fox Park, a large meadow about a day's hike west from the Thorofare Ranger Station. The lone bear was only fifty yards away and probably a subadult (the bear equivalent of a teenager), for it weighed only about two hundred pounds. Being jolted to attention by it eliminated my need for coffee that day, but it reacted with indifference and wandered away.

Fear and indifference are common threads in many of my encounters with Thorofare wildlife. Two seemingly opposite emotions, each reflecting the relative threat of the two animals in a face-to-face encounter. Fear, because there is something more powerful than us in the woods here, and because bear spray and guns do nothing more than reduce the fear level slightly. And indifference, because we mean nothing to the bison or the bear. In their map of daily life, we do not even rise to the significance of insect pests. Mosquitoes and biting flies merit a bear's attention, if in the negative, but we do not even get that, at least at times. More than once, I have had a bear look at me and appear to look right through me. Perhaps that is because bears have poor eyesight, but even if that is the reason, I am still left feeling insignificant to the bear. We are not even a mosquito in the ear to them; we are invisible, less than nothing.

One of those invisible bear encounters in the Thorofare, climbing 12,058-foot Thorofare Mountain at the headwaters of the Yellowstone. Linda and I were carrying full packs, planning to drop over the top into the next drainage (Thorofare Creek) after enjoying lunch on the summit. Still a thousand vertical feet shy of our wilderness table with a view, we were proceeding slowly, the thin air and steep slope slowing our pace to a crawl. Our heads were down, focused on finding secure footholds in this trailless tundra, footholds that did not also entail crushing some of the alpine forget-me-nots perfuming the air. Navigation in this treeless terrain was not difficult, there being no cliffs affecting our route-finding. Nonetheless, looking up took energy at an already taxing point in the climb, so we were only glancing up occasionally to plot a general course.

Suddenly, Linda shouted, "Mike, there's a bear!" Thinking she had said "deer" but wondering why she was so animated, I looked up and saw the cause of her excitement: a subadult grizzly was a hundred yards away and coming straight toward us. At 11,000 feet with forty-five-pound packs on our backs, there was little we could do besides step aside (which is sometimes the best thing to do anyway). Yet, no matter which way we tried, it seemed the topography would funnel the bear right to us. Casting about for some way to get out of harm's way, I saw a snowfield to our right, and suggested to Linda that she follow me out on it, hoping the bear would opt to stay on dry ground. She agreed, and we stepped onto the snow, which the morning sun had softened. Walking as fast as our gasping lungs would allow (a slow walk, which was best because a faster walk or a run could have excited the bear into giving chase), we moved a few yards onto the snow. Turning to face our fate, we watched the griz walk on by at the edge of the snow, no more than fifty feet away. It kept on going, not looking back once. That should not have surprised us, because, for the duration of our interaction (probably only sixty seconds, though my memory makes it more like an hour), it had never even registered our existence. Our fear and excitement was matched by apparent indifference in the bear.

We made the summit an hour later and sat down to a well-deserved repast of bagel, peanut butter, and cheese. To our south, across the valley we had just left, extended an almost unlimited plateau of alpine tundra, an emerald prairie in the sky dotted with patches of blue where flowering lupines or forget-me-nots clustered. It was early August, the peak of the fleeting alpine summer, and the sea of green crested five miles away on the flat summit of Wall Mountain. Linda and I had sat there for lunch yesterday, where the green sea ended atop the 2,000-foot cliff providing the mountain its name (figure 1.8). The wall had earlier framed our view as we had hiked up the South Fork of the Shoshone River canyon the previous two days. Having thus enjoyed the Wall from two perspectives, the view from on top was my favorite, so sweetly scented and colored by the ephemeral wildflower show.

The view to the north whetted our appetites for what was to come: a walk down the Yellowstone River's counterpart, Thorofare Creek. The creek began in the snowfields below us, gathering more aquatic force from springs along the way and entering forest at about the 10,000-foot mark. We would find the forest to be open and easy walking, game trails coalescing into a maintained trail. Hiking down the valley that afternoon, we waited to make camp until green trees gave way to those blackened in 1988. That made for a soggy supper, as naked trees offer little shelter and summer thunderstorms again made their daily appearance. In the high country, though, July (and August!) showers make August flowers, so we took the daily rain in stride and tried to dry our perpetually sodden tent and socks when the sun did shine. Most mornings brought clear skies, giving us a few hours of drying weather, along with mountaintop views of wave upon wave of more mountains. It was summer in the Thorofare: fleeting and wet, colorful and glorious, lush and wild—and home to plenty of bruins.

Ursine indifference to people is often the impression, but another of my bear encounters in the Washakie Wilderness reminds me that vigilance, and possibly aggression, are almost as likely. My friend Bronco and I were hiking out from a couple nights camping in the Absarokas. I was in the lead, and the afternoon was hot, so after climbing a short but steep hill, I stopped in a patch of shade for a sip of water. A few seconds later, he caught up and also paused. Just then, some trailside bushes a hundred feet ahead of us moved, revealing a patch of brown fur. Quickly, Bronco put into words what we both were thinking: "That's a bear!" Shortly thereafter, the patch of fur became a sow grizzly with two cubs standing on their hind legs to see what had made the noise.

Surprising a sow with cubs is just about the most perilous situation for hikers in bear country; the only thing worse is being caught between a sow and her cubs. We both reacted by pulling our cans of bear spray out of their holsters, removing the safety catches so we could discharge the spray if needed, and watching the bear to see if she would charge. If she did, though, I remember clearly thinking that I would drop to the ground and play dead. Doing so was almost guaranteed to save my life, as the sow would perceive that the threat to her cubs had passed, where bear spray was still too new to have an established safety record and would not eliminate the threat to her cubs. Additionally, if we sprayed into the wind, it could blow the spray into our faces, making a bad situation worse.

All these thoughts flashed through my mind in the few seconds before she moved, as well as two other almost conflicting thoughts: first, how thankful I was that, being in the lead, my timing had not been such as to have brought the bears to the brink of that hill just as I topped it. Had that been the case, I surely would have been mauled. Conversely, we had been lax about calling ahead to advertise our presence. Such calls might have alerted the bears and frightened them off the trail, but the heat and associated fatigue had made us drop our guard.

Racing thoughts, suspense, and fear soon gave way to relief as the sow dropped to all fours and slowly—almost indifferently—led her cubs into the shrubbery to the left of the trail. Disappearing from view, a pebble tumbling down the steep hill to our left was our only hint where they had gone: above and around us. The threat each species posed to the other had passed, and both went on their way.

We, however, were hyper-vigilant the rest of the day, practically jumping out of our skins when we rounded a bend in the trail and almost collided with two men on horses. All survived the near collision, but for the rest of the day I thought about one's need to always be alert when hiking in grizzly bear terrain. Watching for tracks on the trail, scanning ahead for patches of brown fur, and calling ahead are not just smart practices, they are virtually required of regular wilderness travelers if they are to return for more trips into bear country. By virtue of necessity, we become more attuned to the surroundings, more aware of the life and beauty through which we travel. In a world full of attention-grabbing distractions, such focus on the natural world is rare. It centers our thoughts on life, both within and without, making us the more alive and deepening our connections to our own place in the Earth's community of life.

Now, looking back on these and other wildlife encounters, I am also struck by their unpredictable nature. Not only do we never know when we will bump into these wild creatures—who would have thought we would encounter those bears in the middle of a hot afternoon, when they were ordinarily bedded down in some shade—but we also never know how they will react. Fight or flight, indifference or wariness: impossible to predict, and indicative of the fact that animals are both sentient and wild. They—especially bears and other large animals—separate the Thorofare (and other wildernesses harboring grizzly bears) from the many others that lack them. They breathe life into wilderness, transforming beautiful scenery into living space, pretty pictures into motion pictures. They are the epitome of wild.[1]

((

It is not just animals that make this place wild—many of them can live in very settled places. A gang of elk, for example, resides year-round amid the many buildings, people, and lawns of Kentucky bluegrass at Yellowstone's headquarters, Mammoth Hot Springs, and most of the park's grizzly bears once fed at several open dumps in the park. Prior to World War II, in fact, the NPS made a show of bears feeding on our garbage, luring them onto a stage covered in food scraps, expectant tourists crowding bleachers on a hill above the stage. Increasingly dissatisfied with the carnival atmosphere that the shows projected, the agency ended them during the war, but the dumps were used by both people and bears into the 1970s. By then, the NPS was actively recreating "vignettes of primitive America" (as a key advisory panel recommended), so park managers closed the dumps to return the bears to a more natural diet.[2] As mentioned, there were some bumps along the way, but the net result is the wilder population of bears that we enjoy today.

As these two cases demonstrate, an equally important contributor to wildness is the setting. Animals do not make a landscape wild if they are in a zoo or, worse, a carnival. As the NPS slowly came to this realization, the architects of the Wilderness Act were doing the same thing, writing those landscape elements that create wildness into the bill that became law in 1964. The importance of these elements in setting the stage for wildness was affirmed for me on my first hike into the Washakie Wilderness with Josh, a nine-day hike in 2002 on which, ironically, we saw few large animals. Nonetheless, signs of wildlife were abundant, and thanks to the landscape itself, wildness was still our constant companion.

Our first day, climbing 3,000 feet from the South Fork of the Shoshone River into Boulder Basin—with sixty-pound packs—was a fitting introduction to the hike. A seventy-five-mile loop, the route featured a mountain pass almost every other day, each with a 2,000- to 3,000-foot climb, as we flitted around the highest peaks of the Absarokas and the headwaters of the Shoshone, Wind, and Greybull Rivers. Moreover, each pass would be higher than the previous one, culminating in a trailless crossing into the Needle Creek drainage that my topographic map suggested could be dicey, with tight contour lines on the downslope slide. Gambling that we would find a safe route through those possible cliff bands, we would pick up a trail along Needle Creek and hike it out to the South Fork of the Shoshone, completing the loop. Both of us were in our mid-thirties and in tip-top shape, so with that as the plan, we took off just after lunch. We made it into Boulder Basin in about four hours, delayed a little by cramps in Josh's legs, but otherwise none the worse for wear. The trail had been rocky and steep, so we called it a day and set up camp in some trees by a small stream. We had the valley to ourselves, and had seen no one on the trail, a pattern that would prevail throughout most of the trip.

The next day, we climbed again, putting another 2,000 feet under us to cross into the Greybull River drainage at Boulder Basin Pass. Along the way, the cold aridity of the Greybull River landscape became apparent, with trees found only on the north- and east-facing slopes, where the less intense sun creates moister conditions (figure 7.3). Elsewhere, grasses dominate, including most of the descent to river level, even in some places where trees would be expected to occur. Winter storms here typically follow the prevailing southwest wind, dropping their load of moisture as they are forced up and over the mountains. With the bulk of the Absaroka massif found southwest, or upwind, of here, storms are mostly spent by the time they arrive here. They drop what moisture they still have around the pass, sustaining trees in their sheltered pockets

7.3. Francs Peak and the Greybull River drainage from Boulder Basin Pass, 2002. Snowfall here is not sufficient to sustain forests on south- and west-facing slopes, where more intense sun favors grasses. Author photo.

there, but by the time they hit the downslope areas of the Greybull River drainage, even some favorable aspects are too dry for trees, replaced by more drought-tolerant grasses. By the time the storms clear the range altogether (farther east of here, and outside of the wilderness), they are so moisture-starved that prairie may extend from mountain base to summit, clothing parts of the range's east front with an unbroken, treeless expanse of grassland. Summer brings thunderstorms throughout the area, but without the meltwater from a deep snowpack, trees still lack the moisture they need. Dominated by this continental-scale weather pattern, this is the driest part of the mountain range and the Washakie Wilderness.

We spent the next three days and nights in the Greybull River drainage, camping on a tributary stream the first night and on the river itself the second two nights, at the base of Francs Peak, the highest peak in the range. Everything about that higher camp spoke of its cold climate, from its 9,000-foot elevation to the spruce-fir forest lining the otherwise open valley (figure 7.4). Driving that point home our first night there was unsettled weather showering us with graupel (pea-sized pellets of

7.4: A cold landscape: the upper Greybull River drainage, 2002. Even during the fleeting summer, snow can fall here, creating a climate that few trees can tolerate. Engelmann spruce and subalpine fir (seen here) dominate in such conditions. Author photo.

soft ice that had been snowflakes a little higher up in the atmosphere) and obscuring the sun with low-hanging clouds. Graupel or not, we needed a rest, having hiked hard for the last three days, so we held up for a day. The next morning, we lazed around camp, a delightful activity that Josh extended to the afternoon while I sauntered farther up the valley for an hour (an equally delightful pastime). Other than the trail itself, I saw neither people nor signs of humanity. The day before, we had passed a Forest Service cabin and an outfitter's camp, but both were unoccupied. We still had yet to see another human, solitude we would continue to enjoy for the rest of the trip but for two days, when we saw a combined total of three other people. Moreover, the Greybull was to be the *most* developed place we would see, for the only human structures we saw for the rest of the hike were modest trail improvements such as water bars. Even bridges at stream crossings were uncommon, making hikers get their feet wet if no creek-spanning logs were handy (figure 3.4). Humans were hardly even visitors here, not remaining for long, and signs of human presence were almost nonexistent.

Due to the cold climate, Native Americans also probably did not remain; their sojourns were more like seasonal residences during the short summers. Certainly, their influence would have been felt at the mid- to lower elevations (perhaps even through the use of fire, due to the drier local climate than that around Yellowstone Lake), though the amount of such influence is not known. At the highest elevations (in the alpine tundra, above treeline), it was probably minor, due to the very short summer season there (and associated fire season), the sheer amount of land that is tundra, the ruggedness of that terrain, and the abundance of natural firebreaks, all of which would have limited the extent and influence of any fires they may have set (figure 7.5). They may also have had some influence through hunting and the associated influences herbivores exert on vegetation, but the extent of such effects is unknown and again probably minor in the higher terrain, where climate strongly limits plant growth.[3] All around Josh and me, then, was a landscape dominated by nonhuman forces, especially in the Thorofare's vast high country. The next day, that was especially evident to us as we ascended 11,350-foot Burwell Pass on our way out of the Greybull. At

7.5. *Francs Peak and the uppermost Greybull River drainage, 2002. These rugged mountains bear the imprint of natural and human forces, though in this cold climate, the Native American influence was probably minor. Author photo.*

the pass, Francs Peak dominated the western horizon, with other barren mountain slopes tumbling down to the partially forested valley up which we had just hiked. The flatter slopes were vegetated with alpine tundra forbs and grasses, curing in the late summer sun (the storm had moved on by this time), while the steeper slopes were naked. It was a view much like the Native Americans themselves might have enjoyed, a cacophony of rugged mountains sculpted by water and ice, the vegetation patterns mostly the result of temperature, precipitation, wind, aspect, and soils.

Josh and I enjoyed an even better view two days later, crossing the divide between Emerald Lake and Needle Creek. The lake was a windswept alpine tarn at the end of a trail and at the base of a rocky ridge separating us from our destination. Arriving at the lake mid-morning, we were disappointed to see that the pass we had hoped to use was not conducive to travel, blocked by cliffs of crumbly volcanic rock. However, we did see another, potentially safer route nearby, with what appeared to be a faint trail leading toward it from the lakeshore—probably a game trail. Having no other options, we decided to trust the local four-footed

7.6. Josh searches for secure footing, 2002. Even on the game trail crossing the divide from Emerald Lake into Needle Creek, we had to watch our step. Author photo.

residents. This would not be the first time I had found a game trail leading me where I wanted to go; topography and common destinations naturally lead to the development of paths beaten in by the hoofs and feet pounding the turf. In this case, not only did their path lead us to a usable alternate crossing, but it also kept going into the Needle Creek valley, down through a gap in the cliff bands I had seen on the map (figure 7.6). It was likely bighorn sheep or elk that usually went this way; that day, the trail provided safe passage for us two bipeds.

Below the cliffs, we paused to have lunch. Spread out before us was the most majestic wilderness tapestry of the trip. To our left, the cliffs grew into a headwall cradling the top of the valley, with snowmelt and springwater tumbling down its face in a few places. Across from us the headwall grew into mountaintops culminating in a 12,242-foot peak with a patch of rust at the summit, called simply Red Tops (figure 1.10). Down the Needle Creek valley to our right was another 12,000-foot mountain bearing the same name as the creek, a mountain that turned the descending stream westward to its confluence with the South Fork and that towered a vertical mile above. And below us was the round, gently sloping basin that once spawned a glacier but now gathered the headwall cascades into the creek we were here to follow. Even the basin was above treeline, clothed with a carpet of tundra grasses and flowers that were still a vibrant green owing to the valley's high, shadow-casting walls and north-facing aspect. Spring arrives later here than to the surrounding mountains and ridges, which keeps the basin in its emerald state later and also keeps the forest away, about two miles down valley. It was another rugged, wild landscape reflecting mostly nonhuman forces; indeed, if there had ever been any human actions altering the course of natural events here, they were likely nothing more than the harvesting of game animals or wild edibles. Vast, high, reflecting nature's many forces, inhospitable to humans but for a few weeks each year, and remote—more so even than we realized at the moment—it was about as untrammeled as landscape as one can find in the country, outside Alaska (figure 7.7).

Our bellies full but our souls still feasting on wildness, we dropped into the basin and strolled down to the edge of the forest. There, we

7.7. A largely untrammeled landscape: the Needle Creek drainage, 2002. Author photo.

found a place to camp and completed the simple wilderness routine for the day, setting up the tent, rinsing off, relaxing with hors d'oeuvres and a snippet of Scotch (on wilderness "rocks"—snow—if available), and having dinner. To end the day, we would watch the setting sun lengthen the shadows and color the mountains with fire, finishing with shades of red the color of wine. It was a comforting routine, with the mornings finding us enjoying coffee and breakfast while we broke camp, beginning the day's hike in the morning coolness, and stopping for a snack around eleven o'clock and a lunch two hours later. For all of this we were ensconced in nature, watching the landscape unfold as we traveled through it, engaging in conversation, meditating, or just being present. It was a simplifying, gratifying, and enriching routine that had no real parallel, at least for me, in my day-to-day life.

The next day, our last full day in wilderness, we turned into the forest and downstream, looking for the trail shown on two of my three maps of the drainage. As we soon realized, though, the third map was correct, for there was no maintained trail to be found. A game trail—a rough one—came to our rescue again, leading us seven miles down to the South Fork. Those were the most difficult miles of the entire hike, more difficult than even the first day, as the barely discernible track led us through dense forest, doubled back on itself to get around deadfalls, and narrowed to just a couple inches wide as it crossed multiple steep talus slopes at the foot of Needle Peak. A misstep there for an ungulate would have been no big deal, with three other hoofs as backup, but for us, potentially deadly, with a long slide on skin-gouging talus and a landing on bone-breaking rocks at the bottom. This was no place for carelessness, so we focused on making every footstep secure and maintaining our balance. We made it through without mishap, making camp as soon as we reached the South Fork and its maintained trail. That seven miles had taken all day, our pace not even a mile an hour. Needle Creek was indeed all but untrammeled, its ruggedness making it all but untraveled, as we now knew personally.

We hiked out the next day, an easy flat walk. That hike was the first of three that Josh and I took into the Thorofare, each one of which provided somewhat different tastes of the area's wildness. Both of the other hikes, for example, brought us more evidence of grizzly bears (tracks, scat piles, and/or actual sightings) as well as indications of other elemental forces like fire (smoke and burned trees), mass wasting, and erosion (figure 7.8). Permeating all of those trips—indeed, every one of my Thorofare trips—was the knowledge and feeling that we were in a truly wild place. Shaped primarily by natural forces (perhaps exclusively in some locales), almost devoid of human development, bigger than our two smallest states, receiving only modest human use, and bearing its own risks and challenges, it is as wild a setting as can be found in the forty-eight contiguous states today. Fittingly, we who hike through are just visitors; those who remain are the thousands of quadrupeds that call the place home. The land and its residents create wildness everywhere one looks in this wilderness. It is the common denominator here, a landscape wherein the most essential forces transcend humanity.

☾

For all that, though, wilderness can be profoundly social. This canoe trip is an excellent case in point: four friends spending a week together, something they would not do in the cities in which they live. Sharing a

7.8. *Bliss Creek Meadows, 2003. The meadows bear witness to some of the geologic forces shaping the Thorofare, for they were created by mass wasting (a large landslide) that impounded the South Fork of the Shoshone River, which then filled in the resulting lake with sediment (over time). Author photo.*

journey together, with communal struggles and moments of joy, gives us an unparalleled opportunity to build and nurture relationships (and to show that wilderness need not exclude the disabled). With all three of my current companions, past weeklong trips into this wilderness had cemented friendships that were already budding. With Josh, it was the Needle Creek hike. With Eric, it was our 2003 canoe trip, the mosquitoes being so ferocious some nights that he and I would eat supper in the boat a hundred yards from shore, the bugs not following us out over open water. And with Sean, it was a fall hike through the Thorofare, the trail disappearing one afternoon under a two-mile-long labyrinth of fire-killed fallen trees so thick that forward movement was only possible by walking logs, jumping from one to the next in a sort of wilderness balance contest, suspended as much as five feet above the actual trail. In each case, though, misery loved company, and the fantastic wilderness made accessible to us by the travails was worth the sweat and blood. More importantly, in overcoming unexpected adversities together, the bonds uniting us as friends strengthened and grew. These first trips grew to be many with each friend, and now this one. Of course, not always do such wilderness pairings become long-term friendships; some wither as life unfolds (as has happened for me with Dave Lee and Linda). For me, though, these exceptions prove the rule: by facilitating diverse experiences toward a common goal, wilderness is an exceptional venue to cement and enrich friendships in a way that is difficult to replicate in the modern world.

Furthermore, some of my fondest memories of times in wilderness have to do with other travelers there, people I never saw again. Perhaps the best illustration is an experience I had with Linda in 1995, on our second trip through the Thorofare. She and I were hiking up the Yellowstone River to its headwaters, an area that we would discover was as convivial as it was wild and beautiful. Reaching the confluence of the river's north and south forks, we turned right and shifted into low gear as we began climbing along the South Fork. The trail in this section was the worst on the whole 110-mile hike, not having been maintained for years—at least not by the cash-starved US Forest Service. On trails such as this, when a tree falls across the trail, outfitters (the majority users of the Thorofare) will just go around if that is the path of least resistance. If it is not, they will clear the tree. On this stretch of trail, they must have regularly found it easier to go around fallen trees, because the trail seemed to be nothing but detours. For this reason, the next two miles became more like three or four.

Thunderheads were gathering as we climbed through the detours, and the first heavy drops of rain were just hitting us as we emerged into the lower of the two large meadows gracing the South Fork (figure 7.9). Two different things immediately grabbed our attention: a tall waterfall tumbling down the cliffs on the south side of the canyon, and an outfitter's canvas tent set up opposite the falls. Inside the tent were some people, who waved us in to get shelter from the storm. We gladly accepted their offer and stepped inside, just as the storm hit. Dropping our packs, we sat down to the company of Triangle X outfitters (from the Jackson Hole area) and two clients, a couple celebrating their fiftieth wedding anniversary. They plied us with coffee and some hotdogs, which we happily devoured, since we had been subsisting on dried food and gorp for

7.9. The lower meadow on the Yellowstone's South Fork, 2003. The waterfall is unnamed. Author photo.

a week and were going through more than three thousand calories a day. Our food supply was being stretched thin (hiking ten to twelve miles a day with a forty-five-pound pack, Linda's appetite had doubled from the norm I had used as calculation in packing the food), so the extra calories were really welcome. Chatting with our hosts, we learned that they had been to this area before, had spent a few days here, and were leaving the next day. We stayed with them until the storm cleared, resuming our journey up the river.

The upper meadow was our destination, and after another hour of uphill hiking, we arrived. Another thunderstorm was looming, so we quickly found a campsite on a knoll overlooking the meadow and set up the tent. A hundred yards away was a whitebark pine with an outstretched branch twenty feet off the ground (a textbook example of a food-hanging branch to use in places like this lacking improved campsites), so we threw a rope over it and hauled our food up, and then dove into the tent for a well-deserved nap. Once that thunderstorm had spent itself, we got out and examined our surroundings. Spread out before us, at 9,900 feet above sea level, was a large meadow blanketed with a patchwork of grass, sedge, and low-growing willow, all in various

7.10. Clearing storm on the upper meadow on the Yellowstone's South Fork, 2003. Younts Peak (left) and Thorofare Mountain rise more than 2,000 feet above the meadow. Author photo.

shades of summertime green (figure 7.10). Framing the meadow was that healthy whitebark pine forest, reaching for the mountaintops where winter's avalanches permitted. Rising above the ribbons of forest were Younts Peak and Thorofare Mountain, each more than 12,000 feet tall and, even in August, adorned with remnant patches of snow. Trickles and cascades of meltwater from the snow coalesced into the stream we would soon stand astride (and drink from), the very headwaters of the Yellowstone River.

Completing this campsite's near-perfect set of amenities was a fire ring at the edge of the meadow: our kitchen and dining room, with that same million-dollar view. The clouds cleared as we cooked my favorite backpacking meal: lentil chili-mac, a satisfying blend of lentil chili mix, macaroni, sun-dried tomatoes, garlic, and sausage, with cheddar cheese melted on top. As we ate, we watched the evening shadows lengthen and planned our route up Younts Peak the next day. We would hop the stream and cross the meadow, then ascend the north wall of the valley (a steep but walkable slope), gain the summit ridge, and walk it up to the top. Like a lot of Absaroka peaks, rock climbing gear was not necessary if one was careful about route-finding. That would be the case for us on the climb the next day, although we found that gaining the ridge was a bit tricky, involving a walk through a gap between a snowfield and the cliff from which it was melting away.

On the summit, we lingered for over an hour, enjoying a commanding view of the headwaters area. Mountains and mountain ranges stretched out before us in every direction. The Absarokas sprawled out of sight to the east and north, a seemingly unending, rumpled quilt of rock, cliff, and summit. West of us and on the horizon were the Tetons, and some of the glaciers in the Wind River Mountains glinted in the sunlight far to the south. At our feet was the green sea of alpine tundra, with more lingering patches of snow capping its emerald waves with white (figure 7.11). We would swim that sea tomorrow, a full-day hike through treeless alpine tundra and an almost endless field of flowers. It was to be a parade of blue, yellow, white, and green, complemented by wafts of efflorescent perfume, golden sunshine, and gentle breezes. We would christen the trail The Yellow-Flowered Road, our Absaroka Oz that ended at a lake only a wizard could have imagined, a cerulean gem of liquid sky called Ferry Lake (figure 7.12). It would be the culmination of three sensual, extraordinary days of wilderness travel, probably the best trio I have had in over fifteen thousand lifetime miles hiked.

Photographing ourselves on the summit before we began our trek down, we were surprised to see a group of three people on horseback approaching. They were not our friends from yesterday, but were equally generous, sharing some cookies with us (by this time we wondered if our hats said "Hungry hiker—please feed"). While we were munching on them, though, we saw a packstring of horses and mules pass through the meadow far below; we assumed it was our friends from yesterday heading home. Descending the mountain on the same route, we arrived back at camp in a couple hours. Preparing to bathe and relax before supper, we opened the tent to get our evening clothes. That is where we came across yet another example of wilderness community, for sitting on our pillows were two very fresh apples, left by our Triangle X friends. We had not noticed them stopping as they passed through, but the evidence before us could not be denied.

Enjoying the fresh fruit for dessert that evening, we contemplated the events of the last two days. On the most basic level, the apples and other food were, of course, sustenance. With these unexpected additions to our larder, we would be able to relax a bit in the hiking we had left to do (in fact, the extra food allowed us to linger a full night longer—but not more, as we still walked out with only enough food for one more snack). More significantly, we had participated in perhaps the most universal act of human community, sharing a meal, with two other parties in as many

7.11. *The view from Younts Peak south to the Buffalo Plateau, 1995. Patches of snow adorn the extensive alpine tundra in this area. Author photo.*

days. The other wilderness explorers may have been complete strangers, but we readily bonded through our travels in this remote wilderness and through our love for things wild and beautiful. I have long forgotten their names, but I will never forget those apples and the wilderness community they symbolize. They were the icing on the rich cake we were already feasting on.

Such acts of kindness happen all the time in our country, though it seems never often enough. In wilderness, they stand out, perhaps because there just are not that many other people around, so there is less opportunity for such gestures. However, if my experiences are any guide, the frequency of their occurrence is higher in wilderness than in our daily lives. This is not unexpected among like-minded people engaged in similar pursuits, but they still seem to mean more, probably because they bespeak our common values and beliefs. Not only do

7.12. Ferry Lake, 1995. This windswept lake captures the sky because it sits at about 10,000 feet. Author photo.

we love nature's beauty and hunger for its wildness, but we also have a profound bond to each other and nature's community of life, a love for community that is nearly universal in humanity. These *three* passions are common to many, if not most, lovers of wilderness; they bring us into wilderness, most often in the company of friends and family, and they motivate acts of kindness there. Rather than being random, such acts are instead celebrations of these shared values and beliefs.

For me, such acts of kindness have multiplied since I came down with ALS. Friends, family, colleagues, and even complete strangers have offered everything from meals to a seat in first class on a recent flight. Certainly, this embrace of community is part of what brought my three friends on this trip; indeed, all such gifts underscore our common love for one another. I accept them with pangs of guilt, wondering if I would do the same were I in the donor's shoes. I want to believe that I would and can recall many times when I did—but others when I did not. For that reason, I sometimes feel unworthy of the generosity, whether it is something simple like cookies on a mountaintop or something more substantial, like the companionship of three friends on an eight-day canoe trip. To be sure, such acts of kindness are reminders that we can always do more to share our mutual passions, whether that is the love of our fellow human being or the call to touch the Earth's beauty and nature's wildness.

Love of community is also implicit in the actions of the rangers who protect this place. Whether they are clearing trail or lobbying in our nation's capital against some threat to the Thorofare's integrity, the desire to secure for future generations a Thorofare as rewarding to explore as it is for us today is at least as strong as the drive to protect its wildness and beauty (figure 7.13). It is manifested through other actions, such as the hospitality of Bob Jackson and his cheese crepes two decades ago or the friendliness and sense of responsibility displayed by two rangers who stopped at our campsite today. In short, our shared values and beliefs, manifested as three passions (for beauty, for wildness, and for community), motivate many of the men and women who steward the Thorofare today, just as they did for their predecessors in Lon Garrison's era and Horace Albright's time.[4]

7.13. Ranger Dave Phillips on patrol in the Thorofare, 1983. Phillips so loved the area that he requested his ashes be scattered there after he died, which came to pass in 2009. Photo by Mark Marschall. Used with permission.

（

The morning on Yellowstone Lake has passed, and it is time for lunch. My three friends have all stuck around the campsite, reading, writing, and reminiscing. Such is the theme of the day, but I sense that there is something more keeping them near. I suspect it is the impending end of the trip and the unspoken desire to make the most of our remaining time together, though no one says as much directly. Rather than depress ourselves by speculating whether tonight will be my last night in the Yellowstone wilderness—ever—we instead dwell on our shared pasts. Doing so is only natural, a way of coping with misfortune. Focus on what we have, not what we have lost or will soon lose. For the meal we eat the last of our bagels and some crackers and cheese, enjoying a view dominated by blue, the lake and sky reflections of each other. There are more clouds than yesterday and a light breeze, but it is still a bluebird day, warm enough to have us seeking shade for the afternoon.

One at a time that afternoon, my companions do take afternoon strolls. Josh checks out a nearby meadow while Sean and Eric climb the short hill to Park Point. A photo I took from there on my previous trip with Eric hangs above my desk, below the one of the upper meadow. It is a study in contrasts and shapes: the meadow grasses in the foreground shine bright gold in the afternoon sun while a looming thunderstorm colors the sky and lake slate gray (figure 7.14). The Promontory forms a black triangular wedge between sky and lake, the latter bounded by a perfect reclining parabola arcing across the center of the view (and past our current camp), the near shore forming the lower half of the curve and the distant shore, its upper half. Complementary contrasts, the lines and colors are a study of natural beauty.

The weather was far different another time I had a memorable encounter with such beauty: it was winter, about twenty degrees, with three feet of snow on the ground, and I was headed to Heart Lake with my friend Bret DeYoung. Following the ski tracks of our colleagues Dennis Young and Rick Hutchinson, who had gone in the day before, we enjoyed a fast five miles through forest to Paycheck Pass. There, we removed our skis and continued on foot, walking on bare, thermally warmed ground

7.14. The view from Park Point, 2006, on a clearer day than that described in the text. The Promontory is the forested hill, center right. Author photo.

along Witch Creek. Hot springs and fumaroles, steaming in the winter air, lined the creek and kept it from freezing. Cyanobacteria in the springs and their runoff channels stained them the colors of the rainbow, while tiny ephydrid flies huddled in the steam for warmth, their egg masses dots of salmon on the cyanobacteria. Here and there, where the balance between cold air and geothermal heat was just right, grew green moss and live plants. Life, in what is usually a season of death: part of the world of contrasts and beauty that is Yellowstone in the winter.

That was just the beginning of our tour of nature's winter beauty. Reaching the end of the bare ground, we strapped our skis back on and slid the final mile to the cabin that had sheltered Linda and me a few months earlier. There, we met up with the two who had broken the trail. Dennis, a ranger in Yellowstone, was assisting Rick, the park geologist, on his annual winter survey of the nearby thermal features; the two were kind enough to let us share the cabin. Skies were clear overnight, dropping the mercury into the single digits and allowing fog from nearby Rustic Geyser to overspread the frozen lake. Knowing we might never come this way again in winter, Bret and I decided to ski a morning loop around the lake before retracing yesterday's steps. Leaving our hosts in the toasty cabin, we stepped out into the bracing air, donned our skis, and slipped down onto the lake and into the fog's embrace. We would soon find that, rather than obscuring the view as I had feared when I first saw it, the fog enhanced the experience in a way we would long remember.

The snow covering the lake ice was wind-packed and firmed by yesterday's sun, making for fast, easy skate-style movement on our skis. At first we paralleled the north shore, staying close enough to it to see trees and, therefore, to stay on course in the featureless gloom. Our skis made the only sound as we approached the eastern shore and turned south. As we made the turn, a warm light above and to our right caught our eye: Mount Sheridan, which looms 3,000 feet above the lake's western shore, was blushing in the rising sun as it broke the horizon. With few trees adorning the mountain's face, the winter's snow caught every last solar pigment, practically glowing in every pastel shade of pink and orange imaginable. The fog shrouded the lower half of the mountain, but its summit was a mirage of color that disappeared and reappeared as we skied on through the fog's hills and swales. In this otherworldly setting, we made our way down the east shore and turned to face the mountain at the lake's south end. The mirage shone brighter there, with the sun now adding hints of yellow and the colors reaching farther down the mountainside. Soon the colors were bright enough to tint the fog itself, even when it shrouded the mountain. It was a fairyland of color, this sunrise landscape.

We finished our ski through the fog and light, taking care to detour widely around Rustic Geyser and the mouth of Witch Creek, their warm water preventing the lake from freezing in that area. Emerging from the magical fog, we retrieved our belongings from the cabin and skied out. On the way, we stopped to enjoy another of Yellowstone's marvels: a quick soak in the warm waters of Witch Creek. The extraordinary natural beauty that morning, however, was easily the highlight of that trip.

That morning jaunt by ski is one of many dozens of encounters I have had with such beauty in the Thorofare wilderness (figure 7.15). Nature's

7.15. Beauty in any season, 1997. The Two Ocean Plateau is reflected in Bridger Lake. Author photo.

beauty infuses all those experiences, whether they were fields of alpine wildflowers, mountaintop views of mountain ranges stretching to the four horizons, or lakes the color of sky. Those experiences are now memories of colors, big space, open space, rocks turned red at sunset, the music of meadows and thunderstorms, and rainbows of alpine wildflowers so rich they perfume the air. Indeed, beauty is everywhere present in the Thorofare.

((

If my experiences are any guide, then, beauty, wildness, and community are alive and well in the Thorofare; we have succeeded in preserving them as essential elements of this singular area. However, these personal experiences—this experiential data, as I called it on day one—are still just that, *personal*, one hiker's memories of time spent in the Thorofare. My selection of stories to include in this book was anything but random; rather, I chose to relate those experiences that were especially illustrative or meaningful. I performed no elaborate statistical analysis on my experiential data, but instead chose the cream of the crop. I left out the run-of-the-mill and, with the exception of the daylong walk in the rain, the negative experiences. Both the humdrum and the negative do exist in my "database"; anyone who has hiked the Thorofare trail south from the Nine-Mile Trailhead knows how dull a lodgepole pine forest can get, and as for bad experiences, on one hike a low-flying Lear jet buzzed Linda and me, and on another, a hiking buddy refused to converse with me as an equal after he discovered I did not share his atheist beliefs. Nonetheless, examples of mediocrity and negativity like these are the exception in my database, not the rule. If it were somehow possible to score each "datum" in that collection on a scale of one to ten, with ten being the best possible experience and one the worst, the average score would be well over five, probably between eight and nine. In other words, the data suggest that there is something happening to make these experiences so rich and rewarding. Some would say that this is to be expected, for a hobbyist will always find his chosen hobby meaningful and enjoyable, the reason he pursues it. True enough, but being woven together by beauty, wildness, and community links these data to fundamental truths in every human immersion in wild nature, for not only are they the same three strands that the more public story of the Thorofare reveals, but they are also common threads in the universal human relationship with nature more generally, as writer Gary Ferguson has found (recall that he is the author of *Hawk's Rest*, the other book about the Thorofare). In his latest book, *The Carry Home*, Ferguson describes surveying over a thousand myths about the creation of Earth's wonders from around the world and finding three common threads, which he calls beauty, mystery, and community. It does not take too much imagination to see wildness as mystery, and, therefore, that my experiences replicate Ferguson's results. In fact, not until after I had delivered my first draft of this book to Oregon State University Press did I discover *The Carry Home*, so our findings can be considered convergent, similar results produced via different methods. They reinforce each other, grounding both in reality, and indicate that my experiential data do have value beyond the personal. Moreover, the three common passions or threads echo the three fundamental relationships that Pope Francis—and, indeed, most world religions—ground human life within: God (wildness/mystery), our neighbor (community), and the Earth (beauty). The wilderness landscape is indeed a rich tapestry with many layers of meaning—some profound—as seen in everything from one man's experiences to those of societies across the globe.[5]

These meanings nest deeply in the hearts and fiber of those fortunate enough to experience wild places, taking root in our values and beliefs and helping define who we are as individuals and, to some extent, as societies. The meanings fire the passions that have long motivated most of the men and women who have fought to protect the Thorofare and places like it. Seeking to protect those same attributes on the ground, those people have consistently risen to the Thorofare's defense, passing it on in much the same condition it was in a century ago. Grizzlies and elk still roam, lake waters still lap at natural levels, and people still take delight in its wonders. Beauty, wildness, and community are still abundant in the Thorofare today, both in the land and in the hearts of most of its users and defenders (as they are in my database). The Thorofare is still the "blank spot on the map" of which Leopold wrote: a place to ramble about, to enjoy companionship, and to contemplate life (figure 7.16).

7.16. A place of wildness, beauty, and community: the Thorofare, 2002. Colter Peak dominates the horizon beyond this sign marking the NPS/USFS Thorofare boundary. Author photo.

Values and beliefs are not just professional motivations; they are guiding principles that we live our lives by. Turning again to my own experience, I have spent most of my adult life embracing the values and beliefs of which I write, personally and professionally. As ardently as I searched out wild country and moving scenery in the land, I did what I could to protect them through my job. Once I found those qualities in the Thorofare, it did not take too long before I found myself taking annual weeklong hikes there. Every one of those trips was in the company of a good friend, who shared with me the tingling of fear and excitement upon seeing bear tracks on the trail. As the Thorofare trips added up, I moved from seasonal Park Service positions into longer-term assignments and eventually into management. Along the way, I pursued graduate studies, writing two books about NPS policymaking and doing my best to put into practice the things I learned. I do not know how successful or influential I have been, but I do know that such job and education trajectories are not uncommon in those who have been touched by nature. Small wonder, then, that the Thorofare's wonders have survived intact.

Moreover, as I pursued my vocation, I began taking similar trips to the Crown of the Continent Ecosystem, the Colorado Plateau, the Sierra, and the northern Idaho wildernesses. The Thorofare, though, was always the wilderness to which I compared the others. They all had beauty galore, but for one reason or another, most of the others never seemed quite as wild. The Colorado Plateau lacked remoteness on the Thorofare's scale, the Sierra was too crowded, and Idaho lacked grizzlies. Only the Crown could compare. Still, for me, the Thorofare was the wildest of the wild, a place of consummate wildness, beauty, and community. In regularly returning there to seek out these attributes, then, some might say that my trips were wilderness pilgrimages, my way of touching what I might call the Divine, what is for me a tangible expression of nature's sacredness. Indeed, it was hard to miss the Divine on Younts Peak, enjoying a hundred-mile view and drinking in the sweetness of tundra flowers in bloom (figure 7.17). And on the Two Ocean Plateau, looking at a pile of fresh grizzly bear scat and watching a gang of elk scatter. And in Needle Creek, wondering if people had *ever*

7.17. Touching the Divine on Younts Peak, 1995. Author photo.

done anything to substantively influence nature's forces there. And skiing around Heart Lake on a foggy morning, catching glimpses of ethereal light. And so many other places in the Thorofare, each time in the company of a friend or two.

((

For the last seven days, I have been blessed to share a little of the Thorofare's essence with three of my closest friends. On this, our last night together, we share a delicious dinner of freeze-dried lasagna, with crème brûlée and wine for dessert. While we ate, the clouds to the north that I had been watching all day finally morphed into a thunderstorm. After finishing supper, we sat on the lakeshore watching the storm slowly approach, the lightning reflected in the lake. That was just a part of the light-show trifecta we watched that evening, as a sliver of moon joined the sun in setting within an hour of each other. We sat in silence, listening to the thunder amplify as the storm drew near (figure 7.18). At the edge of night, with lightning filling the whole northern sky and thunder close behind, we moved inside the tents for the last time.

What a fitting last evening on the lake: wildness, beauty, and community all at once. I could not have asked for a better experience for my

7.18. Last night in the wild, 2014. Together, we watched the sun and moon set and a thunderstorm approach. Photo by Sean Miculka. Used with permission.

last night in the wild. Along with the afternoon at Trail Creek and my hour of natural tranquility, that evening watching the storm overtake us was one of the most enduring and meaningful times of the whole trip. Enduring, because I can still close my eyes and ears and sense the approaching storm. And meaningful, because we touched the Divine that evening.

But, storms can bring change, sometimes violently. For me, this one would signify the change to a discordant future. For nature as well, the storm could signify the same, as tomorrow's travel, the last day of our journey, suggests.

DAY 8 Forever Wild

In every walk with nature one receives far more than he seeks.
—John Muir, 1918

Our morning routine is a little different today: we have a cold breakfast and prepare for an early departure (figure 8.1). The shoreline we have left to paddle has more rocky stretches with a long fetch, and with fifteen- to twenty-five-mile-per-hour winds in the forecast, we do not want to be caught out. Flights in and out tomorrow (in for my twin, coming to visit me, and out for Eric, who has classes starting up the next day) are the real driver, our return to the world of schedules.

By 8:00 a.m., we are under way. The lake is a glassy reflection of sky, the air cool and moist from last night's storm. Soon forest replaces the lakeshore meadows of Park Point. Shafts of low-angle sunlight do their best to find a way between the conifers, highlighting the misty air. Slowly, the sun wins, dispelling the shadows and humidity. Along with them goes the morning chill, so after an hour of paddling we pull in at Clear Creek to shed some layers and grab a snack.

The mood today is bittersweet. Sweet, because it has been a great trip and because tonight holds the promise of hot showers, pizza, and beer (and, for me, because it has been several months since I last saw my twin). But also bitter, for obvious reasons: our time in the Thorofare is over, Josh and Eric will soon be leaving, and I have likely spent my last night in the wild for the year, if not ever. And for a not-so-obvious reason: looking ahead (a natural thing to do on the last day of a wilderness trip), I have only a few weeks left in Yellowstone before I uproot myself and move to Missouri. As is clear by now, I need (or will soon need)

8.1. The last day, 2014. Josh helps load the boats for an early launch. Photo by Eric Compas. Used with permission.

full-time care, and lacking a significant other, my parents have stepped up, but I will have to move in with them.

Looking around here, I see hints that the future for the Thorofare might be as tumultuous as my own. Clear Creek is the site of the cutthroat trout surveys that have tracked their precipitous decline caused by lake trout. Depressing enough, but actually seeing the creek reminds me of global warming, a much more far-reaching challenge not just to trout but to a host of other species. Changes in Yellowstone are already occurring, with higher temperatures, smaller snowpacks that are melting earlier, and matching earlier peaks in stream flows all pivotal changes at Clear Creek. If enough drying occurs, the creek may lose the kinetic energy it needs to keep its mouth to the lake open. Lacking that, wave action will build a sand bar across the mouth, the creek water percolating through the porous sand (figure 8.2). This would cut off trout spawning habitat for the lake-bound cutthroats, adding another survival challenge to those already posed by lake trout and whirling disease. While this sand bar phenomenon has not yet happened to Clear

Creek (it is too big, for now), it was widespread on smaller Yellowstone Lake tributaries in the drought of the early 2000s. Make the droughts longer, drier, and/or hotter with more global warming, and the species may have too little spawning habitat to sustain itself. Like the whitebark pine, it may become overwhelmed, another casualty of a hotter planet.

In the face of such uncertainty, park managers are trying to strengthen the resilience of the cutthroat trout population. The lake trout gill netting program, for example, seeks to minimize the threat from that fish, which will (if it is successful) make the cutthroat population better able to recover from occasional blockage of spawning streams. Similarly, by propagating strains of whitebark pines that are resistant to white pine blister rust, managers seek to improve that species' ability to cope with drought and pine beetles. The common idea in these efforts, then, is to promote resilience by minimizing a different stress to the plant or animal.

Resilience is a buzzword now among academics, conservationists, and land managers searching for ways to cope with climate change and

8.2. The mouth of Clear Creek, 2014. A creek of this size is able to keep wave action from completing the gravel bar across the stream's mouth. Photo by Eric Compas. Used with permission.

its multiplying effects. From conferences to how-to guides and research papers, enhancing the resilience of natural systems is a key strategy for coping with the realities of global warming. Another important approach is reducing our carbon emissions, which some—but too few—are also tackling. Frustrated by society's generally lackadaisical approach to global warming and already seeing significant impacts from it, land managers are increasingly trying to make their resources as resilient as possible to cope with the accelerating disruptions coming our way. The efforts even extend to the landscape level, with concerned individuals and organizations working to ensure that migration corridors link protected areas so that animals and plants can migrate to higher latitudes and altitudes as the planet gets hotter.[1]

The Thorofare has a substantial amount of resilience already. It is large, with a variety of elevation and moisture gradients, so a diversity of habitats will likely persist. It is well connected to other large blocks of protected lands, so wildlife and vegetation will be able to move safely, within the Thorofare, to other places in the Yellowstone area, and beyond. And it has many resilient animals and plants capable of utilizing diverse environments, so animals like elk and grizzly bears and trees like lodgepole pine and Douglas-fir will probably survive. In a number of ways, then, the most remote place is well-positioned to contend with climate disruption, though it is anyone's guess how well it will do, especially if our production of greenhouse gases continues to climb.

In some ways, there is a parallel to my situation and my own need for resilience to counter the ALS onslaught; ALS is to me as global warming is to nature. Recognizing my need for such strength when I was diagnosed, I took a final backpacking trip in Yosemite and began spending more time with family and friends. I took a series of extended and relaxing trips to the places most important to me: I floated the Grand Canyon with my brothers, camped in Glacier and Yosemite National Parks with close friends, and spent a final summer going to my favorite haunts in Yellowstone, including this canoe trip. As my abilities changed, so did the kind of outing, from hikes to bike rides (on a recumbent tricycle that I could mount and dismount safely), and eventually to sitting quietly and enjoying the view, from on a boat or on land. Whatever the activity, the purpose was the same: to soak up as much of nature's magnificence and tranquility as I could, along with the love of friends and family. When I am confined to a wheelchair, the hope is that I will be able to close my eyes, bring that beauty and wildness to mind, feel the conviviality, and smile and relax.

Unfortunately, though, no amount of resilience can fully counter ALS. Resilience can only give me the grace I need to accept the disease's inexorable progression. It cannot prevent the final outcome; the disease is terminal, though some people live with it for years or even decades (Stephen Hawking, for example). Resilience can also help my loved ones cope; really, my most fervent hope is that I can impart some of the resilience I have been given to the family and friends I may soon be leaving.

The same can be said of global warming: no amount of resilience can fully counter it. Using the Thorofare as an example, some species will undoubtedly suffer or disappear altogether, no matter how resilient the landscape may be or how much resilience we try to give the species. Animals and plants that are particularly dependent on snow or cold may be the most vulnerable. Canada lynx, for example, may starve, their prey base of snowshoe hare too reduced by recurring wildfires killing the trees whose needles they eat. Wolverines, too, may be unable to find snow deep enough for denning, and moose might succumb to diseases borne by ticks that formerly found the Thorofare too cold and snowy. Whitebark pine may not be able to fend off pine beetles, despite our efforts to aid the tree. Whatever the species or the exact cause of its disappearance, the speed and extent to which we are heating the globe will overwhelm some, perhaps much, of the resilience we contribute. This does not mean we should abandon our efforts—far from it—but rather that we should not hide the ugly reality behind our hope that resilience boosting will do some good. It will, but global warming, if we do not act now to meaningfully curtail it, promises a long list of woes for the entire community of life on Earth.

What will happen to beauty and wildness? Like me, they will survive, but in a gradually altered and diminished state. That decline in the Thorofare has already begun, for the list of changes we are already observing is long indeed. Dead whitebarks in the remotest corners of the most remote place are silent witnesses that human actions vis-à-vis global warming are now affecting the Thorofare, whittling away at its most fundamental attributes. As with my growing paralysis, the cuts are accumulating. I will steadily weaken, needing more and more life support, especially with breathing, as my diaphragm will eventually be unable to move air into or out of my lungs. The fate of the Thorofare's wildness will be similar: natural processes will increasingly change in function (like precipitation and fire regimes), necessitating ever more life support for the lives dependent on them (like whitebark pine and moose). Nature will increasingly bear humanity's signature, with even the wildest places like the Thorofare becoming significantly trammeled, their wildness more and more compromised. Some wildness will survive, but it may eventually take a back seat to human influence as a shaping force of the wilderness landscape, a marked contrast to the existing situation. Similarly, some beauty will remain, though it will be irrevocably altered.

At this point, the parallel to my own plight breaks down. The difference is choice: I have none with my disease. I can choose how gracefully I accept its frequent setbacks, but not whether ALS will ultimately claim me. It will, unless researchers develop a cure or effective treatment—and soon. They have been trying for twenty years, but their best result is a drug that adds only two or three months to one's life. At least for now, the choice has been made for me.

Conversely, with global warming, we do have a choice. We know what causes it, the calamities it promises for the planet and its inhabitants, and how to prevent those. Some of us are attempting to reduce our carbon footprint, but for others (especially the US Congress), the choice so far has ranged from tepid concern at best to willful ignorance at worst. Some, like my neighbor in a campground a few weeks ago, use one chilly night in an unfamiliar place as sufficient basis to dismiss findings based on billions of data points and peer-reviewed by hundreds of the world's leading climatologists.[2] Others relegate that same science, which is easily as conclusive as that linking smoking to lung disease, to the world of "belief," to the same place where Alice's Wonderland is reality and the sky is pink (or whatever color they "believe" it to be). No matter the excuse, these choices are little better than that of the proverbial ostrich with its head in the ground, hoping the problem will go away if we only hide our eyes from it. It will not, but thankfully there are better, simple, and even easy choices we can make to meaningfully reduce our carbon footprint.

☾

Back at Clear Creek, we have satisfied our hunger, so we embark for the last time. The morning is moving along, the sun well into its arc above us. We pass occasional rock outcrops and walls, one or two of them exuding wisps of steam, evidence that we are approaching the resurgent dome tilting the lake to the south. In the distance we can see cars on the East Entrance Road, their movement catching our eye. Above them is Lake Butte, the high hill from which one can look out over the whole lake. It is much same view as FDR enjoyed a few generations ago, one of wildness and beauty, a sample of what we have enjoyed for the last week. It is also a reminder that having places like the Thorofare is a special gift, bestowed on us by those who went before and who voluntarily gave up their own ability to do what they wanted, whenever they wanted, in that wilderness. They could have laid claim to this or that piece of land or logged its forests, but instead they restrained themselves from personal advantage and limited their own freedom. Everyone then and now is the winner, co-owners of a relatively intact Thorofare and hundreds of other wild places across the globe. Moreover, when threats to the Thorofare's integrity arose, they went to bat for it, advocating for its continued preservation. They kept dams and roads out and tried to keep motorboats out, all for the common good—just as thousands of other wilderness defenders have done, time and again, throughout the world.

To our predecessors and to us, then, places like the Thorofare could not and cannot be all things to all people without losing the fundamental attributes that set them apart. In the same way, our planet cannot be all things to all of its people, absorbing unlimited amounts of greenhouse gases, especially with seven billion of us inhabiting it. If we continue to let global warming amplify unchecked, not only will we see the more dire climate projections become reality, but many of the world's already underprivileged people will also suffer the more, mostly because they lack the resources to cope with increasingly severe storms and climate disruptions.[3] To prevent that injustice from occurring, along with the more draconian changes predicted for the natural world, we can adapt the wilderness legacy of restraint and advocacy, exemplified in the Thorofare, to global warming and the threats it poses to wild places everywhere. Restraint, by voluntarily choosing to forgo things and actions with large carbon footprints, like large vehicles and unnecessarily large homes. And advocacy, by educating ourselves and our youth about nature and climate change, voting for green candidates, and demanding substantive action from all elected politicians and governments to address this threat. Addressing global warming using these two principles may sound simplistic, but they have stood the test of time in effectively protecting wild places around the world.

Still, skeptics might respond that restraint and advocacy will accomplish little more than making one feel pious, because one person's actions, or even those of all wilderness users and writers, are too small a drop in the global sea that needs to change. Changing that sea, they would assert, may be impossible because our existing attitudes are too powerful and entrenched to change, especially that embracing the freedom and independence we find in the automobile. Indeed, that association is certainly one of the reasons we have not seriously addressed global warming thus far, for to do so would be to acknowledge that the most tangible symbol of our freedom—the automobile—is one of its main causes, and therefore that some constraints need to be put on that freedom. Changing the course of this *Titanic*, the skeptics might conclude, is just too difficult, the obstacles too big and numerous. In part, they would be right, at least regarding substantially reducing our carbon footprint through individual actions alone; there are simply too many actors, on too many stages, acting on too many different values and beliefs, to have any hope of bringing about meaningful change in this manner. For example, I would never have convinced my campground neighbor that global warming is real, let alone that he should modify his behavior to address it—much less do the same with everyone else in the campground.

Yet, to do nothing is to let the *Titanic* scrape the iceberg, and we all know how that turned out. Had the captain—indeed, the whole world—not been convinced that the *Titanic* was unsinkable, he could have avoided the iceberg entirely by choosing a more southerly route, where the risk of an iceberg collision would have been reduced or eliminated. Only one person, then, trusted by the passengers to pilot the ship safely, would have had to do something different, shedding the prevailing rose-colored glasses of hubris. Meanwhile, the passengers would have continued making merry, mostly unaware of the added transit time that the safer—but still fast—route entailed. Similarly, there is another way to bring about a meaningful change in our approach to global warming: authorize key leaders to change the policies and rules governing our choices in such a way that, like the *Titanic* passengers, we continue our existing behaviors mostly unchanged while our carbon impact drops. For example, in 2011 President Barack Obama announced new rules, developed in collaboration with thirteen major automakers, requiring all vehicles sold in the United States to average 54.5 miles per gallon by 2025. This fleet average is twice that of the present, and no major consumer behavior will need to change to accomplish it, along with the significant reduction in our carbon footprint that will come with it. Similar fixes are possible, but not yet nationally adopted, for other major pieces of our carbon footprint, from tighter building codes to renewable energy requirements and progressive utility pricing. The common idea in these solutions, then, is to empower key decision-makers (the *Titanic*'s captain, the president, public service commissions, etc.) to implement structural fixes that solve the problem without widespread changes in our behavior (which are unlikely to happen, even with massive media campaigns, according to one source).[4]

Rather than simplistic tools of the pious, restraint and advocacy are the foundations of this approach. Many key decision-makers are elected politicians, so merely casting a vote for green candidates may be the most effective, easy, and widely accepted form of advocacy. Holding them accountable once in office, eliminating roadblocks to their effectiveness (such as by voting out climate change deniers in Congress), and keeping the issue alive (such as by writing op-ed pieces) are more active forms of advocacy for those so inclined. Still another form is to introduce new audiences to and immerse them in nature's wildness and beauty, whether inner city schoolchildren who have never seen a spiderweb adorned with dew, college students who have never studied nature's complexity in the field, or one's own children who have never been to a national park. Whoever they are, by valuing nature personally, they will be more likely to cast their own vote for the green candidate. As for restraint, while the actions of any one individual may indeed be just a drop in the sea needing to be changed, any little bit helps. More importantly, because merely electing a president sympathetic to a structural change is not enough to ensure its success, by choosing to be one of those drops of change, one can both demonstrate that structural fixes are feasible and also create the political climate necessary for structural fixes to work. Returning to the fuel-efficient vehicle example, by demonstrating that a Toyota Prius can comfortably transport a family of four and adopting the car in larger numbers, multiple drops of restraint paved the way for Obama to create a successful fix. In other words, by demonstrating the fix's feasibility, changing a potentially hostile audience into a neutral or even receptive one, and empowering a key individual to implement the fix, simple restraint and advocacy may have produced a sea change that is likely to stick: meaningful reductions of our greenhouse gas emissions and of our climatological hubris.

If we do make broader reductions of our carbon footprint happen, our descendants may be able to embrace wildness as we do now, both the grand wildness of the Thorofare (accessible even to disabled individuals like me, thanks to boats and friends who paddle them) and the more subtle wildness in our backyards, like that of the red-bellied woodpecker flitting around my parents' house in Missouri. Whichever wildness our children and grandchildren connect with, they will touch more than just the focus of our values and beliefs: they may come to understand our place in the global community of life; they may even glimpse the Divine. The universality of that opportunity is, for many of us, the most important reason to stem global warming: so that all our children and grandchildren may have that gateway to understanding and inspiration. Only by restraining ourselves from irreparably damaging our sacred heritage and advocating for its protection will we assure our continued physical, mental, and spiritual health.

(

An hour after we launched from Clear Creek, we beached the boats on the black sand of Sedge Bay and unloaded them one last time (figure 8.3). Our week in the wild was over, so we threw our gear in the cars and loaded the boats on top for the drive home. On the way, we passed the Brink of the Lower Falls trailhead. It was there that, one summer day in 1969, a young couple from Missouri parked their green Ford Falcon station wagon and walked down the switchbacks with their two-and-a-half-year-old twin boys. At the overlook, they admired the view downstream, and then leaned against the railing to look straight down 308 feet at the base of the falls, the river's water blasted into a cold spray upon striking rocks there. Just at that moment, a gust of wind blew the sunglasses off the father's face and over the edge. The twins both erupted in tears at that loss, but their parents consoled them and soon dried up the tears. With no way to retrieve the glasses, the family climbed back up to their car and went on their way.

Incidents like this are unremarkable; they happen all the time in the national parks. Nonetheless, this one is remarkable to me, for I was one of those twins, and the sunglasses incident is, as far as I can identify, my earliest childhood memory. I now have half a lifetime of other memories from Yellowstone, including those from the canoe trip. Many of the richest memories are from the Thorofare, probably because wildness, beauty, and community so deeply permeate them. They, and the ongoing love and support of my family and friends, have indeed become my arsenal of resilience against ALS.

In the time it has taken me to write this book, ALS has continued its consuming progression in my body. My arms have weakened so much that I cannot lift my hands to my mouth, so my mother and father take care of dozens of things most of us do without a thought, everything from feeding to bathing me, scratching an itch to removing food caught in my teeth, turning me over in bed to holding the handkerchief when I blow my nose. My fingers are too weak to type, so I use an on-screen

8.3. *The end of the canoe trip and the end of an era for at least one of us, 2014. Photo by Eric Compas. Used with permission.*

keyboard, tediously moving the cursor to each letter and clicking the mouse to "type." When I lose even this limited typing ability, I will plug in a device that tracks my eyes as they move around the same keyboard, hovering for a second or two on the key I want to strike. I already use a similar eye-tracking device to "speak," allowing others to understand me, my own speech too slurred for even those around me most to comprehend more than half the time. Like the keyboard, the device is slow; I am always two or three subjects behind in the conversation. Even the rudimentary communication that I have with these technologically advanced tools may be taken away if ALS robs me of the ability to keep my eyelids open, as it has done to the woman who gave me the eye-tracking speech device. Thankfully, I am not close to that point, but other muscles in my head (specifically my tongue and throat muscles) have weakened so much that I now derive most of my nutrition from liquids like Ensure, delivered through a port in my stomach wall. I eat only small amounts of food by mouth, for pleasure, and still often choke. As I did on the canoe trip, I wear a neck brace, though weakening neck muscles force me to wear it most of the day now. I can barely walk anymore; not only do I need a walker, but someone also has to hold onto me firmly, and even then my stride is only three or four inches. I expect to be wheelchair-bound by the time this book is published (I already am for anything outside the house). Finally, and perhaps most critically, my diaphragm is progressively weakening; I can inhale only about a third of the air volume expected for someone of my weight, so I sleep attached to another machine that helps me inhale, filling my lungs more than I can on my own.

Sometimes the unyielding progression of this disease makes me wonder if I will reach a point from which I do not wish to go on, where I have reached so low a plain of existence that death, and whatever awaits us on the other side of it, become more attractive. I know that I do not wish to exist in the state of my speech device donor (the poor woman is completely paralyzed, unable to move a single muscle in her body; for that reason, she cannot communicate at all—an unimaginable form of solitary confinement—and depends on a respirator for all of her breathing), but recognizing when I am approaching that threshold may be difficult. For now, I think that as long as I can still meaningfully experience the beauty, wildness, and community of love and life on Earth, I will have the resilience—and desire—to go on. The beauty of just one flower, the wildness of the woodpecker, and the love of just one family member, may individually be enough to make me want to go on; collectively, they should be more than enough. They may not be the overwhelming evidence of the Divine as can be found in the Thorofare, but they are still hints of it, enough to keep me going. Moreover, they keep hope alive, hope for a cure, even if that seems at times like hoping for a miracle.

During the same time as I have been writing, the drought gripping the American West has deepened. Snowfall throughout the West for the winter of 2014–2015 was well below normal, the temperatures well above. In California and the Southwest, the drought has no historic precedent; we are in uncharted terrain. Similarly, wildfires in eastern Washington in summer 2015 were larger than ever, consuming hundreds of square miles of forest parched by that drought. We are right in line with climate change predictions, though, for the entire region will be warmer and drier under virtually any climate model.[5] Also during the same time, gas prices dropped below $2 a gallon, fueling a new round of SUV sales, and the US Congress approved the Keystone pipeline, but failed to summon the votes needed to override President Obama's veto.

In the face of such news, some of us, perhaps many, may despair of ever seeing society take the global warming threat seriously. It will take a societal miracle, they might say, to make us really reduce our carbon emissions, just as it will take a technological miracle to cure me. But such miracles can happen—and already have, not so long ago. In the 1980s, when the ozone hole over Antarctica was traced to our use of chlorofluorocarbon propellants in aerosol sprays, the world's nations devised and implemented a structural fix that solved the problem relatively quickly: the Montreal Protocol banning the production of chlorofluorocarbons.[6] Similarly, we have the knowledge and the means to make a societal climate change miracle become reality. If we look to the people we love and to the beauty and wildness of the nature all around us, we will find the same hope that I find, and the strength we need to act (figure 8.4). Some beauty and wildness will endure no matter the extent of our climate warming, so their inspiration will remain for those who seek it; as Muir suggests, we will continue to receive more than we seek.

And seek we should. As crucial as it is to address global warming, it is even more important to stay inspired, grounded in the Earth's community of life. Western writer Edward Abbey perhaps best expressed this sentiment in a talk he delivered in Montana in 1976:

> One final paragraph of advice: do not burn yourselves out. Be as I am—a reluctant enthusiast . . . a part-time crusader, a half-hearted fanatic. Save the other half of yourselves and your lives for pleasure and adventure. It is not enough to fight for the land; it is even more important to enjoy it. While you can. While it's still here. So get out there and hunt and fish and mess around with your friends, ramble out yonder and explore the forests, climb the mountains, bag the peaks, run the rivers, breathe deep of that yet sweet and lucid air, sit quietly for a while and contemplate the precious stillness, the lovely, mysterious, and awesome space. Enjoy yourselves, keep your brain in your head and your head firmly attached to the body, the body active and alive.[7]

Shortly after my diagnosis, I penned a few words expressing my own coda, one with shades of Abbey but reflecting my new circumstances. Stuck to my refrigerator in California, it made the move to Yellowstone, where it came to grace another fridge, so I would read it daily. It remains my own "final paragraph of advice":

Seek wildness and beauty
Enjoy the love of family and friends
Find joy in the here and now
Be strong, live well, and love deeply.

8.4. The Thorofare and all places wild: inspirations past, present, and future, 2006. Overlook Mountain rises above the meadows on upper Mountain Creek, where evening shadows grow long. Author photo.

Acknowledgments

Writing this book was a way for me to cope with the isolation forced upon me by ALS: not only isolation from the landscape I have always found so invigorating, but also isolation from those that I love, as my speech grew increasingly slurred and unintelligible. The twelve months that I spent writing and revising the book were the longest time period in a quarter century that I did not set foot in Yellowstone, and I have no realistic hope of ever getting there again. Writing, though, transported me through time and space to the trails of the Thorofare and the waterways of Yellowstone Lake, to glorious Absaroka mountaintops and verdant meadows, to scents of dry pine needles and damp grasses, and to the feel of the pack on my back and the tingle of frosty mornings.

Similarly, searching for the book's illustrations in the shoeboxes of photos I accumulated from almost three decades exploring the Yellowstone area impressed upon me the understanding that my journeys were not alone. Even if I was actually hiking by myself, I was part of a rich community of friends and close family that traveled the journey of life together, shouting for joy at our mountains climbed and righting the canoe when it capsized. Writing this book, then, became a way to continue the conversation with those loved ones, to look back on a life lived close to nature, and to contemplate the meanings in those life experiences. I hope that as communication gets more difficult or even impossible for me, this book becomes my voice, allowing me to speak in the way that only a book can, even after the waters of Yellowstone Lake have received my ashes.

Three of the best friends a person could ask for, Josh Becker, Sean Miculka, and Eric Compas, gave me not only the canoe trip, but also a rich setting for the book. I do not know what I ever did to deserve one such friend, let alone three (and several others beyond them), but I do know that I am many times blessed. They did not hesitate to do the trip, even though all of them had been to the Southeast Arm before and had other things they could have (perhaps should have) been doing. In addition to the many camp chores detailed in the narrative, they even lugged my walker around the Southeast Arm. Moreover, they each contributed to the trip in their own personal way, Eric with his quick wit, Josh through his steadfast calmness, and Sean by sharing a tent with me and taking care of me through the night. I am simultaneously humbled and enriched, then and now.

Also making this book possible were my parents, Jim and Jeanne Yochim. In October 2014, they welcomed me into their home to care for me. Caring for an ALS sufferer involves an ever-growing list of physical chores, an unending stream of emotional struggles, and a near-complete loss of personal freedom and privacy. They have stood up to these challenges, helping me turn a road of sadness into a journey of reflection, partly by helping me carve out blocks of time in my day for writing. The journey has not been without tears, but they have given it dignity, love, and even joy, at times.

Keeping me company have also been my three brothers, Jim, Paul, and Brian, and their wives (Nora, Nipa, and Jill) and sons (one each: Matthew, Kieran, and Ellis). Along with my aunts, uncles, and cousins, they bumped along with me on this rough road, helping give me the perseverance to keep typing. Similarly, the friends I have made over the years, especially from my times in Yellowstone and Yosemite National Parks, have helped smooth the road. They are too numerous to name, but a few deserve special mention because they were with me on one of the hikes mentioned in this book: Dave Moser, Dave Lee, Linda Campbell, Bronco Grigg, Mike Stevens, Jim and Eamon Donovan, Bret DeYoung, and Sean, Josh, and Eric (again). Others who joined me regularly on outings not mentioned in this book but who helped develop its ideas include Ann Makley, Mark Baudendistal, Ellen Petrick, Woody and Janet Hesselbarth, Margaret and Charlie Repath, Jim Roche, Erik Skindrud, Jeff Pappas, Brenna Lissoway, Steve and Denice Swanke, Dave

Thoma, Doug Hilborn, David Kirtley, Doug Harrison, Jared White, Mike Tercek, and Donna Sisson. Finally, a few others deserve special mention for other reasons: Missy Miculka helped keep me well-fed my last summer in Yellowstone; Jodi Bailey set up a Facebook page that friends could use to inspire me to keep writing by posting photos from their recent hikes; Bill and Lynn Lowry showed me some of the St. Louis area's natural beauty; Ruth and Leslie Quinn freed me from worrying about my house in Montana; Mark and Joy Marschall provided photos, several samples of the breakfast waffle recipe he perfected when he was a Thorofare ranger, and unflagging enthusiasm for a book about the area where they got engaged; Tom Santi demonstrated that a life with ALS could still be meaningful and productive; and Michelle Gray patiently plowed through those shoeboxes of pictures with me.

A number of colleagues also provided invaluable assistance transforming my ideas into a manuscript. Anne Foster, Jackie Jerla, Jessie Gerdes, and Brandon Sexton helped me plumb the depths of Yellowstone's archives and museum collections, rising above the call of duty to fill in the gaps in my research, in more than one way. Lee Whittlesey and Betsy Watry provided consistent support for the project, even offering to finish the project if ALS made that impossible for me. Eric Compas had already agreed to do that if needed; additionally, he provided the two maps and many of the photos. Graphics master Jim Donovan cleaned up and corrected several of the images, including the cover photo. Mark Fincher, Kathleen Morse, and Don Neubacher schooled me in the fine points of the Wilderness Act, and Wade Vagias provided an office and collegial support my last summer in Yellowstone.

The staff at Oregon State University Press, in turn, helped transform the manuscript into an actual book. Acquisitions Editor Mary Elizabeth Braun saw the potential in a manuscript two other editors had already rejected, expedited the review and publication process to enable me to finish the book before ALS made that impossible, and kindly replied to my badgering emails. Two anonymous reviewers read an imperfect manuscript and provided many suggestions on how to make it less so. Susan Campbell exercised her "sworn duty" as copy editor, turning my many abuses of English into something resembling good prose (any

Notes

Unless otherwise noted, all archival sources are at the Yellowstone National Park Archives, a division of the National Archives, Gardiner, Montana.

Abbreviations used in the endnotes

AHC — Gale W. McGee Collection, Accession #9800, American Heritage Center, University of Wyoming, Laramie

IWL — Izaak Walton League Collection (CONS 41), Conservation Collection, Denver Public Library, Denver, Colorado

LVE — *Livingston (Mont.) Enterprise*

NACP — National Archives, College Park, Maryland

NPAB — *National Parks Association Bulletin*

NPS — National Park Service

TWS — The Wilderness Society Collection (CONS 130), Conservation Collection, Denver Public Library, Denver, Colorado

USDI — United States Department of the Interior

YCR — Yellowstone Center for Resources files, National Park Service, Mammoth Hot Springs, Wyoming

YNPL — Yellowstone National Park Research Library, Gardiner, Montana

Notes to Preface: A Place Called the Thorofare

Thoreau, "Walking," *Atlantic Monthly* 9 (June 1862), 56:657–674.

1. Always spelled that way today, without the *u*, *g*, and *h* found in the more common word.

2   Peter Nabokov and Lawrence Loendorf, *Restoring a Presence: American Indians and Yellowstone National Park* (Norman: University of Oklahoma Press, 2004): 36; and Lee H. Whittlesey, *Yellowstone Place Names* (Gardiner, MT: Wonderland Publishing Co., 2006), second edition, revised.

3   Gary Ferguson, *Hawks Rest: A Season in the Remote Heart of Yellowstone* (Washington, DC: National Geographic, 2003). In most ways, the critique is well deserved; indeed, Ferguson omits discussion of packstock trampling around campsites, an impact I have often observed in the Thorofare. Ferguson, however, also fails to mention that outfitters perform a lot of the trail maintenance that the underfunded US Forest Service would otherwise be unable to do. See days six and seven for more discussion of outfitter use of packstock in the Thorofare.

4   See, for example, Paul Schullery, *Searching for Yellowstone: Ecology and Wonder in the Last Wilderness* (Boston: Houghton Mifflin, 1997); James A. Pritchard, *Preserving Yellowstone's Natural Conditions: Science and the Perception of Nature* (Lincoln: University of Nebraska Press, 1999); Chris Magoc, *Yellowstone: The Creation and Selling of an American Landscape, 1870–1903* (Albuquerque: University of New Mexico Press, 1999); Aubrey L. Haines, *The Yellowstone Story*, rev. ed., 2 vols. (Niwot, CO: Yellowstone Association for Natural Science, History, and Education, in cooperation with the University Press of Colorado, 1996); Susan G. Clark, *Ensuring Greater Yellowstone's Future: Choices for Leaders and Citizens* (New Haven, CT: Yale University Press, 2008); Alice Wondrak Biel, *Do (Not) Feed the Bears: The Fitful History of Wildlife and Tourists in Yellowstone* (Lawrence: University Press of Kansas, 2006); Richard A. Bartlett, *Yellowstone: A Wilderness Besieged* (Tucson: University of Arizona Press, 1985); and Mary Ann Franke, *Yellowstone in the Afterglow: Lessons from the Fires* (Mammoth Hot Springs, WY: National Park Service, 2000).

5   The University of Washington Press in Seattle has published a remarkable series of books providing a comprehensive history of wilderness preservation in America, including James Feldman, *A Storied Wilderness: Rewilding the Apostle Islands* (2013); James Morton Turner, *The Promise of Wilderness: American Environmental Politics since 1964* (2012); David Louter, *Windshield Wilderness:*

Cars, Roads, and Nature in Washington's National Parks (2010); Kevin R. Marsh, *Drawing Lines in the Forest: Creating Wilderness Areas in the Pacific Northwest* (2010); John Miles, *Wilderness in the National Parks: Playground or Preserve* (2009); Mark W. T. Harvey, *Wilderness Forever: Howard Zahniser and the Path to the Wilderness Act* (2007); and Paul Sutter, *Driven Wild: How the Fight against Automobiles Launched the Modern Wilderness Movement* (2005). Complementing these are Daniel Nelson, *Northern Landscapes: The Struggle for Wilderness Alaska* (Washington, DC: Resources for the Future, 2004); and Doug Scott, *The Enduring Wilderness: Protecting Our Natural Heritage through the Wilderness Act* (Golden, CO: Fulcrum Publishing, 2004).

6   Perhaps the most thorough but succinct exploration of wilderness meanings may be found in Thomas R. Vale, *The American Wilderness: Reflections on Nature Protection in the United States* (Charlottesville: University of Virginia Press, 2005), 11–40. Others who explore them include William Cronon, "The Trouble with Wilderness; or, Getting Back to the Wrong Nature," in *Uncommon Ground: Rethinking the Human Place in Nature*, ed. William Cronon, 69–90 (New York: W. W. Norton & Co., 1996); Max Oelschlaeger, *The Idea of Wilderness: From Prehistory to the Age of Ecology* (New Haven, CT: Yale University Press, 1991); Michael L. Johnson, *Hunger for the Wild: America's Obsession with the Untamed West* (Lawrence: University Press of Kansas, 2007); Paul Schullery, *Searching for Yellowstone*, 1997; Roderick Nash, *Wilderness and the American Mind*, 4th ed. (New Haven, CT: Yale University Press, 2001); Wallace Stegner, *The Sound of Mountain Water: The Changing American West* (Lincoln: University of Nebraska Press, 1985); Frederick Turner, *Beyond Geography: The Western Spirit against the Wilderness* (New York: Viking Press, 1980); J. Baird Callicott and Michael P. Nelson, eds., *The Great New Wilderness Debate* (Athens: University of Georgia Press, 1999); and J. Baird Callicott and Michael P. Nelson, eds., *The Wilderness Debate Rages On: Continuing the Great New Wilderness Debate* (Athens: University of Georgia Press, 2008). Scholars from many disciplines have examined conservationist motives and relationships to nature, finding that they view nature as sacred: Evan Berry, *Devoted to Nature: The Religious Roots of American Environmentalism* (Oakland: University of California

Press, 2015); Stephen Fox, *The American Conservation Movement: John Muir and His Legacy* (Madison: University of Wisconsin Press, 1981); Catherine L. Albanese, *Nature Religion in America: From the Algonkian Indians to the New Age* (Chicago: University of Chicago Press, 1990); Linda Graber, *Wilderness as Sacred Space* (Washington, DC: American Association of Geographers, 1976); Thomas R. Dunlap, *Faith in Nature: Environmentalism as Religious Quest* (Seattle: University of Washington Press, 2004); and Justin Farrell, *The Battle for Yellowstone: Morality and the Sacred Roots of Environmental Conflict* (Princeton, NJ: Princeton University Press, 2015).

7   Charles C. Mann, *1491: New Revelations of the Americas before Columbus* (New York: Alfred A. Knopf, 2005); Nabokov and Loendorf, *Restoring a Presence*, 2004; William H. Denevan, "The Pristine Myth: The Landscape of the Americas in 1492," *Annals of the Association of American Geographers* 82 (1992): 369–385; Charles Kay, "Aboriginal Overkill: The Role of Native Americans in Structuring Western Ecosystems," *Human Nature* 5 (1994): 359–398; and "Are Ecosystems Structured from the Top-Down or Bottom-Up? A New Look at an Old Debate," *Wildlife Society Bulletin* 26 (1998): 484–498; Mark David Spence, *Dispossessing the Wilderness: Indian Removal and the Making of the National Parks* (New York: Oxford University Press, 1999); Callicott and Nelson, eds., *The Great New Wilderness Debate*, 1999 (who proclaim its demise in their introduction), and *The Wilderness Debate Rages On*, 2008.

8   Wallace Stegner, *The Sound of Mountain Water*, 1985; Thomas Vale, "The Myth of the Humanized Landscape: An Example from Yosemite National Park," *Natural Areas Journal* 18 (1998): 231–236; Thomas R. Vale, ed., *Fire, Native Peoples, and the Natural Landscape* (Washington, DC: Island Press, 2002); Edward Abbey, *Desert Solitaire: A Season in the Wilderness* (New York: Ballantine Books, 1968); Holmes Rolston, "Biology and Philosophy in Yellowstone," *Biology and Philosophy* 5 (1990): 241–258; and Michael J. Yochim, "Aboriginal Overkill Overstated: Errors in Charles Kay's Hypothesis," *Human Nature* 12 (2001): 141–167 (I used Kay's publications and his references therein as "data" to reach a conclusion very different from his).

9   Michael L. Johnson, *Hunger for the Wild*, 2007; Thomas R. Vale, *Fire, Native Peoples, and the Natural Landscape*, 2002; and Doug Peacock, *The Grizzly Years: In Search of the American Wilderness* (New York: Henry Holt and Co., 1990).

10   Nabokov and Loendorf, *Restoring a Presence*, 2004:5. While basic geographic errors like this can make the reader wonder what other gaffes are present in a book (not to mention erroneous conclusions based on them), the scholarship in this book is otherwise outstanding.

11   I am indebted to my paddling partners not only for this trip, but also for conversations over many years and campfires that helped develop these themes. Sean in particular made me think about the importance of beauty to humanity, while Josh did the same for wildness, and Eric for the management implications of preserving both, although our talks often touched on more than one of the three subjects.

12   Because the term "climate change" seems to understate the severity of humanity's impact on Earth's climate, I will generally use the term "global warming" instead. Even that term seems too benign, given the frightening nature of long-term projections, especially in the American West (see the discussion on day six). Indeed, a more relevant term might be "global overheating."

Note to Day 1: Of Wilds and Men

Ralph Waldo Emerson, "Friendship," in *Essays: First Series*, 1847

Notes to Day 2: Into the Wild

Albright to the Director, October 16, 1920, file "Irrigation—Fall River Reservoir Site, May 22, 1920, to Oct. 30, 1920, Part 3," box 218, General Records/Central Files, 1907–39, Record Group 79, NACP.

1   Dictionary.com, accessed March 12, 2015.

2   Public Law 88-577 (16 U.S. C. 1131-1136), 88th Congress, 2nd session, September 3, 1964. Mark W. T. Harvey provides a comprehensive history of the act and its authorship in *Wilderness Forever* (2007).

3   See note 7 of the preface for a partial list of such authors. See also note 8 for authors providing a different perspective.

4   The Arthur Carhart National Wilderness Training Center, Aldo Leopold Wilderness Research Institute, and the College of Forestry and Conservation's Wilderness Institute at the University of Montana, have volumes of information online about the Wilderness Act. For this analysis, see "What is 'Wilderness'?" http://www.wilderness.net/NWPS/WhatIsWilderness, accessed March 12, 2015. Five of these attributes (everything but size) are so fundamental to wilderness that the center instructs federal land managers to use them as the basis of analysis in evaluating the impacts of prospective management changes.

5   The best overview of fires in Yellowstone is Linda Wallace, ed., *After the Fires: The Ecology of Change in Yellowstone National Park* (New Haven, CT: Yale University Press, 2004). See also Anthony L. Westerling, Monica G. Turner, Erica A. H. Smithwick, William H. Romme, and Michael G. Ryan, "Continued Warming Could Transform Greater Yellowstone Fire Regimes by mid-21st Century," *Proceedings of the National Academy of Sciences* 108 (August 9, 2011) 32:13165–13170.

6   Acreage from peakbagger.com, "Most Remote Spots in USA Wilderness Complexes," http://www.peakbagger.com/PBGeog/..%5Creport%5CReport.aspx?r=w, accessed October 30, 2014. The other three large blocks of wilderness are the Sierra Nevada in California (3,700 square miles), Frank Church/River of No Return complex in Idaho (3,600 square miles) and the Bob Marshall complex in Montana (2,400 square miles). Of the sources I could find online, the Peak Bagger website is the most comprehensive and well documented, listing the various remote sites in wilderness complexes throughout the forty-eight contiguous states, with a map of each area. Note that the map depicts the Yellowstone recommended wilderness, which includes the South and Southeast Arms. Were Congress to adopt the Yellowstone wilderness recommendation, the arms would add about forty-five square miles to the Thorofare total.

7   Because most Americans live in the forty-eight states, this discussion excludes Alaska, which has much more remote places. For example, Alaska's most remote point in wilderness is in the Mollie Beattie Wilderness of the Arctic National Wildlife Refuge in the eastern Brooks Range, with a distance to the nearest road of 42.75 miles.

However, as noted on the Peak Bagger website ("Most Remote Spots in USA Wilderness Complexes," http://www.peakbagger.com/PBGeog/..%5Creport%5CReport.aspx?r=w, accessed October 30, 2014), "Ironically, however, rules for wilderness in Alaska are different, and airplane landings are permitted in most areas. So in some ways you are more remote in the Thorfare [*sic*] area of Wyoming."

8   The majority of this discussion is drawn from the Peak Bagger website, "Most Remote Spots in USA Wilderness Complexes," http://www.peakbagger.com/PBGeog/..%5Creport%5CReport.aspx?r=w, accessed October 30, 2014, which is the source of the shorter distance. The longer distance is from Matt Jenkins, "Destination Nowhere," http://www.backpacker.com/trips/wyoming/yellowstone-national-park/destination-nowhere/7/#bp=0/img1, accessed October 30, 2014 (see also Bonnie Tsui, "A Scientific Search for the Most Remote Places in the United States," http://www.citylab.com/tech/2013/05/scientific-search-most-remote-places-united-states/5591/, accessed November 5, 2014; and Jeff Henry, "Thorofare Country: At the Headwaters of the Yellowstone," *Big Sky Journal*, Summer 1999, 86–90). The closest road to the Thorofare is the South Fork Road southwest of Cody, Wyoming. Note that the most remote point shown on the map is that which results from mapping the South and Southeast Arms as wilderness (i.e., if motorboats were banned from them). Given their presence, the most remote point is currently a few miles southeast, on the west end of the Thorofare Plateau. The most remote points in the Frank Church/River of No Return and Bob Marshall complexes are close competitors to the Thorofare, at 17.2 and 15.6 miles, respectively, but due to the linear shape of the Sierra Nevada wilderness complex, its most remote point is only 12.5 miles from a road. Note that the Peak Bagger website excludes non-wilderness remote areas, but there are few such areas more than ten miles from a road in the forty-eight contiguous states. Also, these are straight-line distances ("as the crow flies"), not distances by trail, which are considerably longer.

9   Per her request, this is a fictitious name to protect her identity.

10 Doug McWhirter "Elk migrations of the Thorofare," Thorofare Lecture Series, July 20, 2005, Coe Auditorium, Cody, Wyoming, DVD recording, YNPL.

11 Most of this paragraph is drawn from NPS Natural Resource Program Center, *Air Quality in National Parks: 2009 Annual Performance & Progress Report* (Denver: NPS, 2010), available at http://www.nature.nps.gov/air/Pubs/pdf/gpra/AQ_Trends_In_Parks_2009_Final_Web.pdf, and from NPS, "Air Pollution Impacts," http://www.nature.nps.gov/air/permits/aris/yell/impacts.cfm?tab=0#TabbedPanels1, both accessed November 3, 2014. Personal experience working in Sequoia and Yosemite National Parks also informed this discussion.

12 This description is drawn from Nabokov and Loendorf, *Restoring a Presence*, 2004 (mostly chapter 3), adapting as needed to reflect the food resources I know to occur in the Thorofare. See notes 7 and 8 from the preface for an overview of the debate about the extent of Native American influence on the pre-Columbian landscape.

13 NPS, "Lake Area Geologic Highlights," http://www.nps.gov/yell/naturescience/geolake.htm, accessed November 5, 2014.

14 As opposed to voluntary risks that one assumes by pursuing high-risk activities, such as any of the extreme sports that use the natural world as their venue (BASE jumping, downhill biking, and free climbing being typical examples).

Notes to Day 3: Keepers of the Thorofare

Curtis K. Skinner, "Thoroughfare: Yellowstone National Park's Wilderness Ranger Station," n.d. (but probably in the 1950s), unpublished manuscript, vertical files, YNPL.

1 *Report of the Superintendent*, 1904 (map), YNPL; Item 99B, file "Items Reported," documents "Schedule for Rationing Snowshoe Cabins, 1903," and "Articles Needed at S.S. Cabins for Fall of 1915," Item 99B, loose maps dated 1912–13 and 1914; Item 99B, file "Chart list of Snowshoe Cabin Supplies 1910–17," documents "Record of Snowshoe Cabins Winter 1912–13" and "Cabin Supplies Fall 1914." Quote from Horace Albright, *Report of Superintendent, 1920*, 53–54. Reconditioning from C. A. Lord, "Final Report: Reconstruction and Equipment, Thorofare Ranger Station," [1937], file "Thorofare—Patrol Cabin/barn," YCR Register files, NPS, Mammoth Hot Springs, Wyoming.

2 Curtis K. Skinner, "Thoroughfare: Yellowstone National Park's Wilderness Ranger Station," n.d., unpublished manuscript, vertical files, YNPL.

3   Curtis K. Skinner, "Winter Wallowing in Yellowstone Park's Cold Loose Snow Prior to the 1950's," n.d., unpublished manuscript, vertical files, YNPL.

4   Robert Miller to Major Pitcher, January 13, 1906, document 7633, Item 28.

5   *Pocatello Tribune,* May 11, 1907, as quoted in USFS, [untitled], http://www.fs.usda.gov/Internet/FSE_DOCUMENTS/stelprdb5189934.pdf, accessed July 11, 2015. The USFS document states the cabin was built in the early 1900s.

6   Bert McLaren, October 4–8, 1958, Thorofare Ranger Station logbooks.

7   Dave Phillips, September 5, 1975, Thorofare Ranger Station logbooks.

8   Bob Marshall, August 1, 1939, Thorofare Ranger Station logbooks. On Marshall, see Wikipedia, http://en.wikipedia.org/wiki/Bob_Marshall_%28wilderness_activist%29, accessed November 28, 2014. On the wilderness areas, see Arthur Carhart National Wilderness Training Center, Aldo Leopold Wilderness Research Institute, and the College of Forestry and Conservation's Wilderness Institute at the University of Montana, "List Wilderness Areas by Name," http://www.wilderness.net/NWPS/AtoZ, accessed November 28, 2014.

9   Curtis K. Skinner, "Thoroughfare: Yellowstone National Park's Wilderness Ranger Station," n.d., unpublished manuscript, vertical files, YNPL. Another account (Eugene Young to Mother, October 23, 1938, T. Eugene Young Papers, msc 129, box 1) dubbed him the "Phantom." Because these two accounts are very similar but off by a year, they probably refer to the same character and events, with 1938 being the likely year.

10 [Lee Shrum], September 11, 1940, Thorofare Ranger Station logbooks.

11 Curtis K. Skinner, "Thoroughfare: Yellowstone National Park's Wilderness Ranger Station," n.d., unpublished manuscript, vertical files, YNPL.

12 Murie also completed a more abbreviated study of moose in the Thorofare that same year, describing their movements and estimating the population in the Yellowstone River Valley at about two hundred (Olaus Murie, "Report on Game Animals in Upper Yellowstone-Thorofare Region," 1929, YNPL). Murie published the

results of his elk study in *The Elk of North America* (Harrisburg, PA: Wildlife Management Institute, 1951).

13 Margaret and Olaus Murie, *Wapiti Wilderness* (Boulder: Colorado Associated University Press, 1985). The passages are all from chapter 5 (specifically pages 52, 57, and 62), which Mardy wrote.

14 Wikipedia, "Margaret Murie," https://en.wikipedia.org/wiki/Margaret_Murie, and Arthur Carhart National Wilderness Training Center, Aldo Leopold Wilderness Research Institute, and the College of Forestry and Conservation's Wilderness Institute at the University of Montana, "Wilderness Statistics Reports," http://www.wilderness.net/NWPS/chartResults?chartType=legislatedAcreage, both accessed July 14, 2015.

15 Terry Small, July 13, 1974, Thorofare Ranger Station logbooks.

16 Curtis K. Skinner, "Thoroughfare: Yellowstone National Park's Wilderness Ranger Station," n.d., unpublished manuscript, vertical files, YNPL.

17 Vincent H. Hunter, "The Winter Job of a Yellowstone Park Forest Ranger," *Union Pacific Magazine* (February 1931): 13+.

18 John Jay, interview by Herb Evison, September 20, 1962, Estes Park, Colorado. In John Jay and Curtis K. Skinner, "Transcripts of Interviews with Jay and Skinner," Manuscript Collection, Rare Book Room, YNPL.

19 Ibid.

20 Ibid.

21 Curtis K. Skinner, "Winter Wallowing in Yellowstone Park's Cold Loose Snow Prior to the 1950's," n.d., unpublished manuscript, vertical files, YNPL.

22 Vincent H. Hunter, "The Winter Job of a Yellowstone Park Forest Ranger," *Union Pacific Magazine* (February 1931): 13+.

23 Harry V. Reynolds Jr., "Thorofare Ski Patrol, February 27–March 11, 1956," file "Thorofare Patrol Cabin, YELL #HS-0291, LCS #51027," YCR National Register files, NPS, Mammoth Hot Springs, Wyoming.

24 Ibid.

25 Reynolds, March 4 and 6, 1956, Thorofare Ranger Station logbooks.

26 Curtis K. Skinner, interview by Herb Evison, September 16, 1972, Moose, Wyoming. In John Jay and Curtis K. Skinner, "Transcripts of Interviews with Jay and Skinner," Manuscript Collection, Rare Book Room, YNPL.

27 Bob Murphy, August 25, 1996 (but recorded on page 62 of the 1938–1956 logbook), Thorofare Ranger Station logbooks. Murphy was stationed in the Thorofare from 1944 to 1946.

Notes to Day 4: Beauty and the Beet

David E. Folsom, *The Folsom-Cook Exploration of the Upper Yellowstone in the Year 1869* (St. Paul, MN: H. L. Collins Co., 1894).

1 The dam story is adapted from my article "Beauty and the Beet: The Dam Battles of Yellowstone," *Montana the Magazine of Western History* 53 (Spring 2003): 14–27. Reprinted here with permission.

2 Gifford Pinchot, *Breaking New Ground* (New York: Harcourt Brace Jovanovich, 1947), 325–326 (first quote); Gifford Pinchot, *The Fight for Conservation* (New York: Doubleday, Page & Company, 1910), 42; and "The Beauty of Use," *Electrical World*, December 18, 1920 (second quote).

3 John Muir, "The Wild Parks and Forest Reservations of the West," *Atlantic Monthly* 81 (January 1898): 483.

4 This phrase was previously used as a subtitle in "The Yellowstone Grab: Beauty and the Beet," *The Outlook* 144 (November 3, 1926).

5 Michael Cohen credits Hetch Hetchy with the precedent that national parks were not inviolable in *The History of the Sierra Club, 1892–1970* (San Francisco: Sierra Club, 1988), 29. There are many accounts of the Hetch Hetchy crisis: Robert Righter, *The Battle over Hetch Hetchy: America's Most Controversial Dam and the Birth of Modern Environmentalism* (New York: Oxford University Press, 2005); Roderick Nash, *Wilderness and the American Mind,* 4th ed. (New Haven, CT: Yale University Press, 2001), ch. 10; Elmo Richardson, "The Struggle for the Valley: California's Hetch Hetchy Controversy, 1905–1913," *California Historical Society Quarterly* 38 (September 1959): 249–258; and Holway Jones, *John Muir and the Sierra Club: The Battle for Yosemite* (San Francisco: Sierra Club, 1965), 82–169.

6 Mark Fiege, *Irrigated Eden: The Making of an Agricultural Landscape in the American West* (Seattle: University of Washington Press, 1999), 91. Reservoirs such as Jackson Lake Reservoir in Wyoming (upstream on the Snake River) were built during this period.

7 "George Sees City of 50,000 Here If Dam Is Completed," *LVE*, March 19, 1920; and Yellowstone Irrigation Association, *The Lake*

Yellowstone Project: What Is It? Why Is It?, copy in Irrigation and Dam Proposals, 1920–1921 Scrapbooks.

8   "Montana Men to Fight for Water," *LVE*, December 7, 1919; *A Bill for the Erection and Maintenance of a Dam across the Yellowstone River, in the State of Montana*, 66th Congress, 3rd session, S.R. 459; and [Stephen Mather], *Annual Report of Director of National Park Service, 1920* (Washington, DC: US Government Printing Office, 1920), 22–30.

9   United States Geological Survey, *Second Annual Report of the Reclamation Service* (Washington, DC: US Government Printing Office, 1904), plate 34; M. Hillman to Colonel Lloyd Brett, April 16, 1916; D. G. Martin to Chester A. Lindsley, July 30, 1917; A. E. Berlin to United States General Land Office, November 7, 1915; Colonel of Cavalry to Secretary of the Interior, December 1, 1915; M. Hillman to Colonel Lloyd Brett, April 6, 1916; and D. G. Martin to Chester A. Lindsley, July 30, 1917, all in file "480—Waters and Sanitation," box D-46. See also Fiege, *Irrigated Eden*, 97–112; Horace M. Albright, as told to Robert Cahn, *The Birth of the National Park Service: The Founding Years, 1913–33* (Salt Lake City: Howe Brothers, 1985), 100; and Richard A. Bartlett, *Yellowstone: A Wilderness Besieged* (Tucson: University of Arizona Press, 1985), 349.

10   Addison T. Smith, "Yellowstone Park and the Nation," *The Outlook* 145 (January 19, 1927): 78.

11   Hugh T. Lovin, "Fighting over the Cascade Corner of Yellowstone National Park, 1919–1935," *Annals of Wyoming* 72 (Spring 2000): 14–29; [Stephen Mather], *Annual Report of Director of National Park Service, 1920*, 28–29; John Ise, *Our National Park Policy* (New York: Arno Press, 1979), 310–311; and *A Bill Authorizing the Granting of Certain Irrigation Easements in the Yellowstone National Park, and for Other Purposes*, 66th Congress, 2nd session, S.R. 3895 and H.R. 12466.

12   16 U.S.C. 791-828c; Chapter 285, June 10, 1920; 41 Stat. 1063. The Federal Water Power Commission is today's Federal Energy Regulatory Commission.

13   Bartlett, *Yellowstone*, 349–352.

14   Stephen Mather to Mr. Secretary, January 31, 1920, Irrigation Projects No. 1, July 1919–May 31, 1920 (Fall River Basin). Mather also argued against the dams in the annual report he filed almost simultaneously as NPS director.

15 J. J. Cotter to Horace M. Albright, July 31, 1919, telegram; Paul S. A. Bickel to Franklin K. Lane, n.d.; Arno Cammerer to Horace Albright, July 29, 1919, telegram; and Horace Albright to Director, July 30, 1919 (source of quote), all in Irrigation Projects No. 1, July 1919–May 31, 1920 (Fall River Basin); Bartlett, *Yellowstone,* 347–352; and Albright, *The Birth of the NPS,* 101–102.

16 The organization was known as the National Parks and Conservation Association after 1970 and as the National Parks Conservation Association since 2000.

17 In a special edition of the organization's journal, Yard editorialized against the dams and urged association members and the public "to the defense": Robert Sterling Yard, "Hands Off the National Parks," *The Nation's Parks* 1 (Summer 1920): 11, copy in Irrigation Scrapbooks, 1921–28; and Robert Sterling Yard, "The Water Power Bill and the National Parks," *NPAB* 10 (June 25, 1920): 1–2.

18 Robert Sterling Yard to Editor, *Philadelphia Public Ledger,* May 23, 1922, and Yard, "Snatching Our Public Parks from Private Spoilers," *Philadelphia Public Ledger,* July 23, 1922 (source of quote).

19 Yard gave special thanks to the women's organizations in "National Protest against the Walsh Bill," *NPAB* 17 (March 20, 1921): 1–2; and "Progress of the War on the National Parks," *NPAB* 13 (November 20, 1920): 1–3.

20 "Report on the National Parks Situation," *Bird Lore* 23 (March-April 1921): 111–112; William E. Colby and William Frederic Bade, "Fellow Member of the Sierra Club," *Sierra* (November 10, 1920), copy in Irrigation and Dam Proposals, 1920–1921 Scrapbooks; "Locke Nails Lies about Dam," *LVE,* December 12, 1920; and Yard, "National Protest against the Walsh Bill," 1–2. John C. Miles asserted Yard was the "ringleader" in *Guardians of the Parks* (Washington: Taylor & Francis, 1995), 34.

21 Yellowstone National Park Organic Act, "An Act to Set Apart a Certain Tract of Land Lying Near the Headwaters of the Yellowstone River as a Public Park," 17 Stat. 32, approved March 1, 1872.

22 [Mather], *Annual Report of Director of National Park Service, 1920,* 26. See also [Yard], "Now to Defeat the Dangerous Walsh Bill," *NPAB* 19 (May 23, 1921): 1; J. Horace McFarland, "Exploiting the Yellowstone: Is It Necessary—or Merely Cheaper?" *The Outlook* 126 (October 6, 1920): 255–257; Stephen Mather, "Do You Want to Lose Your Parks?" *The Independent* 104 (November 13, 1920);

Emerson Hough, "Pawning the Heirlooms," *Saturday Evening Post* 193 (September 25, 1920) 13:12–13, 90, 95, 96, 98, 102; "The Rape of the Yellowstone," *Field and Stream,* June 1920; and George Shiras III, "The Proposed Yellowstone Dam," *Forest and Stream,* February 1921.

23 William C. Gregg, "The Cascade Corner of Yellowstone Park," *The Outlook* 129 (November 23, 1921): 469–476, with a very similar second quote in Gregg, "Cornering Cascades," *Saturday Evening Post* 193 (November 20, 1920): 11, 78, 83. Gregg's findings were widely reported; see, for example, Mather's *Annual Report of Director of National Park Service, 1921* (Washington, DC: US Government Printing Office, 1921), 18–19.

24 [Mather], *Annual Report of Director of National Park Service, 1920,* 23; McFarland, "Exploiting the Yellowstone," 255 (source of quote); J. Horace McFarland, "The Yellowstone Park Question," *The Outlook* 125 (July 28, 1920): 578; and [Mather], *Annual Report of Director of National Park Service, 1920,* 23.

25 Warren G. Swendsen, "'Preserving' the Heirloom," 6, and P. S. A. Bickel, "What the Fall River Bill Means," 8, both in *New West Magazine* 11 (November 1920); and Yellowstone Irrigation Association, *Lake Yellowstone Project,* 8.

26 Swendsen, "'Preserving' the Heirloom," 5–6; and Bickel, "What the Fall River Bill Means," 8.

27 J. Horace McFarland, "Primrose by the River's Brim," *The Independent* 102 (May 8, 1920): 211; [Robert Sterling Yard], "The Work Before Us," *NPAB* 11 (September 30, 1920): 6 (source of quote); and [Robert Sterling Yard], "Now to Defeat the Dangerous Walsh Bill," *NPAB* 19 (May 23, 1921): 1.

28 The parallel to Hetch Hetchy was noted in "Another Hetch Hetchy," *The Outlook* 125 (July 7, 1920): 448; and J. Horace McFarland, "The Yellowstone Park Question," *The Outlook* 125 (July 28, 1920): 578.

29 See, generally, Swendsen "'Preserving' the Heirloom"; and Yellowstone Irrigation Association, *Lake Yellowstone Project.*

30 Hough, "Pawning the Heirlooms," 98; and [Yard], "Now to Defeat the Dangerous Walsh Bill," 1–4.

31 [Warren G. Swendsen], "'Desecrating' Yellowstone Park," *New West Magazine,* 11 (November 1920): 7 (source of quote); and "Eastern Fiction," *LVE,* May 11, 1920. See also *Boise (Id.) Statesman,* April 26, 1920; and "Nature Fakers to the Rescue!" *LVE,* June 4, 1920.

32 T. J. Walsh, "Are Special Interests Trying to Exploit the Yellowstone Park?" *The Outlook* 126 (September 8, 1920): 68 (source of quote); and Frank A. Waugh, "The Market Price on Landscape," *The Outlook* 127 (March 16, 1921): 428–429.

33 Horace M. Albright, "Memorand[a] for the Files re Yellowstone Lake dam—Walsh Bill No. 4529," February 23, 24, 1921, in Irrigation Projects No. 3, January 3, 1921–April 30, 1921, box L-57; Frederick Law Olmsted, "Fundamental Objections to the Walsh Bill," *National Municipal Review* 10 (May 1921): 270–271; Robert Sterling Yard, "One Substantial Victory for National Parks," *NPAB* 16 (March 20, 1921) (Payne quote); Ise, *Our National Park Policy,* 313; Aubrey L. Haines, *The Yellowstone Story,* rev. ed., 2 vols. (Niwot, CO: Yellowstone Association for Natural Science, History, and Education, in cooperation with the University Press of Colorado, 1996), 2:343–44; and [Yard], "Now to Defeat the Dangerous Walsh Bill," 1–4.

34 Miles, *Guardians of the Parks,* 33; *An Act To Amend an Act Entitled An Act to Create a Federal Power Commission. . . ,* 66th Congress, 1st session, S.R. 369, March 3, 1921; and Yard, "One Substantial Victory for National Parks," 1. See also Robert Shankland, *Steve Mather of the National Parks* (New York: Alfred A. Knopf, 1970), 214.

35 As quoted in [Robert Sterling Yard], "Harding and Work to Protect National Parks," *NPAB* 34 (July 6, 1923): 1–2; and Haines, *Yellowstone Story,* 2:344. See Irrigation Scrapbooks, 1921–28, page 59, for copies of many of the Associated Press articles.

36 Yellowstone National Park Boundary Commission, *Message from the President Transmitting the Final Report of the Yellowstone National Park Boundary Commission. . . ,* 71st Congress, 3rd session, 1931, H. Doc. 710, p. 9; and Lovin, "Fighting over the Cascade Corner," 28.

37 Robert Sterling Yard, "New Tricks to Grab Yellowstone," *NPAB* 14 (June 1938): 11–12. The tunneling idea had been discussed in the first dam battle as a contingency plan for the Idaho irrigators if the Bechler dams failed; see H. C. McMillen, "Would Put Dams in Yellowstone Park," *New York Evening Post,* September 9, 1920; and "Montana Men to Fight for Water," *LVE,* December 7, 1919.

38 Edmund Rogers to NPS Director Arno Cammerer, October 5, 1937, file "Yellowstone National Park, September 15, 1937 thru December 31, 1939," box 13, Records of Arno B. Cammerer, 1922–40, RG 79, NACP.

39 Dan W. Greenburg, "Study of Proposed Damming of Yellowstone Lake," report submitted to Wyoming governor Leslie A. Miller, copy in file "660-05.4, Proposed Damming of Yellowstone Lake," box D-225; [Robert Sterling Yard], "Save the Yellowstone," *NPAB* 65 (June 1938): 9; [Robert Sterling Yard], "The Fight for Yellowstone," *NPAB* 66 (December 1938): 9; and Bartlett, *Yellowstone*, 358.

40 Gregg, "The Cascade Corner of Yellowstone Park," 469–476; Hough, "Pawning the Heirlooms," 12; and Yard, "Water Power Bill and the National Parks," 1–2.

41 See note 6 of the preface for a list of scholars who find nature to be sacred for conservationists.

42 There are eighteen terminal values (the goals that a person would like to achieve during his or her lifetime) and the same number of instrumental values (the means of achieving the terminal values). The terminal values are true friendship, mature love, self-respect, happiness, inner harmony, equality, freedom, pleasure, social recognition, wisdom, salvation, family security, national security, a sense of accomplishment, a world of beauty, a world at peace, a comfortable life, and an exciting life. The instrumental values are cheerfulness, ambition, love, cleanliness, self-control, capability, courage, politeness, honesty, imagination, independence, intellect, broad-mindedness, logic, obedience, helpfulness, responsibility, and forgiveness. See Wikipedia, "Rokeach Value Survey," https://en.wikipedia.org/wiki/Rokeach_Value_Survey, accessed September 2, 2015; and Milton Rokeach, *The Nature of Human Values* (New York: Free Press, 1973).

43 The causative influence of values and beliefs on our attitudes and actions is widely documented and accepted. I based this discussion primarily on Thomas Heberlein, *Navigating Environmental Attitudes* (New York: Oxford University Press, 2012).

44 Tom Barker to NPS, August 13, 1991, YCR; Stanley L. Ponce to Tom Barker, August 28, 1991, YCR; and [Robert Sterling Yard], "The Fight for Yellowstone," 25.

Notes to Day 5: To Drive or Not to Drive

Albright to the Director, October 16, 1920, file "Irrigation—Fall River Reservoir Site, May 22, 1920, to October 30, 1920, Part 3," box 218, General Records/Central Files, 1907–39, Record Group 79, NACP.

1   See, for example, Emily Underwood, "New Map Shows America's Quietest Places," http://news.sciencemag.org/environment/2015/02/new-map-shows-americas-quietest-places, accessed March 18, 2015; and Peter A. Coates, "The Strange Stillness of the Past: Toward an Environmental History of Sound and Noise," *Environmental History* 10 (2005): 636–665.

2   For the story of the road that was never built, I relied on two sources: Aubrey L. Haines, *The Yellowstone Story: A History of Our First National Park,* rev. ed. (Niwot, CO: Yellowstone Association for Natural Science, History, and Education, in cooperation with the University Press of Colorado, 1996) 2:319–336; and John J. Cameron, "The Proposed Upper Yellowstone-Thorofare Extension," unpublished manuscript, box L-10, loose within box. Haines's account is quite comprehensive, though Cameron has many additional details. Because Haines's account is so thorough, published, and widely available, there is no need to retell the complete road proposal/boundary adjustment story here. Therefore, this overview does not provide the same level of detail as the Yellowstone Lake zoning controversy later in this chapter.

3   Greeley, as quoted in Cameron, "The Proposed Upper Yellowstone-Thorofare Extension."

4   Robert W. Righter thoroughly describes the effort to create Grand Teton National Park in his two histories of the park: *Crucible for Conservation: The Struggle for Grand Teton National Park* (Jackson, WY: Grand Teton Natural History Association, 1982), and *Peaks, Politics and Passion: Grand Teton National Park Comes of Age* (Jackson, WY: Grand Teton Association, 2014).

5   David Louter, in *Windshield Wilderness: Cars, Roads, and Nature in Washington's National Parks* (Seattle: University of Washington Press, 2006), uses the historical geography of the three national parks in Washington to demonstrate the changing NPS understanding of the relationship of roads and cars to wilderness preservation in the parks.

6   One of the most common themes in NPS discussions and histories is the balance between preservation and visitor accommodation that the agency is directed to negotiate in its Organic Act. Some good discussions of this tension can be found in Lary M. Dilsaver, *Cumberland Island National Seashore: A History of Conservation*

Conflict (Charlottesville: University of Virginia Press, 2004); Richard West Sellars, *Preserving Nature in the National Parks: A History* (New Haven, CT: Yale University Press, 1997); Lary M. Dilsaver and William C. Tweed, *Challenge of the Big Trees: A Resource History of Sequoia and Kings Canyon National Parks* (Three Rivers, CA: Sequoia Natural History Association, 1990); Alfred Runte, *National Parks: The American Experience*, 4th ed. (New York: Taylor Trade Publishing, 2010); and Ronald A. Foresta, *America's National Parks and Their Keepers* (Washington, DC: Resources for the Future, 1984).

7 Yi-Fu Tuan, in *Space and Place: The Perspective of Experience* (Minneapolis: University of Minnesota Press, 1977), argues that machines confer a sense of freedom: "Being free has several levels of meaning. Fundamental is the ability to transcend the present condition, and this transcendence is most simply manifest as the elementary power to move. . . . Tools and machines enlarge man's sense of space and spaciousness" (52–53).

8 Several ex-NPS directors call for reduced political influence on the NPS, including William C. Everhart, *The National Park Service* (Boulder, CO: Westview Press, 1983); George B. Hartzog Jr., *Battling for the National Parks* (Mount Kisco, NY: Moyer Bell, 1988); and James M. Ridenour, *The National Parks Compromised: Pork Barrel Politics and America's Treasures* (Merrillville, IN: ICS Books, 1994). Political scientist William R. Lowry has published three books demonstrating that the NPS is subject to a high amount of political influence: *The Capacity for Wonder: Preserving National Parks* (Washington, DC: Brookings Institution Press, 1994); *Preserving Public Lands for the Future: The Politics of Intergenerational Goods* (Washington, DC: Georgetown University Press, 1998); and *Repairing Paradise: The Restoration of Nature in America's National Parks* (Washington, DC: Brookings Institution Press, 2009). My other two books make the same point: *Yellowstone and the Snowmobile: Locking Horns over National Park Use* (Lawrence: University Press of Kansas, 2009); and *Protecting Yellowstone: Science and the Politics of National Park Management* (Albuquerque: University of New Mexico Press, 2013).

9 Several scholars examine interest group influence—primarily that of conservationists—including Fox, *The American Conservation Movement*; Sellars, *Preserving Nature in the National Parks*; James

A. Pritchard, *Preserving Yellowstone's Natural Conditions: Science and the Perception of Nature* (Lincoln: University of Nebraska Press, 1999); and Alston Chase, *Playing God in Yellowstone: The Destruction of America's First National Park* (San Diego: Harcourt Brace Jovanovich, 1986). See Don Hummel, *Stealing the National Parks: The Destruction of Concessions and Park Access* (Bellevue, WA: Free Enterprise Press, 1987) for an argument in favor of continued motorized access.

10 The story is based on my article "A Water Wilderness: Battles over Values and Motorboats on Yellowstone Lake," *Historical Geography* 35 (2007): 185–213. Reprinted with permission.

11 Lemuel A. Garrison, *The Making of a Ranger: Forty Years with the National Parks* (Salt Lake City, UT: Howe Brothers, 1983).

12 Lon Garrison, "A Conversation with an Osprey," Rare Separates Files, Rare Book Room, YNPL; Senate Committee on Appropriations, *Proposed Boating Regulations for Yellowstone Lake, Hearings before a Subcommittee of the Committee on Appropriations,* 86th Congress, 2nd session 1960: 148; Richard A. Crysdale, "An Analysis of Lake Zoning Factors, Objectives and Problems on Yellowstone Lake" (master's thesis, Utah State University, 1965): 115–116; Advisory Committee on Boating (Luis A. Gastellum, Otto M. Brown, David del Condon, Frank E. Mattson, and Ernest K. Field) to Superintendent, November 21, 1958, file "[untitled]," box W-156; Warren F. Hamilton to Regional Director, October 5, 1956, and E. T. Scoyen to Senator Mike Mansfield, August 7, 1957, file "W4624 #1 Sept. 1953–June 1959 2 of 2," box W-254; and "Yellowstone Lake Zoning Proposal," unpublished timeline of key events, file "W4624—Boating (Lake Zoning) January-February 1960," box W-158.

13 The zoning idea had actually originated with a committee suggested by NPS director Conrad Wirth on a visit to Yellowstone a few weeks earlier (Luis Gastellum, "Chronology of Events Leading to the Zoning of Yellowstone Lake," unpublished report, file "Chronology of Events Leading to Hearing and Miscellaneous Correspondence," and Garrison to Regional Director, December 12, 1958, file "[untitled]," both in box W-156).

14 Crysdale, "An Analysis of Lake Zoning Factors," 54–55, 115–120.

15 Lemuel Garrison, "A Conversation with an Osprey" (source of first

quote), and another untitled memoir of the controversy written in August 1974, file "Lon Garrison—Miscell. Items," box A-1 (source of last quote).

16 Advisory Committee on Boating to Superintendent, November 21, 1958, and Garrison to Regional Director, December 12, 1958, both in file "[untitled]," box W-156; M. H. Harvey to the Director, January 16, 1959, Garrison to Regional Director, March 17, 1959, Howard W. Baker to Superintendent, June 19, 1959, Conrad Wirth to Senator James E. Murray, June 30, 1959, and Garrison to Regional Director, June 13, 1959, all in file "W4624 Book #1, Sept. 1953–June 1959, 1 of 2," box W-254.

17 Joseph R. Murphy, "The Molly Island Nesting Colonies of Yellowstone Lake," 1960, vertical files, YNPL, V, 5–9; Paul D. Sebesta, "Wildlife Census and Effects of Power Boating in the Arms of Yellowstone Lake," unpublished report, and Otto M. Brown to Superintendent, September 11, 1959, both in file "W4624 Book #3, Jan–Mar. 1960, 1 of 3," box W-254 (Sebesta used the same data in his master's thesis, "The Effects of Human Disturbance on the Ecology of the Yellowstone Lake Shore Wilderness Areas," University of Nebraska, 1961). The canoe group also weathered a Richter-scale 7.5 earthquake, the largest ever recorded in the northern Rockies, which struck at night on August 17 (John Montagne, personal interview by author, Bozeman, Montana, June 18, 2003).

18 Garrison to Regional Director, December 12, 1958, file "[Untitled]," box W-156; Superintendent to Gastellum, Sylvester, McIntyre, and Beal (first names not provided on original), January 16, 1960, file "W4624-Boating (Lake Zoning) January–February 1960," box W-158; John Q. Nichols to Sherman Jones, January 29, 1959, Thomas J. Hallin to Sherman D. Jones, January 12, 1959, and Sherman D. Jones, "A Report on the NPS Proposal for Zoning of Yellowstone Lake as Related to the Yellowstone Park Company Boat Division Operation and Private Boat Owners," unpublished report, in a file of the same name, all three in box YPC-79; and Milton Rees, testimony at Senate Committee, *Proposed Boating Regulations*, 86.

19 Curtis E. Lees to Lon Garrison, November 29, 1958, and C. L. Conaway to Harrell F. Mosbaugh, June 3, 1959, both in file "W4624 Book #1, Sept. 1953–June 1959, 1 of 2," box W-254.

20 The Billings Boat Club, "A Memorandum in Opposition . . . ," file

"Chronology of Events Leading to Hearing and Miscellaneous Correspondence," box W-156. The "benefit and enjoyment" and "pleasuring ground" quotes are from the Yellowstone National Park Organic Act, "An Act to Set Apart a Certain Tract of Land Lying Near the Headwaters of the Yellowstone River as a Public Park," 17 Stat. 32, approved March 1, 1872.

21 Conaway to Mosbaugh, June 3, 1959, Mike Mansfield to Conrad Wirth, April 29, 1959, and E. T. Scoyen to Mike Mansfield, May 7, 1959, all in file "W4624 Book #1, Sept. 1953–June 1959, 1 of 2," box W-254; Garrison to Regional Director, August 13, 1959, file "W4624 #2, July 1959–Jan. 1960, 2 of 2," box W-254; and The Billings Boat Club, "A Memorandum in Opposition."

22 Garrison to Regional Director, September 17, 1959, Baker to Superintendent, October 13, 1959, Garrison to Regional Director, November 21, 1959, and Baker to the Director, December 18, 1959, all in file "W4624 Book #2, July 1959–Jan. 1960, 1 of 2," box W-254; and E. T. Scoyen to Regional Director, January 16 or 18, 1960 (date is indistinguishable on original), file "W4624 #3 Jan.–Mar. 1960, 2 of 3," both in box W-254.

23 Many authors discuss Mission 66, and all argue that it was the consuming focus of the NPS and Director Wirth in the late 1950s. See Ethan Carr, *Mission 66: Modernism and the National Park Dilemma* (Amherst: University of Massachusetts Press, 2007); Louter, *Windshield Wilderness*, 2006; Sellars, *Preserving Nature in the National Parks*, 1997, 180–212; Runte, *National Parks*, 1997, 173; Foresta, *America's National Parks and Their Keepers*, 1984, 52–57; and Garrison, *The Making of a Ranger*, 1983, 254–265.

24 Conservationist correspondence: Garrison to E. Sue Gloriod, June 12, 1959, file "W4624 Book #1, Sept. 1953–June 1959, 1 of 2," box W-254; Hillory A. Tolson to Joseph W. Penfold, September 4, 1959, file "Boat Regulations on Yellowstone Lake," box 7:4, IWL; and Hillory A. Tolson to John H. Baker, September 4, 1959 and Anthony Wayne Smith to Wirth, November 20, 1959, both in file W4624 Book #2, July 1959–Jan. 1960, 1 of 2," box W-254. Political correspondence: Duane D. Jacobs, "Brief Summary of [Washington Office] Replies to Congressmen and Senators Concerning Proposed Yellowstone Lake Zoning," James E. Murray to Wirth, October 16, 1959, Curtis E. Lees to Mike Mansfield, September 20, 1959, Mike

Mansfield to Wirth, September 23, 1959, and Director [Wirth] to Mike Mansfield, [n.d.], all in file "W4624 Book #2, July 1959–Jan. 1960, 1 of 2," box W-254. Constituent letters to Gale McGee in 1959 in Folder 14, box 561, AHC.

25 Information on McGee from T. A. Larson, Preface to "The Gale W. McGee Papers: A Guide," finding aid to the Gale W. McGee collection, available online at http://ahc.uwyo.edu/mcgee/mcgee. pdf, accessed December 10, 2003. Information on the hearing from Carl Hayden to Fred A. Seaton, January 11, 1960, and M. H. Harvey to Superintendent, January 22, 1960, both in file "W4624 #3 Jan.– Mar. 1960, 2 of 3," box W-254; and Gale McGee to James E. Murray, Frank Church, Mike Mansfield, and Frank E. Moss, January 15, 1960, Folder "Yellowstone Lake Correspondence," box 836, AHC.

26 John C. Borzea, testimony at Senate Committee, *Proposed Boating Regulations*, 42.

27 Senate Committee, *Proposed Boating Regulations*.

28 Phil Empey to Gale McGee, February 9, 1960 (source of quote), Folder 3, box 570, AHC.

29 Senate Committee, *Proposed Boating Regulations*; and Olaus J. Murie, "Wilderness on Yellowstone Lake," *National Parks Magazine* (December 1959), 2, which was commonly quoted in 1960, such as in "FLASH: Yellowstone Boating Hearing, February 3, Cody, Wyoming," January 19, 1960, file "W4624—Boating (Lake Zoning), January-February 1960," box W-158.

30 Senate Committee, *Proposed Boating Regulations*; Horace M. Albright to McGee, January 22, 1960, file "W4624—Boating (Lake Zoning), January-February 1960," box W-158; and see the letters in Folder 4, box 570, AHC for examples of letters to McGee in support of zoning from his constituents.

31 J. D. Love to Olaus Murie, January 27, 1960, file "W4624—Boating (Lake Zoning), January-February 1960," box W-158.

32 Senate Committee, *Proposed Boating Regulations*, 33–36; and Howard W. Baker to the Director, February 4, 1960, Luis A. Gastellum to Superintendent, February 6, 1960, and Garrison to Regional Director, February 12, 1960, all in file "W4624 #3 Jan.– Mar. 1960, 2 of 3," box W-254.

33 Garrison to Regional Director, February 10, 1960, and February 12, 1960, E. T. Scoyen to Regional Director, February 29, 1960,

and Howard W. Baker to the Director, February 16, 1960, all in file "W4624 #3, Jan.–Mar. 1960, 2 of 3," box W-254; Baker to the Director, February 16, 1960, file "[Untitled]", box W-156; Wirth to Secretary of the Interior, April 6, 1960, file "Office of the Secretary—Parks & Sites—Yellowstone National Park, Part 3—January 6, 1960 to September 3, 1960," box 337, Central Classified Files, 1959–1963, Record Group 48, NACP; and 25 *Federal Register* 101: 4554–4555, May 24, 1960.

34 L. F. Cook to The Director, March 3, 1960, file "W4624 Book #4, Mar.–July 1960, 2 of 2," box W-255; Keith Thomson to Roger C. Ernst, February 2, 1960, file "Office of the Secretary—Parks & Sites—Yellowstone National Park, Part 3—Jan. 6, 1960, to Sept. 3, 1960," box 337, Central Classified Files, 1959–1963, Record Group 48, NACP; Henry Dworshak to Roger Ernst, March 3, 1960, and Roger Ernst to Henry Dworshak, March 29, 1960, both in file "W4624—Boating (Lake Zoning), March–June 1960," box W-157; and 25 *Federal Register* 101:4554–4555, May 24, 1960.

35 Robert N. McIntyre to Acting Superintendent, February 18, 1960, and Garrison to Regional Director, February 20, 1960, both in file "[Untitled]," box W-156; Garrison to Regional Director, February 19, 1960, file "W4624 Book #3, Jan.–Mar. 1960, 1 of 3," box W-254; William R. Lorenzen to Garrison, March 7, 1960, file "W4624 Book #4, Mar.–July 1960, 2 of 2," box W-255; Robert N. McIntyre, "Proposal for Zoning Yellowstone Lake to Motor Boat Use with the Protection of Primary Wilderness Values," address given to Bonneville County Sportsmens' Association, Idaho Falls, Idaho, March 12, 1960, YNPL; and "Statement of Lemuel A. Garrison for Interior Department Hearing on Zoning of Yellowstone Lakes, Salt Lake City, Utah—July 17, 1961," file "Lake Zoning—Salt Lake Hearing W4624," box W-156.

36 Garrison to Charles L. Barron, October 10, 1960, file "W4624—Boating (Lake Station), September–December 1960"; "Proposed Public Use Plan for Yellowstone Lake," file "W4624—Lake Zoning, 1960"; and "Statement of Lemuel A. Garrison for Interior Department Hearing on Zoning of Yellowstone Lakes, Salt Lake City, Utah—July 17, 1961," file "Lake Zoning—Salt Lake Hearing W4624," all in box W-156.

37 Information on Outboard Boating Club (OBC) comes from Ron

Stone to McGee, February 17, 1960, in Folder 5, box 570, AHC; OBC, "Special Legislative Report—Glacier and Yellowstone National Parks," file "W4624 Book #4, Mar.–July 1960, 2 of 2," box W-255; OBC, "Proposed Zoning of Yellowstone Lake" (source of quote), file "W4624—Boating (Lake Zoning) August 1960," box W-157; USDI-NPS, "Hearings on Proposed Motorboat Restrictions on Yellowstone Lake," 1960, 376, unpublished transcripts, file "W4624—Lake Zoning Hearings," box D-154; "Yellowstone Boating," *National Parks Magazine* (April 1960): 15; Wirth to Howard Zahniser, April 1, 1960, file "Correspondence: USDI-NPS, 1960–1966," box 4:300, TWS; and David M. Abbott to McGee, February 2, 1960, file "W4624 Book #3, Jan.–Mar., 1960, 1 of 3," box W-254.

38 Murie's involvement in Murie to Howard Baker, May 6, 1960, file "Members: Olaus J. Murie, 1960," box 3:201, TWS; Olaus J. Murie, "Canoe Wilderness in Yellowstone," *The Living Wilderness* (Spring 1960): 15–20; and Thomas B. Hyde to Superintendent, June 1, 1960, file "W4624—Boating (Lake Zoning), March–June 1960," box W-157. MWA's involvement in Kenneth K. Baldwin, "New Yellowstone Lake Zoning Proposal Hearing," August 10, 1960, file "W4624—Boating (Lake Zoning), August, 1960," box W-157. Izaak Walton League's involvement in Garrison to Charlie Piersall, February 12, 1960, file "W4624 #3, Jan.–Mar. 1960, 2 of 3," box W-254.

39 Robert N. McIntyre to F. M. Paulson, March 15, 1960, and E. T. Scoyen to David R. Brower, March 30, 1960, both in file "W4624—Boating (Lake Zoning), March–June 1960," box W-157; Brower to Scoyen, March 28, 1960, and Wirth to Brower, June 7, 1960, both in file "W4624 Book #4, March–July 1960, 1 of 2," box W-255; Scoyen to Brower, March 16, 1960, file "W4624 Book, #4, Mar.–July 1960, 2 of 2," box W-255; Garrison to Charlie Piersall, February 12, 1960, and Director [Wirth] to D. K. Bradley, date illegible, both in file "W4624 #3 Jan.–Mar. 1960, 2 of 3," box W-254; and Thomas B. Hyde to Burton W. Marston, July 13, 1960 (source of quote) and Garrison to Devereux Butcher, July 19, 1960, both in file "W4624—Boating (Zoning), July 1960," box W-157.

40 Bruce M. Kilgore to Garrison, August 12, 1960, file "W4624—Boating (Lake Zoning), August 1960, box W-157; Sierra Club,

"Motorboats Have Been Given a Place, BUT Canoes, Wildlife and Wilderness Deserve Room on Yellowstone Lake, Too!" *Outdoor Newsletter*, August 10, 1960, in file "Chronology of Events Leading to Hearing and Miscellaneous Correspondence," box W-156. See the numerous articles and updates on the topic in 1960 issues of *National Parks Magazine, The Living Wilderness, Outdoor America*, and *The Sierra Club Bulletin*. Most conservation groups, and the General Federation of Women's Clubs, sent letters supporting zoning to the August hearings.

41 Olaus J. Murie, "Wilderness Conference on Yellowstone Lake," *The Living Wilderness* (Summer-Fall 1961): 14–16.

42 L. F. Cook to The Director, March 3, 1960, file "W4624—Boating (Lake Zoning), March–June 1960," box W-157, and Luis A. Gastellum to Superintendent, February 6, 1960, file "W4624 #3, Jan.–Mar. 1960, 2 of 3," box W-254. Garrison and Murie were certainly not the first conservationists to struggle with this difficulty; as Robert Righter records in *The Battle over Hetch Hetchy: America's Most Controversial Dam and the Birth of Modern Environmentalism* (New York: Oxford University Press, 2005), 206–208, John Muir and the defenders of the famous valley in Yosemite faced the same challenge several decades earlier, and also lost their battle.

43 Garrison to Regional Director, February 20, 1960, file "[Untitled]," box W-156; Garrison to Regional Director, June 17, 1960, file "W4624 Book #4, Mar.–July 1960, 1 of 2," box W-255 (source of quote); USDI-NPS, "Hearings on Proposed Motorboat Restrictions on Yellowstone Lake," 1960, unpublished transcripts, file "W4624—Lake Zoning Hearings," box D-154, and "Statement of Superintendent Garrison, Yellowstone National Park Departmental Hearings, Yellowstone Lake Zoning, August 23–26, 1960," file "W4624—Lake Zoning 1960," box W-156. By this time Garrison was informing new arriving staff members to focus on other reasons for zoning, not erosion (John Good, interview by author, Mammoth Hot Springs, March 21, 2003), as Garrison himself did at each hearing.

44 USDI-NPS, "Hearings on Proposed Motorboat Restrictions on Yellowstone Lake," 1960, with Gardner's quote on page 57.

45 USDI-NPS, "Hearings on Proposed Motorboat Restrictions on Yellowstone Lake," 1960, 191–350.

46 USDI-NPS, "Hearings on Proposed Motorboat Restrictions on Yellowstone Lake," 1960, 351–541; Garrison, "Superintendent's Annual Report for 1961," Section VIII (2), YNPL; L. F. Cook to Superintendent, September 15, 1960, file "W4624—Boating (Lake Station), Sept.–Dec. 1960," box W-156; Nelson Murdock, "Progress Report—Proposed Zoning of Yellowstone Lake," presentation to the Montana Outfitters and Guides Association, December 7–10, 1960, file "W4624 Book #5, July 1960–Jan. 1961, 2 of 2," box W-255; Nelson Murdock to Superintendent, September 30, 1960, file "W4624—Lake Zoning 1960," box W-156; and Garrison to Kenneth Black, August 30, 1960, file "W4624—Boating (Lake Zoning) August 1960," box W-157.

47 McGee to Fred A. Seaton, November 15, 1960, Press Release from the Office of Senator Gale W. McGee, November 15, 1960, and McGee to Fred A. Seaton, November 18, 1960, all in Folder 4, box 38, AHC; McGee to Associated Press and United Press International, telegram, November 17, 1960, in Folder 2, box 38, AHC; and McGee, "A Compromise Proposal Pertaining to the Status of the South and Southeast Arms of Yellowstone Lake in Yellowstone National Park," in Folder 6, box 593, AHC.

48 Margaret E. Murie to McGee, November 30, 1960, file "Members: Margaret E. Murie 1960–1964," box 3:200, TWS; F. Howard Brady to Fred A. Seaton, December 1, 1960, file "Boat Regulations on Yellowstone Lake," box 7:4, IWL; USDI, "Interior Department Regulates Motorboats in Yellowstone National Park," Press Release, December 29, 1960, and Garrison to Regional Director, December 8, 1960, both in file "W4624 Book #5, July 1960–Jan. 1961, 2 of 2"; and 25 *Federal Register*: 13970–13972, December 30, 1960.

49 Garrison to Ken Baldwin and other conservationists, all dated January 5 or 6, 1961 and in file "W4624—Boating (Lake Zoning), 1961," box W-158; NPS Press Release, February 8, 1961, file "W4624 #6, Jan.–July 1961, 2 of 2," box W-255; and "Statement of Lemuel A. Garrison for Interior Department Hearing on Zoning of Yellowstone Lakes, Salt Lake City, Utah—July 17, 1961," file "Lake Zoning—Salt Lake Hearing W4624," box W-156.

50 Rumor discussions found in Florence W. Baldwin to Lon [Garrison], March 23, 1961, file "L48—Wilderness Areas (Research Reserve) (Wilderness Assoc.) 1961 thru 1962," box L-52, and J. W. Penfold

to Stewart L. Udall,　May 15, 1961, file "W4624a Salt Lake City Hearings Lake Zoning," box W-157. McGee's efforts in his letters to John H. Larsen, January 6, 1961 (source of first two quotes), to Lee Underbrink, January 10, 1961, to P. M. Cooper, January 17, 1961, to Frank Hicks, January 16, 1961, and January 24, 1961 (source of third quote), to Stewart Udall, January 26, 1961, and to R. L. Bradford, February 22, 1961, all in Folder 2, box 38, AHC; and Stewart L. Udall to "Gale" (McGee), February 6, 1961, Folder 4, box 38, AHC.

51 McGee to Stewart L. Udall, March 9, 1961, in Folder 4, box 38, AHC; McGee to "Frank," April 19, 1961, and June 9, 1961 (source of first quote), and McGee to "Bert" Reinow, June 21, 1961 (source of second quote), Folder 2, box 38, AHC; and USDI, Press Release, "Interior Department Reaffirms Controls on Yellowstone Boating," June 9, 1961, file "W4624 Book #6, Jan.–July 1961, 1 of 2," box W-255.

52 McGee, "A Compromise Proposal" (source of quote), and McGee to Seaton, November 15, 1960, both in Folder 4, box 38, AHC; Crysdale, "An Analysis of Lake Zoning Factors ," 62–63; McGee to Robert Rose, August 18, 1960, in Folder 7, box 570, AHC; McGee to Associated Press and UPI, telegram, November 17, 1960, Folder 2, box 38, AHC; and "Statement of Lemuel A. Garrison for Interior Department Hearing on Zoning of Yellowstone Lakes, Salt Lake City, Utah—July 17, 1961," file "Lake Zoning—Salt Lake Hearing W4624," box W-156. While shipping food by plane is commonly done today, it was uncommon at the time, especially from remote Cody.

53 Howard Zahniser to Stewart L. Udall, June 16, 1961, and John A. Carver Jr. to Howard Zahniser, June 22, 1961, both in file "States/Wyoming: Yellowstone National Park, 1959–1963," box 7:195, TWS; and 26 *Federal Register*: 5632, June 23, 1961.

54 Some letters contesting the decision are Kenneth B. Pomeroy to Stewart L. Udall, June 28, 1961, file "W4624a Salt Lake City Hearings Lake Zoning," box W-157 (there are others in the same file); and Ira N. Gabrielson to John A. Carver Jr., July 14, 1961, and Carl W. Buchheister to Frank Barry, July 12, 1961, both in file "Boat Regulations on Yellowstone Lake," box 7:4, IWL. Conservationist letters rallying members to the hearing include Michael Nadel to Members and Friends of The Wilderness Society, July 7, 1961,

file "W4624a Salt Lake City Hearings Lake Zoning," box W-157; Anthony Wayne Smith to All Organizations Cooperating with National Parks Association, file "Boat Regulations on Yellowstone Lake," box 7:4, IWL; and Bruce M. Kilgore to Burton W. Marston, July 3, 1961, file "Yell. & Grand Teton National Park," box 62, Izaak Walton League Papers, Accession #301, American Heritage Center, University of Wyoming-Laramie. *New York Times* opinion, "Motorboats vs. the Parks," July 13, 1961.

55 Harrell F. Mosbaugh to Charles H. Stoddard, July 19, 1961, and "Statement of the Izaak Walton League of America, Inc., in Regard to Motor Boat Zoning Regulations in Yellowstone National Park," both in file "W4624 Book #7, July–Aug. 1961," box W-255; "Testimony of National Parks Association at Hearings Held by the Solicitor, . . . " July 17, 1961, file "W4624—Lake Zoning 1960," box W-156; Howard W. Baker to The Director, July 24, 1961, and E. T. Scoyen to Regional Director, August 9, 1961, both in file "W4624a Salt Lake City Hearings Lake Zoning," box W-157; and Hartt Wixom, "No More Yellowstone Talks Set, Barry Says," *Deseret News and Telegram* (Salt Lake City), July 19, 1961.

56 "Statement of Lemuel A. Garrison for Interior Department Hearing on Zoning of Yellowstone Lakes, Salt Lake City, Utah—July 17, 1961," file "Lake Zoning—Salt Lake Hearing W4624," box W-156, and Garrison to Director, November 9, 1961 (source of quote), file "W4624 Book #8, Aug. 1961–Jan. 1962, 1 of 2," box W-255.

57 "Deathly silence" from "The Editorial Page," *National Parks Magazine* (December 1962): 2; and Garrison, *The Making of a Ranger*, 289–290.

58 Garrison, *Making of a Ranger*, 289–290.

59 Frank J. Barry to the Secretary, March 28, 1962, file "Office of the Secretary—Parks and Sites—Yellowstone National Park, Part 6—March 6, 1962 to March 22, 1963," box 338, Central Classified Files, 1959–1963, Record Group 48, NACP.

60 John A. Carver Jr. to Secretary Udall, February [date of month illegible] 1962, and John A. Carver Jr. to Secretary, January 29, 1962, both in file "Office of the Secretary—Parks & Sites—Yellowstone National Park, Part 5—Aug. 1, 1916 to Feb. 22, 1962," box 337, Central Classified Files, 1959–1963, Record Group 48, NACP; and Office of the Secretary, draft press release entitled "Yellowstone

Boating Regulations Revised to Protect Two Wilderness Areas,"
[n.d.], Folder 4, box 53, AHC.

61 "Yellowstone National Park Boating Regulations Still in Doubt,"
National Wildlands News (June 1962):1; Dave Toeppen,
"Conservation Report on Yellowstone Park," *AYH Byways* (journal
of American Youth Hostels) (September 1962):2; and Lon
Garrison, untitled memoir of the controversy, August 1974, file
"Lon Garrison—Miscell. Items," box A-1. The NACP, YNPA, the
American Heritage Center, and the Kennedy Presidential Library
contain no written correspondence with Udall on the issue. Perhaps
Kennedy took Udall aside before or after some cabinet meeting and
told him to stand down, but there is no record of it.

62 Complaints to President and Udall from Ralph A. Dungan to
Secretary of the Interior, August 16, 1962, Folder "Public Affairs,
June 21, 1962 to Aug. 25, 1962," box 657, John F. Kennedy
Presidential Library, National Archives; and John A. Carver Jr. to
Leo Drey, October 15, 1962 (source of first quote), John A. Carver
Jr. to Thomas D. Mulhern Jr., November 21, 1962, and Robert M.
Mangan to Lindsay Hoben, January 23, 1963, all in file "Office of
the Secretary—Parks and Sites—Yellowstone National Park, Part
6—March 6, 1962 to March 22, 1963," box 338, Central Classified
Files, 1959–1963, Record Group 48, NACP. Quote to Brooks in
Oscar T. Dick to Acting Superintendent, October 22, 1962, file
"W4624—Boating (Lake Zoning General), 1962," box W-156. Calls
for investigation from David R. Toeppen to Mr. President, July 29,
1962, and Betty Groth to John F. Kennedy, August 8, 1962, both in
Folder 6, box 593, AHC.

63 USDI-NPS, "Yellowstone National Park Wilderness Proposal
Hearing," 1972, unpublished transcripts (each) for the March 11,
1972, Jackson, Wyoming, hearing, the March 13, 1972, Idaho Falls
hearing, and the March 15, 1972, Livingston, Montana, hearing,
all in YNPL; USDI-NPS, *Wilderness Recommendation, Yellowstone
National Park* (Washington, DC: US Government Printing Office,
August 1972), 12–15 and 25–28; Stanley W. Hulett to Legislative
Counsel, August 15, 1972, file "Wilderness Areas and Research
Reserves, May thru December 1972," box L-29; Rogers B. Morton
to Mr. President, September 14, 1972, file "EIS—Wilderness,"
Management Assistant's Office files, NPS, Yellowstone National

Park; and William Ringle, "Yellowstone Plans Largest Wilderness," *The [Boise] Idaho Statesman*, September 22, 1972.

64 Although conservationists arguably derive the most value from the spiritual meanings, they also enjoy its recreation potential, although often in ways different than motorized users. Similarly, motorized users also appreciate the special nature of Yellowstone and other preserves. However, each group seems to find primary value in the meanings with which they are commonly identified, such as in this story. See also Judith Layzer, *The Environmental Case: Translating Values into Policy* (Washington, DC: CQ Press, 2006), who argues that this is the primary value conflict underlying many contemporary federal land management controversies, and Justin Farrell, *The Battle for Yellowstone: Morality and the Sacred Roots of Environmental Conflict* (Princeton, NJ: Princeton University Press, 2015), who makes a similar argument specifically about Yellowstone controversies.

65 The other two issues were the effort to remove tourist developments from grizzly bear habitat at Fishing Bridge in the 1980s and to close Sylvan Pass to snowmobile traffic in the early 2000s. For more detail on them, see my article, "Yellowstone City Park: The Dominating Influence of Politicians in National Park Service Policymaking," *Journal of Policy History* 23 (2011): 381–398.

66 Garrison, *The Making of a Ranger*, 293; and untitled memoir of the controversy, August 1974, file "Lon Garrison—Misc. Items," box A-1.

67 Others canoeists report similar experiences with motorboat noise on Yellowstone Lake (Orville Bach, personal communication with the author, Old Faithful, July 20, 2004).

Notes to Day 6: On the Edge

Aldo Leopold, *A Sand County Almanac: And Sketches Here and There* (New York: Oxford University Press, 1949), 224–225.

1 The lake trout–cutthroat trout discussion is drawn from the following sources: Robert E. Gresswell and Lusha M. Tronstad, "Altered Processes and the Demise of Yellowstone Cutthroat Trout in Yellowstone Lake," in *Yellowstone's Wildlife in Transition*, ed. P. J. White, Robert A. Garrott, and Glenn E. Plumb, 209–225 (Cambridge, MA: Harvard University Press, 2013); NPS, "Preservation of

Yellowstone Lake Cutthroat Trout," available at http://www.nps. gov/yell/planyourvisit/upload/fishar9-18.pdf; NPS, "Whirling Disease," available at http://www.nps.gov/yell/learn/nature/ whirlingdisease.htm; and Pat Bigelow and Todd Koel, "Yellowstone Cutthroat Trout" and "Lake Trout," both available at http://www. nps.gov/yell/planyourvisit/upload/RI_2014_10_Wildlife.pdf, and all accessed January 7, 2015; NPS Fisheries and Aquatics Section, "Draft Summary of 2014 Accomplishments on Yellowstone Lake," attached to Pat Bigelow to author, email, January 5, 2015; and Pat Bigelow to author, email, October 22, 2015.

2 The grizzly bear discussion is drawn from the following sources: P. J. White and Kerry A. Gunther, "Population Dynamics: Influence of Resources and Other Factors on Animal Density," in *Yellowstone's Wildlife in Transition* (2013), ed. White, Garrott, and Plumb, 47–68; and Wikipedia, "Grizzly Bear," http://en.wikipedia.org/wiki/Grizzly_bear, and NPS, "Grizzly Bears and the Endangered Species Act," http://www.nps.gov/yell/naturescience/bearesa.htm, both accessed January 10, 2015.

3 "Saving Species in Peril," *National Wildlife* (April/May 2014): 44.

4 See Justin Farrell, *The Battle for Yellowstone: Morality and the Sacred Roots of Environmental Conflict* (Princeton, NJ: Princeton University Press, 2015), for a cogent (but sometimes self-congratulatory) examination of the bison and wolf management controversies, as well as my own *Protecting Yellowstone: Science and the Politics of National Park Management* (Albuquerque: University of New Mexico Press, 2013).

5 Moose sightings from Thorofare Ranger Station logbooks, with the seventy-six sighting from Eugene Young to Mother, October 23, 1938, T. Eugene Young Papers, msc 129, box 1. Moose population from Olaus Murie, "Report on Game Animals in Upper Yellowstone-Thorofare Region," 1929, YNPL. Murie's estimate of two hundred was for the Yellowstone River Valley only; undoubtedly, moose in the rest of the Thorofare would have swelled that number to a few hundred or more. Remainder of paragraph from Scott A. Becker, "Habitat Selection, Condition, and Survival of Shiras Moose in Northwest Wyoming" (master's thesis, University of Wyoming, 2008); John C. Henningsen, Amy L. Williams, Cynthia M. Tate, Steve A. Kilpatrick, and W. David Walter, "Distribution and Prevalence of

Elaeophora schneideri in Moose in Wyoming," *Alces* 48 (2012): 35–44; Laura Zuckerman, "Brain-Attacking Worm Linked to Decline of Wyoming Moose," http://www.reuters.com/article/2011/10/08/us-moose-wyoming-idUSTRE79706B20111008, accessed July 14, 2015; Cory Hatch, "Worm Infests Area Moose," *Jackson Hole News & Guide*, October 14, 2013, http://www.jhnewsandguide.com/news/environmental/worm-infests-area-moose/article_658ffa38-a0dd-570c-bfa1-9ed69b6ee51d.html, accessed July 14, 2015; and NPS, "Moose Information Continued," http://www.nps.gov/yell/naturescience/mooseinfo.htm, accessed January 12, 2015.

6   Unless otherwise noted, the discussion of river boating is based on my article "Kayaking Playground or Nature Preserve: Whitewater Boating Conflicts in Yellowstone National Park," *Montana the Magazine of Western History* 55 (Spring 2005): 52–64. This paragraph is also drawn from American Whitewater, "Yellowstone and Grand Teton," https://www.americanwhitewater.org/content/Project/view/id/124/, accessed January 15, 2015; and Forrest McCarthy, "Snake River Headwaters," http://forrestmccarthy.blogspot.com/2013/06/snake-river-headwaters.html, accessed January 14, 2015.

7   Joseph L. Sax, *Mountains without Handrails: Reflections on the National Parks* (Ann Arbor: University of Michigan Press, 1980), and Edward Abbey, *Desert Solitaire: A Season in the Wilderness* (New York: McGraw-Hill, 1968). Sax discusses Olmsted's thinking about the national parks.

8   Forrest McCarthy, "Du'Mor'—Packrafting Wyoming's Wildest Corner," http://forrestmccarthy.blogspot.com/2013/07/dumor-packrafting-wyomings-wildest.html, and "Snake River Headwaters," http://forrestmccarthy.blogspot.com/2013/06/snake-river-headwaters.html, both accessed January 14, 2015. See also Forrest McCarthy, "Wilderness Paddling: The Thorofare," http://www.explorebigsky.com/newspost/2014-06-28-wilderness-paddling-the-thorofare, accessed January 14, 2015.

9   USDI/NPS, *NPS Management Policies 2006* (Washington, DC: US Government Printing Office, 2006), 98–103; and The Wilderness Act, 16 U.S.C. 1133(c). See also Doug Scott, "Mechanization in Wilderness Areas: Motors, Motorized Equipment, and Other Forms of Mechanical Transport," 2003, published online at https://www.wilderness.net/toolboxes/documents/tools/Mechanization%20

in%20Wilderness.pdf, accessed January 21, 2015. On noise effects on wildlife, see Frank Turina and Jesse Barber, "Annotated Bibliography Impacts of Noise on Wildlife," https://www.nature.nps.gov/sound/assets/docs/Wildlife_AnnotatedBiblio_Aug2011.pdf, accessed November 20, 2015.

10 USDI/NPS, *NPS Management Policies 2006*, 98–99.

11 I personally observed all these problems between 1993 and 2007, mostly in the Teton Wilderness but also in the park and Washakie Wilderness. See also Gary Ferguson, *Hawks Rest: A Season in the Remote Heart of Yellowstone* (Washington, DC: National Geographic, 2003).

12 See Todd Wilkinson, "One Murie's Position on Paddling Bill Clear," *Jackson Hole News & Guide*, February 19, 2014, http://www.jhnewsandguide.com/opinion/columnists/the_new_west_todd_wilkinson/one-murie-s-position-on-paddling-bill-clear/article_2a8ab502-b1df-5fcf-840b-48924e77b40e.html, especially the remarks by Edward Abbey, for a similar argument.

13 Bart Melton, "Paddling Bill Is Bad News for Yellowstone and Grand Teton Parks," *High Country News,* March 26, 2014, at https://www.hcn.org/wotr/paddling-bill-is-bad-news-for-yellowstone-and-grand-teton-parks; Todd Wilkinson, "One Murie's Position on Paddling Bill Clear," *Jackson Hole News & Guide*, February 19, 2014, http://www.jhnewsandguide.com/opinion/columnists/the_new_west_todd_wilkinson/one-murie-s-position-on-paddling-bill-clear/article_2a8ab502-b1df-5fcf-840b-48924e77b40e.html; US Congress, "HR 3492 (113th): River Paddling Protection Act," https://www.govtrack.us/congress/bills/113/hr3492; American Rivers, "American Rivers Statement on HR 3492, The River Paddling Protection Act," February 19, 2014, http://www.americanrivers.org/newsroom/press-releases/hr3492-river-paddling-protection-act/, all accessed July 12, 2015; and Lisa Rein, "Bill Advances to Open Some National Parks to Paddlers, Drawing Battle Lines with Environmentalists," *Washington Post*, October 9, 2015, https://www.washingtonpost.com/news/federal-eye/wp/2015/10/09/bill-advances-to-open-some-national-parks-to-paddlers-drawing-battle-lines-with-environmentalists/; and US Congress, "HR 974 (114th): Yellowstone and Grand Teton Paddling Act," https://www.govtrack.us/congress/bills/114/hr974, both accessed November 30, 2015.

14 The whitebark pine discussion is drawn from S. Thomas Olliff, Roy A. Renkin, Daniel P. Reinhart, Kristin L. Legg, and Emily M. Wellington, "Exotic Fungus Acts with Natural Disturbance Agents to Alter Whitebark Pine Communities," in *Yellowstone's Wildlife in Transition* (2013), ed. White, Garrott, and Plumb, 236–251; Greater Yellowstone Coordinating Committee Whitebark Pine Subcommittee, "Whitebark Pine Strategy for the Greater Yellowstone Area," 2011, http://fedgycc.org/documents/WBPStrategyFINAL5.31.11.pdf; "Whitebark Pine Publications and Reports," http://fedgycc.org/WhitebarkPinePublicationsandArticles.htm; NPS, "Whitebark Pine," http://www.greateryellowstonescience.org/ topics/biological/vegetation/whitebarkpine; and Stephanie Pappas, "Grizzlies Should Stay on Endangered Species List, Scientists Say," 2013, http://www.livescience.com/41915-scientists-contest-grizzly-bear-delisting.html, all accessed January 25, 2015.

15 Intergovernmental Panel on Climate Change [Core Writing Team, R. K. Pachauri, and L. A. Meyer, eds.], *Climate Change 2014: Synthesis Report: Contribution of Working Groups I, II and III to the Fifth Assessment Report of the Intergovernmental Panel on Climate Change* (Geneva, Switzerland: IPCC, 2015), available at http://ar5-syr.ipcc.ch/ipcc/ipcc/resources/pdf/IPCC_SynthesisReport.pdf, accessed August 28, 2015; William H. Romme and Monica G. Turner, "Ecological Implications of Climate Change in Yellowstone: Moving into Uncharted Territory?" *Yellowstone Science* 23 (March 2015): 6–13; Tony Chang and Andrew Hansen, "Historic & Projected Climate Change in the Greater Yellowstone Ecosystem," *Yellowstone Science* 23 (March 2015): 14–19; Mike Tercek, Ann Rodman, and David Thoma, "Trends in Yellowstone's Snowpack," *Yellowstone Science* 23 (March 2015): 20–28; and NPS, "Climate Change," http://www.nps.gov/yell/naturescience/climatechange.ht, and Roy Renkin and Tom Olliff, "Climate Change in Greater Yellowstone," http://www.nps.gov/yell/planyourvisit/upload/RI_2014_05_GYE.pdf, both accessed January 28, 2015.

16 Intergovernmental Panel on Climate Change, *Climate Change 2014,* 2015, page 47 (first two quotes) and page v (last quote), available at http://ar5-syr.ipcc.ch/ipcc/ipcc/resources/pdf/IPCC_SynthesisReport.pdf, accessed August 28, 2015.

17 On the Paris accord: Coral Davenport, "Nations Approve Landmark

Climate Accord in Paris," *New York Times*, December 12, 2015, http://www.nytimes.com/2015/12/13/world/europe/climate-change-accord-paris.html?_r=0, and Oliver Milman, "James Hansen, Father of Climate Change Awareness, Calls Paris Talks 'a Fraud,'" *The Guardian*, December 12, 2015, http://www.theguardian.com/environment/2015/dec/12/james-hansen-climate-change-paris-talks-fraud, both accessed December 13, 2015. On the effects on the Thorofare: Chang and Hansen, "Historic and Projected Climate Change"; Andrew Hansen, Nate Piekielek, Tony Chang, and Linda Phillips, "Changing Climate Suitability for Forests in Yellowstone and the Rocky Mountains," *Yellowstone Science* 23 (March 2015): 36–43; Romme and Turner, "Ecological Implications of Climate Change in Yellowstone"; Mike Tercek, "A Seemingly Small Change in Average Temperature Can Have Big Effects," *Yellowstone Science* 23 (March 2015): 70–71; Anthony L. Westerling, H. G. Hidalgo, D. R. Cayan, and T. W. Swetnam, "Warming and Earlier Spring Increase Western US Forest Wildfire Activity," *Science* 313 (2006) 5789: 940–943; and Anthony L. Westerling, Monica G. Turner, Erica A. H. Smithwick, William H. Romme, and Michael G. Ryan, "Continued Warming Could Transform Greater Yellowstone Fire Regimes by Mid-21st Century," *Proceedings of the National Academy of Sciences* 108 (August 9, 2011) 32:13165–13170.

18 The ice bucket challenge discussion is drawn from ALS Association, "The ALS Ice Bucket Challenge," http://www.alsa.org/fight-als/ice-bucket-challenge.html?gclid=CLKmvJmTtcMCFeXm7AodDRsAFg, and Wikipedia, "Ice Bucket Challenge," http://en.wikipedia.org/wiki/Ice_Bucket_Challenge, both accessed January 27, 2015.

19 Whitney Bermes, "Once More into the Wild," *Bozeman Daily Chronicle,* August 23, 2014.

Notes to Day 7: The Journey of a Lifetime

Aldo Leopold, *A Sand County Almanac: And Sketches Here and There* (New York: Oxford University Press, 1949), 148–149.

1 Doug Peacock makes much the same point in *The Grizzly Years: In Search of the American Wilderness* (New York: Henry Holt and Co., 1990).

2 For more on the history of bear management in Yellowstone, see Alice Wondrak Biel, *Do (Not) Feed the Bears: The Fitful History of*

Wildlife and Tourists in Yellowstone (Lawrence: University Press of Kansas, 2006); and James A. Pritchard, *Preserving Yellowstone's Natural Conditions: Science and the Perception of Nature* (Lincoln: University of Nebraska Press, 1999). Quote from A. Starker Leopold, S. A. Cain, C. M. Cottam, I. N. Gabrielson, and T. L. Kimball, "Wildlife Management in the National Parks," reprinted in *America's National Park System: The Critical* Documents, ed. Lary Dilsaver (Lanham, MD: Rowman & Littlefield, 1994), 239.

3   Peter Nabokov and Lawrence Loendorf, *Restoring a Presence: American Indians and Yellowstone National Park* (Norman: University of Oklahoma Press, 2004); and Thomas R. Vale, ed., *Fire, Native Peoples, and the Natural Landscape* (Washington, DC: Island Press, 2002).

4   Certainly, not all who manage the Thorofare are motivated by these values and beliefs. Turning again to my own experience, my thoughts go quickly to Suzanne Lewis, superintendent of Yellowstone from 2001 to 2010. While she adequately held the line against the George W. Bush administration's assaults on our public lands, she was not as protective toward her own employees. A deeply suspicious person, she distrusted any employee below the mid-management level, especially if they had an advanced degree. Most such employees just tried to stay out of her way, but I could not easily avoid her because I worked in the same building, on the same floor, and on the snowmobile issue, which had her ongoing attention. Worse, I had a PhD and was writing a book on the snowmobile issue. The book was part of my job description—and that was the worst part of my situation, as my position was temporary, not to last more than four years. The NPS has a lot of such positions; its supervisors usually reward high-performing employees in them with permanent jobs or, at worst, new four-year positions. Not for me, though; when my position ended in 2009, I found myself out of a job. I lost my job because I did my job, and did it well: my book, *Yellowstone and the Snowmobile*, was published by the University Press of Kansas two months before my job ended. I will never know if Lewis ordered my boss to let me go, but I do know that she did not care for me (colleagues told me so) and that she did nothing to help me. I doubt she ever read my book, and losing my job was good evidence that her love of community did not include all of her employees.

5   Gary Ferguson, *The Carry Home: Lessons from the American Wilderness* (Berkeley, CA: Counterpoint Press, 2014: 118–126); and Pope Francis, "Laudato Si': Encyclical Letter on Care for our Common Home," May 24, 2015, paragraph 66, http://w2.vatican.va/content/francesco/en/encyclicals/documents/papa-francesco_20150524_enciclica-laudato-si.html, accessed September 29, 2015. Note that I adopted Ferguson's term "community" for what I had more awkwardly been calling "love of others." See also note 6 of the preface.

Notes to Day 8: Forever Wild

"Mormon Lilies," *San Francisco Daily Evening Bulletin* (part 4 of the 4 part series "Notes from Utah") dated July 1877, published July 19, 1877; reprinted in *Steep Trails* (New York: Houghton Mifflin, 1918), chapter 9.

1   A simple Google search for the words "climate change resilience" will produce dozens of hits on such documents. See, for example, Craig Moritz and Rosa Agudo, "The Future of Species under Climate Change: Resilience or Decline?" *Science* 341 (August 2, 2013) 6145: 504–508; Ian Thompson, B. Mackey, S. McNulty, and A. Mosseler, *Forest Resilience, Biodiversity, and Climate Change. A Synthesis of the Biodiversity/Resilience/Stability Relationship in Forest Ecosystems* (Montreal: Secretariat of the Convention on Biological Diversity, 2009); NPS, "Climate Change Action Plan 2012–2014," http://www.nps.gov/jeca/learn/management/upload/NPS-Climate-Change-Action-Plan-2012-2014.pdf; National Wildlife Federation, *Green Works for Climate Resilience: A Community Guide to Climate Planning,* 2014, http://www.nwf.org/~/media/PDFs/Global-Warming/Climate-Smart-Conservation/2014/green-works-final-for-web.pdf; and NPS, "12th Biennial Scientific Conference," http://www.nps.gov/yell/learn/management/12thbiennialscienceconferen ce.htm, all accessed March 8, 2015.

2   Intergovernmental Panel on Climate Change [Core Writing Team, R. K. Pachauri, and L. A. Meyer, eds.], *Climate Change 2014: Synthesis Report: Contribution of Working Groups I, II and III to the Fifth Assessment Report of the Intergovernmental Panel on Climate Change* (Geneva, Switzerland: IPCC, 2015), available at http://ar5-syr.ipcc.ch/ipcc/ipcc/resources/pdf/IPCC_SynthesisReport.pdf,

accessed August 28, 2015. See also the wealth of information at the IPCC website, http://www.ipcc.ch/.

3   Intergovernmental Panel on Climate Change, *Climate Change 2014*, 2015, p. 64, available at http://ar5-syr.ipcc.ch/ipcc/ipcc/resources/pdf/IPCC_SynthesisReport.pdf, accessed August 28, 2015; and Pope Francis, "Laudato Si': Encyclical Letter on Care for our Common Home," May 24, 2015 (see especially paragraphs 48–52), http://w2.vatican.va/content/francesco/en/encyclicals/documents/papa-francesco_20150524_enciclica-laudato-si.html, accessed September 29, 2015.

4   The White House, "President Obama Announces Historic 54.5 mpg Fuel Efficiency Standard," press release, July 29, 2011, https://www.whitehouse.gov/the-press-office/2011/07/29/president-obama-announces-historic-545-mpg-fuel-efficiency-standard, accessed September 9, 2015. The term "structural fix" is from Thomas Heberlein, *Navigating Environmental Attitudes* (New York: Oxford University Press, 2012), who strongly influenced this discussion. Heberlein shows that education campaigns, which he calls "cognitive fixes," usually fail; in contrast, structural fixes and technological fixes often succeed (he would probably consider Obama's hike in fuel efficiency standards a technological fix, since it is based on new technology).

5   Cally Carswell, "Scientists Strengthen Link between Climate Change and Drought," August 20, 2015, and Sarah Tory, "Canadian Water for California's Drought?" April 28, 2015, both in *High Country News*, available at www.hcn.org; [State of California], "California Drought," http://ca.gov/drought/; and Greg Toppo, "Washington Wildfires Now Largest in State's History," *USA Today*, August 25, 2015, http://www.usatoday.com/story/news/2015, all accessed August 28, 2015; and Western Water Assessment, "Climate Change and Projections: Recent Climate Changes and their Causes," http://wwa.colorado.edu/climate/change.html; and Brian Clark Howard, "Worst Drought in 1,000 Years Predicted for American West," February 12, 2015, http://news.nationalgeographic.com/news/2015/02/150212-megadrought-southwest-water-climate-environment/, both accessed September 29, 2015.

6   National Science Foundation, "Ozone Hole over Antarctica,"
    http://www.nsf.gov/about/history/nsf0050/arctic/ozonehole.htm,
    accessed September 11, 2015.

7   From a speech to environmentalists in Missoula, Montana, and in
    Colorado, which was published in *High Country News*, September
    24, 1976, under the title "Joy, Shipmates, Joy!"

Bibliography

Archival Collections

American Rivers Collection (CONS 147), Conservation Collection, Denver
Public Library (ARC)

Gale W. McGee Collection, Accession #9800, American Heritage Center,
University of Wyoming, Laramie (AHC)

Izaak Walton League Collection (CONS 41), Conservation Collection, Denver
Public Library (IWL)

National Archives, College Park, Maryland (NACP)

National Archives, Yellowstone National Park, Gardiner, Montana (YNPA)

The Wilderness Society Collection (CONS 130), Conservation Collection,
Denver Public Library (TWS)

Yellowstone Center for Resources files, National Park Service, Mammoth Hot
Springs, Yellowstone (YCR)

Yellowstone National Park Research Library, Gardiner, Montana (YNPL)

Books and Articles

Abbey, Edward. *Desert Solitaire: A Season in the Wilderness.* New York:
McGraw-Hill, 1968.

Albanese, Catherine L. *Nature Religion in America: From the Algonkian
Indians to the New Age.* Chicago: University of Chicago Press, 1990.

Albright, Horace M., as told to Robert Cahn. *The Birth of the National Park
Service: The Founding Years, 1913–33.* Salt Lake City, UT: Howe Brothers,
1985.

Bartlett, Richard A. *Yellowstone: A Wilderness Besieged.* Tucson: University of
Arizona Press, 1985.

Becker, Scott A. "Habitat Selection, Condition, and Survival of Shiras Moose
in Northwest Wyoming." Master's thesis, University of Wyoming, 2008.

Berry, Evan. *Devoted to Nature: The Religious Roots of American
Environmentalism.* Oakland: University of California Press, 2015.

Biel, Alice Wondrak. *Do (Not) Feed the Bears: The Fitful History of Wildlife and Tourists in Yellowstone*. Lawrence: University Press of Kansas, 2006.

Callicott, J. Baird, and Michael P. Nelson, eds. *The Great New Wilderness Debate*. Athens: University of Georgia Press, 1999.

Callicott, J. Baird, and Michael P. Nelson, eds. *The Wilderness Debate Rages On: Continuing the Great New Wilderness Debate*. Athens: University of Georgia Press, 2008.

Carr, Ethan. *Mission 66: Modernism and the National Park Dilemma*. Amherst: University of Massachusetts Press, 2007.

Chang, Tony, and Andrew Hansen. "Historic and Projected Climate Change in the Greater Yellowstone Ecosystem." *Yellowstone Science* 23 (March 2015): 14–19.

Chase, Alston. *Playing God in Yellowstone: The Destruction of America's First National Park*. San Diego: Harcourt Brace Jovanovich, 1986.

Clark, Susan G. *Ensuring Greater Yellowstone's Future: Choices for Leaders and Citizens*. New Haven, CT: Yale University Press, 2008.

Coates, Peter A. "The Strange Stillness of the Past: Toward an Environmental History of Sound and Noise." *Environmental History* 10 (2005): 636–665.

Cohen, Michael. *The History of the Sierra Club, 1892–1970*. San Francisco: Sierra Club, 1988.

Cronon, William. "The Trouble with Wilderness; or, Getting Back to the Wrong Nature." In *Uncommon Ground: Rethinking the Human Place in Nature*, ed. William Cronon, 69–90. New York: W. W. Norton & Co., 1996.

Crysdale, Richard A. "An Analysis of Lake Zoning Factors, Objectives and Problems on Yellowstone Lake." Master's thesis, Utah State University, 1965.

Denevan, William H. "The Pristine Myth: The Landscape of the Americas in 1492." *Annals of the Association of American Geographers* 82 (1992): 369–385.

Dilsaver, Lary M. *Cumberland Island National Seashore: A History of Conservation Conflict*. Charlottesville: University of Virginia Press, 2004.

Dilsaver, Lary M., and William C. Tweed. *Challenge of the Big Trees: A Resource History of Sequoia and Kings Canyon National Parks*. Three Rivers, CA: Sequoia Natural History Association, 1990.

Dunlap, Thomas R. *Faith in Nature: Environmentalism as Religious Quest*. Seattle: University of Washington Press, 2004.

Everhart, William C. *The National Park Service*. Boulder, CO: Westview Press, 1983.

Farrell, Justin. *The Battle for Yellowstone: Morality and the Sacred Roots of Environmental Conflict.* Princeton, NJ: Princeton University Press, 2015.

Feldman, James. *A Storied Wilderness: Rewilding the Apostle Islands.* Seattle: University of Washington Press, 2013.

Ferguson, Gary. *The Carry Home: Lessons from the American Wilderness.* Berkeley, CA: Counterpoint Press, 2014.

———. *Hawks Rest: A Season in the Remote Heart of Yellowstone.* Washington, DC: National Geographic, 2003.

Fiege, Mark. *Irrigated Eden: The Making of an Agricultural Landscape in the American West.* Seattle: University of Washington Press, 1999.

Folsom, David E. *The Folsom-Cook Exploration of the Upper Yellowstone in the Year 1869.* St. Paul, MN: H. L. Collins Co., 1894.

Foresta, Ronald A. *America's National Parks and Their Keepers.* Washington, DC: Resources for the Future, Inc., 1984.

Fox, Stephen. *The American Conservation Movement: John Muir and His Legacy.* Madison: University of Wisconsin Press, 1981.

Franke, Mary Ann. *Yellowstone in the Afterglow: Lessons from the Fires.* Mammoth Hot Springs, WY: National Park Service, 2000.

Garrison, Lemuel A. *The Making of a Ranger: Forty Years with the National Parks.* Salt Lake City, UT: Howe Brothers, 1983.

Graber, Linda. *Wilderness as Sacred Space.* Washington, DC: American Association of Geographers, 1976.

Gresswell, Robert E., and Lusha M. Tronstad. "Altered Processes and the Demise of Yellowstone Cutthroat Trout in Yellowstone Lake." In *Yellowstone's Wildlife in Transition*, ed. P. J. White, Robert A. Garrott, and Glenn E. Plumb, 209–225. Cambridge, MA: Harvard University Press, 2013.

Haines, Aubrey L. *The Yellowstone Story.* Rev. ed. 2 vols. Niwot, CO: Yellowstone Association for Natural Science, History, and Education, in cooperation with the University Press of Colorado, 1996.

Hansen, Andrew, Nate Piekielek, Tony Chang, and Linda Phillips. "Changing Climate Suitability for Forests in Yellowstone and the Rocky Mountains," *Yellowstone Science* 23 (March 2015): 36–43.

Hartzog, George B., Jr. *Battling for the National Parks.* Mount Kisco, NY: Moyer Bell, 1988.

Harvey, Mark W. T. *Wilderness Forever: Howard Zahniser and the Path to the Wilderness Act.* Seattle: University of Washington Press, 2007.

Heberlein, Thomas. *Navigating Environmental Attitudes.* New York: Oxford University Press, 2012.

Henningsen, John C., Amy L. Williams, Cynthia M. Tate, Steve A. Kilpatrick, and W. David Walter. "Distribution and Prevalence of *Elaeophora schneideri* in Moose in Wyoming." *Alces* 48 (2012): 35–44.

Hummel, Don. *Stealing the National Parks: The Destruction of Concessions and Park Access.* Bellevue, WA: Free Enterprise Press, 1987.

Ise, John. *Our National Park Policy.* New York: Arno Press, 1979.

Johnson, Michael L. *Hunger for the Wild: America's Obsession with the Untamed West.* Lawrence: University Press of Kansas, 2007.

Jones, Holway. *John Muir and the Sierra Club: The Battle for Yosemite.* San Francisco: Sierra Club, 1965.

Kay, Charles. "Aboriginal Overkill: The Role of Native Americans in Structuring Western Ecosystems." *Human Nature* 5 (1994): 359–398.

———. "Are Ecosystems Structured from the Top-Down or Bottom-Up? A New Look at an Old Debate." *Wildlife Society Bulletin* 26 (1998): 484–498.

Layzer, Judith. *The Environmental Case: Translating Values into Policy.* Washington, DC: CQ Press, 2006.

Leopold, Aldo. *A Sand County Almanac: And Sketches Here and There.* New York: Oxford University Press, 1949.

Leopold, A. Starker, S. A. Cain, C. M. Cottam, I. N. Gabrielson, and T. L. Kimball. "Wildlife Management in the National Parks." Reprinted in *America's National Park System: The Critical Documents,* ed. Lary Dilsaver. Lanham, MD: Rowman & Littlefield, 1994.

Louter, David. *Windshield Wilderness: Cars, Roads, and Nature in Washington's National Parks.* Seattle: University of Washington Press, 2010.

Lovin, Hugh T. "Fighting over the Cascade Corner of Yellowstone National Park, 1919–1935." *Annals of Wyoming* 72 (Spring 2000): 14–29.

Lowry, William R. *Repairing Paradise: The Restoration of Nature in America's National Parks.* Washington, DC: Brookings Institution Press, 2009.

———. *Preserving Public Lands for the Future: The Politics of Intergenerational Goods.* Washington, DC: Georgetown University Press, 1998.

———. *The Capacity for Wonder: Preserving National Parks.* Washington, DC: Brookings Institution Press, 1994.

Magoc, Chris. *Yellowstone: The Creation and Selling of an American Landscape, 1870–1903.* Albuquerque: University of New Mexico Press, 1999.

Mann, Charles C. *1491: New Revelations of the Americas before Columbus.* New York: Alfred A. Knopf, 2005.

Marsh, Kevin R. *Drawing Lines in the Forest: Creating Wilderness Areas in the Pacific Northwest.* Seattle: University of Washington Press, 2010.

Miles, John. *Wilderness in the National Parks: Playground or Preserve.* Seattle: University of Washington Press, 2009.

———. *Guardians of the Parks.* Washington, DC: Taylor & Francis, 1995.

Moritz, Craig, and Rosa Agudo. "The Future of Species under Climate Change: Resilience or Decline?" *Science* 341 (2 August 2013) 6145:504–508.

Murie, Margaret, and Olaus Murie. *Wapiti Wilderness.* Boulder: Colorado Associated University Press, 1985.

Murie, Olaus. *The Elk of North America.* Harrisburg, PA: Wildlife Management Institute, 1951.

Nabokov, Peter, and Lawrence Loendorf. *Restoring a Presence: American Indians and Yellowstone National Park.* Norman: University of Oklahoma Press, 2004.

Nash, Roderick. *Wilderness and the American Mind.* 4th ed. New Haven, CT: Yale University Press, 2001.

Nelson, Daniel. *Northern Landscapes: The Struggle for Wilderness Alaska.* Washington, DC: Resources for the Future, 2004.

Oelschlaeger, Max. *The Idea of Wilderness: From Prehistory to the Age of Ecology.* New Haven, CT: Yale University Press, 1991.

Olliff, S. Thomas, Roy A. Renkin, Daniel P. Reinhart, Kristin L. Legg, and Emily M. Wellington. "Exotic Fungus Acts with Natural Disturbance Agents to Alter Whitebark Pine Communities." In *Yellowstone's Wildlife in Transition,* ed. P. J. White, Robert A. Garrott, and Glenn E. Plumb, 236–251. Cambridge, MA: Harvard University Press, 2013.

Peacock, Doug. *The Grizzly Years: In Search of the American Wilderness.* New York: Henry Holt and Co., 1990.

Pinchot, Gifford. *Breaking New Ground.* New York: Harcourt Brace Jovanovich, 1947.

———. *The Fight for Conservation.* New York: Doubleday, Page & Co., 1910.

Pritchard, James A. *Preserving Yellowstone's Natural Conditions: Science and the Perception of Nature.* Lincoln: University of Nebraska Press, 1999.

Richardson, Elmo. "The Struggle for the Valley: California's Hetch Hetchy Controversy, 1905-1913." *California Historical Society Quarterly* 38 (September 1959): 249–258.

Ridenour, James M. *The National Parks Compromised: Pork Barrel Politics and America's Treasures.* Merrillville, IN: ICS Books, 1994.

Righter, Robert. *Peaks, Politics and Passion: Grand Teton National Park Comes of Age.* Jackson, WY: Grand Teton Association, 2014.

———. *The Battle over Hetch Hetchy: America's Most Controversial Dam and the Birth of Modern Environmentalism.* New York: Oxford University Press, 2005.

———. *Crucible for Conservation: The Struggle for Grand Teton National Park.* Jackson, WY: Grand Teton Natural History Association, 1982.

Rokeach, Milton. *The Nature of Human Values.* New York: Free Press, 1973.

Rolston, Holmes. "Biology and Philosophy in Yellowstone." *Biology and Philosophy* 5 (1990): 241–258.

Romme, William H., and Monica G. Turner. "Ecological Implications of Climate Change in Yellowstone: Moving into Uncharted Territory?" *Yellowstone Science* 23 (March 2015): 6–13.

Runte, Alfred. *National Parks: The American Experience.* 4th ed. New York: Taylor Trade Publishing, 2010.

Sax, Joseph L. *Mountains without Handrails: Reflections on the National Parks.* Ann Arbor: University of Michigan Press, 1980.

Schullery, Paul. *Searching for Yellowstone: Ecology and Wonder in the Last Wilderness.* Boston: Houghton Mifflin, 1997.

Scott, Doug. *The Enduring Wilderness: Protecting Our Natural Heritage through the Wilderness Act.* Golden, CO: Fulcrum Publishing, 2004.

Sebesta, Paul D. "The Effects of Human Disturbance on the Ecology of the Yellowstone Lake Shore Wilderness Areas." Master's thesis, University of Nebraska, 1961.

Sellars, Richard West. *Preserving Nature in the National Parks: A History.* New Haven, CT: Yale University Press, 1997.

Shankland, Robert. *Steve Mather of the National Parks.* New York: Alfred A. Knopf, 1970.

Spence, Mark David. *Dispossessing the Wilderness: Indian Removal and the Making of the National Parks.* New York: Oxford University Press, 1999.

Stegner, Wallace. *The Sound of Mountain Water: The Changing American West.* Lincoln: University of Nebraska Press, 1985.

Sutter, Paul. *Driven Wild: How the Fight against Automobiles Launched the Modern Wilderness Movement.* Seattle: University of Washington Press, 2005.

Tercek, Mike. "A Seemingly Small Change in Average Temperature Can Have Big Effects." *Yellowstone Science* 23 (March 2015): 70–71.

Tercek, Mike, Ann Rodman, and David Thoma. "Trends in Yellowstone's Snowpack." *Yellowstone Science* 23 (March 2015): 20–28.

Thompson, Ian, B. Mackey, S. McNulty, and A. Mosseler. *Forest Resilience, Biodiversity, and Climate Change: A Synthesis of the Biodiversity/ Resilience/Stability Relationship in Forest Ecosystems*. Montreal: Secretariat of the Convention on Biological Diversity, 2009.

Tuan, Yi-Fu. *Space and Place: The Perspective of Experience*. Minneapolis: University of Minnesota Press, 1977.

Turner, Frederick. *Beyond Geography: The Western Spirit against the Wilderness*. New York: Viking Press, 1980.

Turner, Morton. *The Promise of Wilderness: American Environmental Politics since 1964*. Seattle: University of Washington Press, 2012.

Vale, Thomas R. *The American Wilderness: Reflections on Nature Protection in the United States*. Charlottesville: University of Virginia Press, 2005.

Vale, Thomas R., ed. *Fire, Native Peoples, and the Natural Landscape*. Washington, DC: Island Press, 2002.

Vale, Thomas R. "The Myth of the Humanized Landscape: An Example from Yosemite National Park." *Natural Areas Journal* 18 (1998): 231–236.

Wallace, Linda, ed. *After the Fires: The Ecology of Change in Yellowstone National Park*. New Haven, CT: Yale University Press, 2004.

Westerling, Anthony L., H. G. Hidalgo, D. R. Cayan, and T. W. Swetnam. "Warming and Earlier Spring Increase Western US Forest Wildfire Activity." *Science* 313 (2006) 5789: 940–943.

Westerling, Anthony L., Monica G. Turner, Erica A. H. Smithwick, William H. Romme, and Michael G. Ryan. "Continued Warming Could Transform Greater Yellowstone Fire Regimes by mid-21st Century." *Proceedings of the National Academy of Sciences* 108 (August 9, 2011) 32:13165–13170.

White, P. J., and Kerry A. Gunther. "Population Dynamics: Influence of Resources and Other Factors on Animal Density." In *Yellowstone's Wildlife in Transition*, ed. P. J. White, Robert A. Garrott, and Glenn E. Plumb, 47–68. Cambridge, MA: Harvard University Press, 2013.

Whittlesey, Lee H. *Yellowstone Place Names*. Rev. 2nd ed. Gardiner, MT: Wonderland Publishing Co., 2006.

Yochim, Michael J. *Protecting Yellowstone: Science and the Politics of National Park Management*. Albuquerque: University of New Mexico Press, 2013.

———. "Yellowstone City Park: The Dominating Influence of Politicians in National Park Service Policymaking." *Journal of Policy History* 23 (2011): 381–398.

———. *Yellowstone and the Snowmobile: Locking Horns over National Park Use*. Lawrence: University Press of Kansas, 2009.

———. "A Water Wilderness: Battles over Values and Motorboats on Yellowstone Lake." *Historical Geography* 35 (2007): 185–213.

———. "Kayaking Playground or Nature Preserve: Whitewater Boating Conflicts in Yellowstone National Park." *Montana the Magazine of Western History* 55 (Spring 2005): 52–64.

———. "Beauty and the Beet: The Dam Battles of Yellowstone." *Montana the Magazine of Western History* 53 (Spring 2003): 14–27.

———. Aboriginal Overkill Overstated: Errors in Charles Kay's Hypothesis." *Human Nature* 12 (2001): 141–167.

Government Documents

[Albright, Horace]. *Report of Superintendent, 1920.*

Federal Register.

Intergovernmental Panel on Climate Change [Core Writing Team, R. K. Pachauri, and L. A. Meyer, eds.]. *Climate Change 2014: Synthesis Report: Contribution of Working Groups I, II and III to the Fifth Assessment Report of the Intergovernmental Panel on Climate Change.* Geneva, Switzerland: IPCC, 2015.

[Mather, Stephen]. *Annual Report of Director of National Park Service, 1921.* Washington, DC: US Government Printing Office, 1921.

———. *Annual Report of Director of National Park Service, 1920.* Washington, DC: US Government Printing Office, 1920.

NPS Natural Resource Program Center. *Air Quality in National Parks: 2009 Annual Performance and Progress Report.* Denver, CO: NPS, 2010.

Senate Committee on Appropriations. *Proposed Boating Regulations for Yellowstone Lake, Hearings before a Subcommittee of the Committee on Appropriations.* 86th Congress, 2nd session, 1960.

USDI/NPS. *NPS Management Policies 2006.* Washington, DC: US Government Printing Office, 2006.

———. *Wilderness Recommendation, Yellowstone National Park.* Washington, DC: US Government Printing Office, August 1972.

United States Geological Survey. *Second Annual Report of the Reclamation Service.* Washington, DC: US Government Printing Office, 1904.

Periodicals, Newspapers, and Newsletters

Atlantic Monthly

AYH Byways

Big Sky Journal

Bird Lore

Boise (Id.) Statesman
Bozeman (Mont.) Daily Chronicle
Deseret News and Telegram
Electrical World
Field and Stream
Forest and Stream
High Country News
The Independent
Jackson Hole (Wyo.) News & Guide
Livingston (Mont.) Enterprise
The Living Wilderness
National Municipal Review
National Parks Association Bulletin/National Parks Magazine
National Wildlands News
National Wildlife
New West Magazine
New York Evening Post
New York Times
Outdoor America/Outdoor Newsletter
The Outlook
Philadelphia Public Ledger
Pocatello (Id.) Tribune
Saturday Evening Post
Sierra/The Sierra Club Bulletin
Union Pacific Magazine

Index